DATA COMMUNICATION COMPONENTS

DATA COMMUNICATION COMPONENTS

CHARACTERISTICS, OPERATION, APPLICATIONS

Gilbert Held

Office of Personnel Management
United States Government
Chief, Data Communications

HAYDEN BOOK COMPANY, INC.
Rochelle Park, New Jersey

To Beverly, Jonathan, and Jessica
for their patience and especially to
Milton for his encouragement and support

ISBN   0-8104-5126-3
Library of Congress Catalog Card Number   79-2041

2   3   4   5   6   7   8   9   PRINTING

80 81 82 83 84 85 86 87   YEAR

preface

This book has been written to provide the reader with an intimate awareness of the numerous devices which can be used for the design, modification, or optimization of a data communications network.

The development of this book resulted from the response I received to a series of articles I wrote for *Data Communications*. Personnel responsible for data communications at over 30 industrial firms and government agencies, both in the United States and abroad, have contacted me during the last 2 years for additional information on specific devices and knowledge about other devices which were briefly mentioned. Using the previous articles as a foundation, I have attempted to develop a book which is designed to provide the reader with an insight to how such devices operate, where they can be employed in networks, and the cost and performance parameters which should be considered in selecting such equipment.

Through the use of numerous schematic diagrams, I believe the reader will easily be able to see how different devices can be integrated into networks, and some examples should stimulate new ideas for even the most experienced person. From a personal observation, a schematic diagram I encountered gave me the idea of incorporating manual switches into a network I was designing when employed by Honeywell Information Systems, Incorporated. The use of these switches resulted in a systems cost reduction of almost $1 million and permitted Honeywell to win a competitive procurement in excess of $9.7 million.

To permit the maximum number of people to use this book profitably, an introductory section is included which covers the fundamental concepts common to all phases of data communications, explaining the interrelationships between computers, lines, data communications components, and terminals. Thereafter, each section is written to cover a group of components based upon a common function. Those familiar with the fundamental concepts of data communications may bypass or skim through the introductory section and begin their reading with the appropriate section commensurate with their interest, if they require knowledge about some particular component, or they may read the remainder of the book in sequence.

GILBERT HELD

Macon, Georgia

acknowledgments

The author is indebted to Mr. Harry R. Karp, Editor-in-Chief of *Data Communications,* for permission to utilize extracts and illustrations from articles I previously wrote for that magazine. I would also like to thank Mr. Thomas R. Marshall for contributing specific advice and assistance in preparing the chapters covering limited distance modems and line drivers.

contents

list of abbreviations

ACB   Asynchronous communications base
ACK   Acknowledgment
ACU   Automatic calling unit
ASCII   American Standard Code for Information Interchange
AWG   American wire gauge

BCD   Binary-coded decimal
BISYNC   Binary synchronous
bps   Bits per second
BTAM   Basic telecommunications access method

cps   Characters per second
CPU   Central processing unit
CRT   Cathode-ray tube
CSU   Channel service unit
CTS   Clear to send

DAA   Data access arrangement
DCE   Data communications equipment
DDD   Direct distance dialing
DDS   Dataphone® digital service
DMA   Direct memory access
DMC   Data multiplexed control
DSR   Data set ready
DSU   Digital service unit
DTE   Data terminal equipment
DTR   Data terminal ready

EBCDIC   Extended binary coded decimal interchange code
EIA   Electronic Industry Association

FCC   Federal Communications Commission
FDM   Frequency division multiplexer
FDX   Full duplex
FX   Foreign exchange

GPCB	General purpose communications base
h	Hours
HDX	Half duplex
Hz	Hertz
IDDS	International Digital Data Service
kbps	Thousand bits per second
Mbps	Million bits per second
MLC	Multiline controller
ms	Milliseconds
NAK	Negative acknowledgment
NBS	National Bureau of Standards
ns	Nanoseconds
PAR	Positive acknowledgment
PND	Present next digit
RCD	Receiver-carrier detect
RI	Ring indicator
RJE	Remote job entry
RNP	Remote network processor
RTS	Request to send
s	Second
SDLC	Synchronous data link control
SLC	Single line controller
SSU	Split-stream unit
TDM	Time division multiplexer
TTL	Transistor-transistor logic
WATS	Wide area telephone service

DATA COMMUNICATION
COMPONENTS

chapter 1
fundamental concepts

In order to transmit information between two locations, it is necessary to have a transmitter, a receiver, and a transmission medium that will provide a path or link between the transmitter and the receiver. In addition to transmitting signals, a transmitter must be capable of translating information from a form created by humans or machines into a signal suitable for transmission over the transmission medium. The transmission medium provides a path to convey the information to the receiver without introducing a prohibitive amount of signal distortion that could change the meaning of the transmitted signal. The receiver then converts the signal from its transmitted form into a form intelligible to humans or machines.

From and including the transmitter, to and including the receiver, a variety of data communications components can be utilized to perform specialized functions, reduce network costs, increase network reliability, and provide additional levels of transmission redundancy. The utilization of these components is a function of the characteristics which govern computer-to-computer and computer-to-terminal connections. These characteristics will be examined in this chapter.

1.1. Line Connections

Of line connections available to connect terminals to computers or other terminals, three basic types include dedicated, switched, and leased lines. A dedicated line is similar to a leased line in that the terminal is always connected to the device on the distant end, transmission always occurs on the same path, and, if required, the line can be easily tuned to increase transmission performance. The key difference between a dedicated and a leased line is that a dedicated line refers to a transmission medium internal to a user's facility, where the customer has the right of way for cable laying, whereas a leased line provides an interconnection between separate facilities. The term facility is usually employed to denote a building, office, or industrial plant. Dedicated lines are also referenced as direct connect lines and normally link a terminal or business machine on a direct path through the facility to another terminal or computer located at that facility. The dedicated line can be a wire conductor installed by employees of a company or by the computer manufacturer's personnel, or it can be a local line installed by the telephone company.

A leased line is commonly called a private line and is obtained from a communications company to provide a transmission medium between two facilities which could be in separate buildings in one city or in distant cities.

A switched line, often referred to as a dial-up line, permits contact with all parties having access to the telephone network. If the operator of a business machine wants access to a computer, he or she dials the telephone number of a telephone which is connected to the computer. In using switched or dial-up transmission, telephone company switching centers establish a connection between the dialing party and the dialed party. After the connection is set up, the terminal and the computer conduct their communications. When communications are completed, the switching centers disconnect the path that was established for the connection and restore all paths used so they become available for other connections.

Cost, speed of transmission, and degradation of transmission are the primary factors used in the selection process between leased and switched lines. If data communications requirements to a computer involve occasional random contact from a number of terminals at different locations, and each call is of short duration, dial-up service is normally employed. If a large amount of transmission occurs between a computer and a few terminals, leased lines are usually installed between the terminal and the computer. Since a leased line is fixed as to its routing, it can be conditioned to reduce errors in transmission as well as permit ease in determining the location of error conditions since its routing is known. Normally, switched circuits are used for transmission at speeds up to 4,800 bits per second (bps). Different categories of leased lines are available which permit transmission from under 100 bps to many hundreds of thousands of bits per second. This is discussed in the Sec. 1.8, "Transmission Rate." Table 1.1

Table 1.1. Line Selection Guide

Line type	Distance between transmission points	Speed of transmission	Use for transmission
Dedicated (direct connect)	*Local*	Limited by conductor	Short or long duration
Switched (dial-up)	Limited by telephone access availability	Normally less than 4,800 bps*	Short-duration transmission
Leased (private)	Limited by telephone company availability	Limited by type of facility*	Long-duration or frequent short-duration calls

* Refer to Sec. 1.2 for additional information.

lists some of the limiting factors involved in determining the type of line to use for transmission between business machines and computers.

1.2. Types of Service

If the distance between the terminal and the computer is relatively short, the transmission of digital information between the two devices may be obtained simply by cabling the devices together. As the distance between the two devices increases, the pulses of the digital data distort until they become nonrecognizable by the receiver. Of all transmission services, two types are available for the transmission of data: analog and digital service. Each type of service requires specialized equipment when transmission exceeds a short distance.

Since telephone lines were originally designed to carry analog, or voice signals, the digital signals to be transmitted from a terminal to a computer or from the computer to a terminal must be converted into a signal that is acceptable for transmission by the telephone line. To effect transmission between distant points, a data set or modem is used. A modem is a contraction of the compound modulation-demodulator and is an electronic device used to convert the digital signals generated by computers and business machines into analog tones for transmission over telephone network analog facilities. At the receiving end, a similar device accepts the transmitted tones, reconverts them to digital signals, and delivers these signals to the connected device. Signal conversion performed by modems is illustrated in Fig. 1.1. This illustration shows the interrela-

Fig. 1.1. Signal Conversion Performed by Modems
A modem converts (modulates) the digital signal produced by a terminal or business machine into an analog tone for transmission over an analog facility.

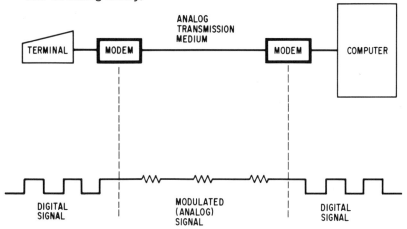

tionship of terminals, computers, and transmission lines when an analog transmission service is used. Both leased lines and switched lines employ analog service; therefore, modems can be used for transmission of data over both types of analog line connection. Although an analog transmission medium used to provide a transmission path between modems can be a direct connect, leased, or switched line, modems are directly connected (hard wired) to direct connect and leased lines, whereas they are interfaced to a switched facility. Thus, a terminal user can only communicate with the one distant location on a leased line but can communicate with many devices when he or she has access to a switched line. Most low-speed terminals utilize an acoustic coupler which is a modem whose connection to the telephone line is obtained by acoustically coupling the telephone headset to the coupler. The primary advantage in the utilization of an acoustic coupler is that no hard-wired connection to the switched network is required and a terminal employing such devices for data transmission becomes portable.

The acoustic coupler converts the signals generated by the terminal into a series of audible tones, which are then passed to the mouthpiece or transmitter of the telephone and then onto the switched telephone network. Information transmitted by the computer to the terminal is converted into audible tones at the earpiece of the telephone connected to the terminal's acoustic coupler. The coupler then converts those tones into the appropriate electrical signals recognized by the terminal. One of the significant advantages provided by the utilization of acoustic couplers is that the light weight permits portable terminals to be transported from location to location and used to access a computer anywhere a telephone capable of reaching the computer network is available. The interrelationship of modems, acoustic couplers, terminals, and analog transmission mediums is illustrated in Fig. 1.2.

Analog Facilities

Several types of analog switched facilities are offered by communications carriers. Each type of facility has its own set of characteristics and rate structure. Normally, an analytic study is conducted to determine which type or types of service should be utilized to provide an optimum cost-effective service for the user. The common types of analog switched facilities are direct distance dialing, wide area telephone service, and foreign exchange service.

Direct distance dialing (DDD) permits the user to dial directly any telephone connected to the public switched telephone network. The dialed telephone may be connected to a computer, another terminal, or some type of data communications component. The charge for this service, in addition to installation costs, may be a fixed monthly fee if no long distance calls

Fig. 1.2. Interrelationship of Modems, Acoustic Couplers, Terminals, Computers, and Analog Transmission Mediums

When using modems on an analog transmission medium, the line can be a dedicated, leased, or switched facility. Terminals can use acoustic couplers to transmit via the switched network.

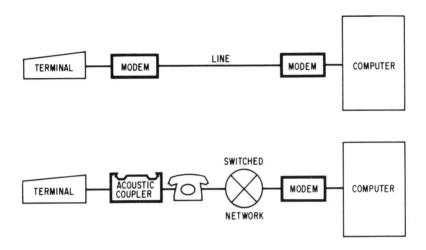

are made, a message unit basis based upon the number and duration of local calls, or a fixed fee plus any long distance charges incurred. Depending upon the time of day a long distance call is initiated and its destination (intrastate or interstate), discounts from normal long distance tolls are available for selected calls made without operator assistance.

Wide area telephone service (WATS) may be obtained in two different forms, each designed for a particular type of communications requirement. Outward WATS is used when a specific location requires placing a large number of outgoing calls to geographically distributed locations. Inward WATS service provides the reverse capability, permitting a number of geographically distributed locations to communicate with a common facility. Calls on WATS are initiated in the same manner as a call placed on the public switched telephone network. However, instead of being charged on an individual call basis, the user of WATS facilities pays a flat rate per block of communications hours per month. Communications in excess of the block are billed on an overtime basis.

A voice-band trunk called an access line is provided to the WATS user. This line links the facility to a telephone company central office. Other than cost considerations and certain geographical calling restrictions which are a function of the service area of the WATS line, the user may place as many calls as desired on this trunk if the service is outward WATS or receive as many calls as desired if the service is inward. Inward WATS, the well-known "800" area code, permits remotely located personnel to call your facility toll free from the service area provided by the particular inward WATS-type of service selected. The charge for WATS is a function of the service area, which can be intrastate WATS, a group of states bordering the user's state where the user's main facility is located, or a grouping of distant states. Recently, WATS service was extended from the continental United States to Alaska, Hawaii, Puerto Rico, and the Virgin Islands.

Foreign exchange (FX) service may provide a method of transmission from a group of terminals remotely located from a computer facility at less than the cost of direct distance dialing. An FX line can be viewed as a mixed analog switched and leased line. To use an FX line, a terminal user dials a local number which is answered if the FX line is not in use. From the FX, the information is transmitted via a dedicated voice line to a permanent connection in the switching office of a communications carrier near the facility with which communication is desired. A line from the local switching office which terminates at the user's home office is included in the basic FX service. This is illustrated in Fig. 1.3.

The use of an FX line permits the elimination of long distance charges that would be incurred by terminal users directly dialing the distant computer facility. Since only one terminal at a time may use the FX line, normally only groups of terminals whose usage can be scheduled are suitable for FX utilization. In Fig. 1.4, possible connections between remote terminals and a central computer where transmission occurs over an analog facility are illustrated.

The major difference between an FX line and a leased line is that any terminal dialing the FX line provides the second modem required for the

Fig. 1.3. Foreign Exchange (FX) Service

A foreign exchange line permits many terminals to use the facility on a scheduled or on a contention basis.

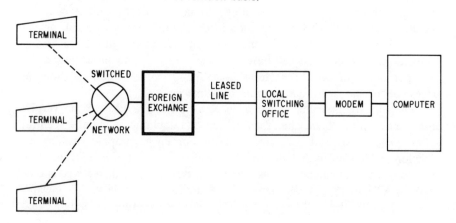

Fig. 1.4. Terminal-to-computer Connections via Analog Mediums

A mixture of dedicated, dial-up, leased lines, and foreign exchange lines can be employed to connect local and remote terminals to a central computer facility.

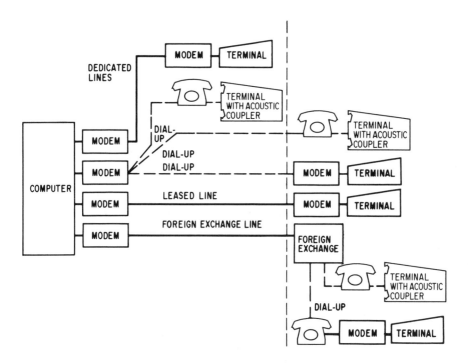

transmission of data, over that line, whereas a leased line used for data transmission normally has a fixed modem attached at both ends of the circuit.

Digital Facilities

In addition to analog service, digital service offerings have been implemented by communications carriers over the last several years. Using digital service, data is transmitted from source to destination in its original digital form without the necessity of converting the signal into an analog form for transmission over analog facilities as is the case when modems or acoustic couplers are interfaced to analog facilities.

In place of modems, users can choose one of two basic interface arrangements to connect their terminal or computer to a digital medium. A digital service unit (DSU) can be installed which will provide a standard interface to a user's terminal which is compatible with modems and handles such functions as signal translation, regeneration, reformating, and timing. The DSU is designed to operate at one of four speeds: 2,400, 4,800, 9,600, and 56,000 bps. The transmitting portion of the DSU processes the customers' signal into bipolar pulses suitable for transmission over the digital facility. The receiving portion of the DSU is used both to extract timing information and to regenerate mark and space information from the received bipolar signal. The second interface arrangement is called a channel service unit (CSU) and is provided by the communication carrier to those customers who wish to perform the signal processing to and from the bipolar line, as well as to retime and regenerate the incoming line signals through the utilization of their own equipment.

As data is transmitted over digital facilities, the signal is regenerated by the communications carrier numerous times prior to its arrival at its destination. In general, digital service gives data communications users improved performance and reliability when compared to analog service, due to the nature of digital transmission and the design of digital networks. Although digital service is offered in many locations, for those locations outside the serving area of a digital facility, the user will have to employ analog devices as an extension in order to interface to the digital facility. The utilization of digital service via an analog extension is illustrated in Fig. 1.5. As depicted in Fig. 1.5, if the closest city to the terminal located in city 2 that offers digital service is city 1, then to use digital service to communicate with the computer an analog extension must be installed

Fig. 1.5. Analog Extension to Digital Service

Although data is transmitted in digital form from the computer to city 1, it must be modulated by the modem at that location for transmission over the analog extension.

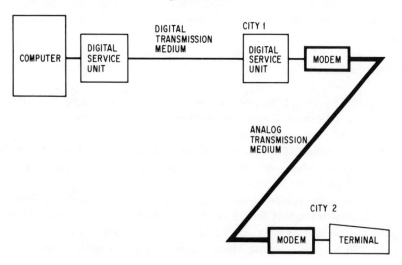

between the terminal location and city 1. In such cases, the performance, reliability, and possible cost advantages of using digital service may be completely dissipated. Digital service is currently only available for leased service. A leased digital line is similar to a leased analog line in that it is dedicated for full-time use to a particular user.

1.3. Transmission Mode

One method of characterizing lines, terminals, computer channels, and communications components such as modems is by their transmission or communications mode. The three classes of transmission modes are simplex, half-duplex, and full-duplex.

Simplex transmission is that transmission which occurs in one direction only, disallowing the receiver of information a means of responding to a transmission. A home AM radio which receives a signal transmitted from a radio station is an example of a simplex communications mode. In a data transmission environment, simplex transmission might be used to turn on or off specific devices at a certain time of the day or when a certain event occurs. An example of this would be a computer-controlled environmental system where a furnace is turned on or off depending upon the thermostat setting and the current temperature in various parts of a building. Normally, simplex transmission is not utilized where human-machine interaction is required due to the inability to turn the transmitter around so that the receiver can reply to the originator.

Half-duplex transmission permits transmission in either direction; however, transmission can occur in only one direction at a time. Half-duplex transmission is used in citizen band (CB) radio transmission where the operator can either transmit or receive but cannot perform both functions at the same time on the same channel. When the operator has completed a transmission, the other party must be advised that he or she is through transmitting and is ready to receive by saying the term "over." Then, the other operator can begin transmission. When data is transmitted over the telephone network, the transmitter and the receiver of the modem or acoustic coupler must be appropriately turned on and off as the direction of the transmission varies. Both simplex and half-duplex transmission require two wires to complete an electrical circuit. The top of Fig. 1.6 illustrates a half-duplex modem interconnection while the lower portion shows a typical sequence of events in the terminal's sign-on process to access a computer. In the sign-on process, the terminal user first transmits the word NEWUSER to inform the computer that a newuser wishes a connection to the computer. The computer responds by asking for the user's password, which is then furnished by the terminal user. In the top portion of Fig. 1.6, when data is transmitted from the computer to the terminal, control signals are sent from the computer to modem A which

Fig. 1.6. Half-duplex Transmission

Top: Control signals from the computer and terminal operate the transmitter and receiver sections of the attached modems. When the transmitter of modem A is operating, the receiver of modem B operates; when the transmitter of modem B operates, the receiver of modem A operates. However, only one transmitter operates at any one time in the half-duplex mode of transmission. Bottom: During the sign-on sequence, transmission is turned around several times.

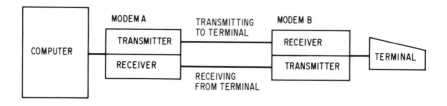

turns on the modem A transmitter and causes the modem B receiver to respond. When data is transmitted from the terminal to the computer, the modem B receiver is disabled and its transmitter is turned on while the modem A transmitter is disabled and its receiver becomes active. The time necessary to effect these changes is called transmission turnaround time, and during this interval transmission is temporarily halted. Half-duplex transmission can occur on either a 2-wire or 4-wire circuit. The switched network is a 2-wire circuit, whereas leased lines can be obtained as either 2-wire or 4-wire links. A 4-wire circuit is essentially a pair of 2-wire links which can be used for transmission in both directions simultaneously. This type of transmission is called the full-duplex mode. Half-duplex communication can use either a 2-wire or a 4-wire circuit; however, full-duplex transmission must normally be accomplished over a 4-wire connection.

Full-duplex transmission is often used when large amounts of alternate traffic must be transmitted and received within a fixed time period. If two

Fig. 1.7. Transmission Modes

Top: Simplex transmission is in one direction only; transmission cannot reverse direction. Center: Half-duplex transmission permits transmission in both directions but only one way at a time. Bottom: Full-duplex transmission permits transmission in both directions simultaneously.

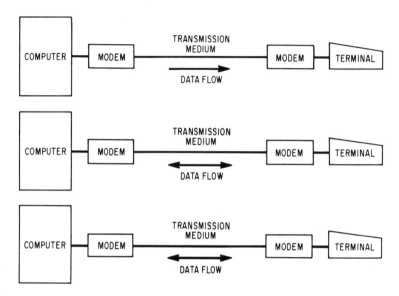

channels were used in our CB example, one for transmission and another for reception, two simultaneous transmissions could be effected. While full-duplex transmission provides more efficient throughput, this efficiency may be negated by the cost of 2-way lines and more complex equipment required by this mode of transmission. In Fig. 1.7, the three types of transmission modes are illustrated.

When referring solely to terminal operations, the terms half-duplex and full-duplex operation take on meanings different from the communications mode of the transmission medium. Terminal manufacturers often use the terms half duplex and full duplex to denote whether local copy (printing on the terminal as messages are transmitted) is provided or if the device on the distant end retransmits that which was transmitted. Half/full-duplex operations as applied to terminals are illustrated in Fig. 1.8.

1.4. Transmission Techniques

Data can be transmitted either synchronously or asynchronously. Asynchronous transmission is commonly referred to as start-stop transmission where one character at a time is transmitted or received. Start and stop bits are used to separate characters and synchronize the receiver with the trans-

Fig. 1.8. Terminal Operation Modes

Top: The term half-duplex terminal operation implies that data transmitted is also printed on the local terminal. This is known as local copy. Bottom: The term full-duplex terminal operation implies that no local copy is provided.

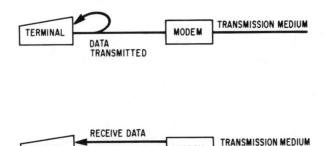

mitter, thus providing a method of reducing the possibility that data becomes garbled. Most terminals designed for human-machine interaction that are teletype compatible transmit data asynchronously. As characters are depressed on the terminal's keyboard they are transmitted to the computer, with idle time occurring between the transmission of characters. This is illustrated in the bottom portion of Fig. 1.9.

In asynchronous transmission, each character to be transmitted is encoded into a series of pulses. The transmission of the character is started by a start pulse equal in length to a code pulse. The encoded character (series of pulses) is followed by a stop pulse that may be equal to or longer than the code pulse, depending upon the transmission code used. As illustrated in the top portion of Fig. 1.9, the transmission of an 8-bit

Fig. 1.9. Asynchronous (Start-stop) Transmission

(A) Transmission of one 8-bit character. (B) Transmission of many characters. STB = start bit; CB = character bits; SPB = stop bit(s); Idle time is time between character transmission.

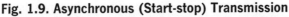
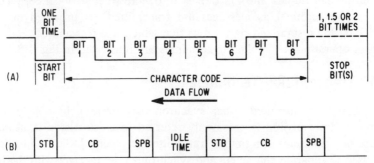

character requires either 10 or 11 bits, depending upon the length of the stop bit. In the start-stop mode of transmission, transmission starts anew on each character and stops after each character. This is indicated in the lower portion of Fig. 1.9. Since synchronization starts anew with each character, any timing discrepancy is cleared at the end of each character, and synchronization is maintained on a character-by-character basis. Asynchronous transmission normally is used for transmission at speeds under 2,000 bps. The use of potential data bit positions for the start and stop pulses is the price one pays when using this type of transmission.

A second type of transmission involves sending a grouping of characters in a continuous bit stream. This type of transmission is referred to as synchronous or bit-stream synchronization. In the synchronous mode of transmission, modems located at each end of the transmission medium normally provide a timing signal or clock that is used to establish the data transmission rate and enable the terminals to identify the appropriate characters as they are being transmitted or received. In some instances, timing may be provided by the terminal itself or other communication components such as multiplexers and front-end processor channels. No matter what timing source is used, prior to beginning the transmission of data, the transmitting and receiving devices must establish synchronization among themselves. In order to keep the receiving clock in step with the transmitting clock for the duration of a stream of bits that may represent a large number of consecutive characters, the transmission of the data is preceded by the transmission of one or more special characters. These special synchronization or "sync" characters are at the same code level (number of bits per character) as the coded information to be transmitted. However, they have a unique configuration of zero and one bits which are interpreted as the sync character. Once a group of sync characters is transmitted, the receiver recognizes and synchronizes itself onto a stream of those sync characters. When synchronization is achieved, then actual data transmission can proceed. Synchronous transmission is illustrated in Fig. 1.10. Since characters must be grouped or blocked into groups of characters for synchronous transmission, terminals must have a buffer or memory area so characters can be grouped for transmission in blocks. In addition to having

Fig. 1.10. Synchronous Transmission
In synchronous transmission, one or more sync characters are transmitted to establish clocking prior to the transmission of a block of data.

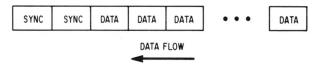

Table 1.2.   Transmission Technique Characteristics

Asynchronous
1. Each character is prefixed by a start bit and followed by one or more stop bits.
2. Idle time (period of inactivity) can exist between transmitted characters.
3. Bits within a character are transmitted at prescribed time intervals.
4. Timing is established independently in the computer and terminal.
5. Transmission speeds normally do not exceed 1,800 bps over switched facilities or leased lines and 9,600 bps over dedicated links.

Synchronous
1. Sync characters prefix transmitted data.
2. Sync characters are transmitted between blocks of data to maintain line synchronization.
3. No gaps exist between characters.
4. Timing is established and maintained by the transmitting and receiving modems, the terminal, or other devices.
5. Terminals must have buffers.
6. Transmission speeds normally are in excess of 2,000 bps.

a buffer area, more complex circuitry is required for synchronous terminals, since the receiving terminal must remain in phase with the transmitter for the duration of the transmitted block of information. Synchronous transmission is normally used for data transmission rates in excess of 2,000 bps. The major characteristics of synchronous and asynchronous transmission are denoted in Table 1.2.

1.5. Types of Transmission

The two types of data transmission that one can consider are serial and parallel. For serial transmission, the bits which comprise a character are transmitted in sequence over one line, whereas in parallel transmission, characters are transmitted serially but the bits that represent the character are transmitted in parallel. If a character consists of eight bits, then parallel transmission would require a minimum of eight lines. Additional lines may be necessary for control signals or for the transmission of a parity bit. Although parallel transmission is used extensively in computer-to-peripheral unit transmission, it is not normally employed other than in dedicated data transmission usage due to the cost of the extra circuits required. A typical use of parallel transmission is the in-plant connection of badge readers and similar devices to a computer in that facility. Parallel transmission can reduce the cost of terminal circuitry since the terminal does not have to convert the internal character representation to a serial data stream for transmission. However, the cost of the transmission medium and interface will increase due to the additional number of conductors and connectors required. Since the total character can be transmitted at the same moment in time using parallel transmission, higher data transfer rates can be obtained than possible with serial transmission facilities. For this reason most

Fig. 1.11. Types of Data Transmission

In serial transmission, the bits that comprise the character to be transmitted are sent in sequence over one line. In parallel transmission, the characters are transmitted serially but the bits that represent the character are transmitted in parallel.

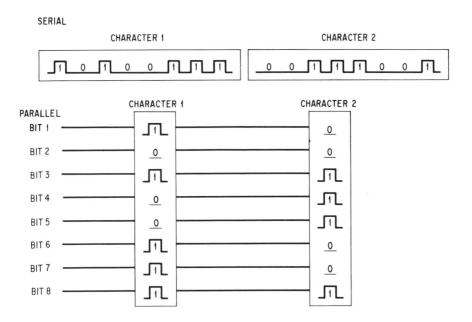

local facility intercomputer communications are accomplished using parallel transmission. Figure 1.11 illustrates the two types of transmission.

1.6. Line Structure

Both the geographical distribution of terminals and the distance between each terminal and the device it transmits to are important parameters that must be considered in developing a network configuration. The method used to interconnect terminals to computers or to other terminals is known as line structure and results in a computer's network configuration. The two types of line structure used in networks are point-to-point and multipoint, the latter also commonly referred to as multidrop lines. Communications lines that only connect two points are point-to-point lines. An example of this line structure is depicted at the top of Fig. 1.12. As illustrated, each terminal transmits and receives data to and from a computer via an individual connection that links a specific terminal to the computer. The point-to-point connection can utilize a dedicated circuit, a leased line, or can be obtained via a connection initiated over the switched (dial-up) telephone network.

Fig. 1.12. Line Structures in Networks

Top: Point-to-point line structure. Center: Multipoint (multidrop)
line structure. Bottom: Mixed network line structure.

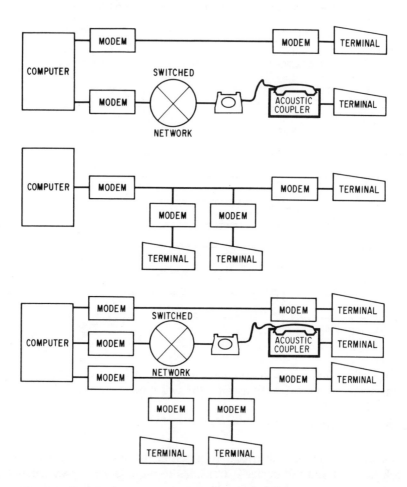

When two or more terminal locations can share portions of a common
line, the line is a multipoint or multidrop line. Although no two terminals
on such a line can transmit data at the same time, two or more terminals
may receive a message at the same time. The number of terminals receiving
such a message is dependent upon the addresses assigned to the message
recipients. In some systems a "broadcast" address permits all terminals
connected to the same multidrop line to receive a message at the same
time. When multidrop lines are employed, overall line costs may be reduced
since common portions of the line are shared for use by all terminals connected to that line. To prevent data transmitted from one terminal interfering with data transmitted from another terminal, a line discipline or

control must be established for such a link. This discipline controls terminal transmission so no two terminals transmit data at the same time. A multidrop line structure is depicted in the second portion of Fig. 1.12. For a multidrop line linking n terminals to a computer, $n + 1$ modems are required, one for each terminal as well as one located at the computer facility.

Both point-to-point and multipoint lines may be intermixed in developing a network, and transmission can be either in the full- or halfduplex mode. This mixed line structure is shown in the lower portion of Fig. 1.12.

1.7. Line Discipline

When several devices share the use of a common, multipoint communications line, only one device may transmit at any one time, although one or more devices may receive information simultaneously. To prevent two or more devices from transmitting at the same time, a technique known as poll and select is utilized as the method of line discipline for multidrop lines. To utilize poll and select, each terminal on the line must have a unique address of one or more characters as well as circuitry to recognize a message sent from the computer to that address. When the computer polls a line, in effect it asks each terminal in a predefined sequence if the terminal has data to transmit. If the terminal has no data to transmit, it informs the computer of this fact and the computer continues its polling sequence until it encounters a terminal on the line that has data to send. Then the computer acts on that data transfer. As the computer polls each terminal, the other terminals on the line must wait until they are polled before they can be serviced. Conversely, transmission of data from the computer to each terminal on a multidrop line is accomplished by the computer selecting the terminal address to which that data is to be transferred, informing the terminal that data is to be transferred to that terminal, and then transmitting data to the selected terminal. Polling and selecting can be used to service both asynchronous or synchronous terminals connected to independent multidrop lines. Due to the control overhead of polling and selecting terminals, synchronous high-speed terminals are normally serviced in this type of environment. By the use of signals and procedures, polling and selecting line control insures the orderly and efficient utilization of multidrop lines. An example of a computer polling the second terminal on a multipoint line and then receiving data from that terminal is shown at the top of Fig. 1.13. At the bottom of that illustration, the computer first selects terminal number three on the line and then transfers a block of data to that terminal. When terminals transmit data on a point-to-point line to a computer or another terminal, the transmission of that data occurs at the discretion of the terminal operator. This method of line control is known as non-poll-and-select or free-wheeling transmission.

Fig. 1.13. Poll and Select Line Discipline

Poll and select is a line discipline which permits several devices to use a common line facility in an orderly manner.

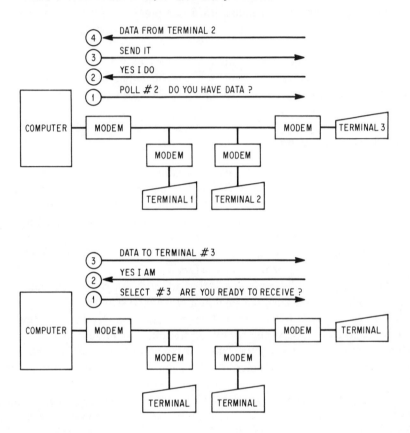

1.8. Transmission Rate

Many factors can affect the transmission rate at which data is transferred. While the types of modems and acoustic couplers used, as well as the line discipline and the type of computer channel to which a terminal is connected via a transmission medium, all play governing roles that affect transmission rates, the transmission medium itself is a most important factor in determining transmission rates.

Data transmission services offered by communications carriers such as American Telephone and Telegraph Company (AT&T) and Western Union are based on their available plant facilities. Depending upon terminal and computer locations, two types of transmission services may be available. The first type of service, analog transmission, is most readily available and can be employed on switched or leased telephone lines. Digital transmission is only available in most large cities, and analog extensions are required to connect to this service from nondigital service locations, as illustrated in Fig. 1.5. Within each type of service several grades of transmission are available for consideration.

In general, analog service offers the user three grades of transmission: narrowband, voice band, and wideband. The data transmission rates capable on each of these grades of service is dependent upon the bandwidth and electrical properties of each type of circuit offered within each grade of service. Basically, transmission speed is a function of the bandwidth of the communications line: the greater the bandwidth, the higher the possible speed of transmission.

Narrowband facilities are obtained by the carrier subdividing a voice-band circuit or by grouping a number of transmissions from different users onto a single portion of a circuit by time. Transmission rates obtained on narrowband facilities range between 45 and 300 bps. Teletype terminals that connect to message switching systems may use narrowband facilities.

While narrowband facilities have a bandwidth in the range of 200 to 400 Hz, voice-band facilities have a bandwidth in the range of 3,000 Hz. Data transmission speeds obtainable on voice-band facilities are differentiated by the type of voice-band facility utilized—switched dial-up transmission or transmission via a leased line. For transmission over the switched telephone network, maximum data transmission is between 4,800 and 7,200 bps, with 9,600-bps transmission occurring very infrequently. Since leased lines can be conditioned, a speed of 9,600 bps is employed frequently on such voice lines. Although low data speeds can be transmitted on both narrowband and voice-band circuits, one should not confuse the two since a low data speed on a voice circuit is transmission at a rate far less than the maximum permitted by that type of circuit, whereas a low data rate on a narrowband facility is at or near the maximum transmission rate permitted by that type of circuit.

Facilities which have a higher bandwidth than voice band are termed wideband or group-band facilities since they provide a wider bandwidth through the grouping of a number of voice-band circuits. Wideband facilities are available only on leased lines and permit transmission rates in excess of 9,600 bps. Transmission rates on wideband facilities vary with the offerings of communications carriers. Speeds normally available include 19,200, 40,800, 50,000, and 230,400 bps.

For direct connect circuits, transmission rates are a function of the distance between the terminal and the computer as well as the gauge of the conductor used.

In the area of digital service, one offering is currently available for user consideration. Digital data service, offered by AT&T as DATA-PHONE® digital service (DDS) provides interstate, full-duplex, point-to-point, and multipoint leased line, synchronous digital data transmission at

Table 1.3.   Transmission Facilities

Facility	Transmission speed	Use
Analog		
Narrowband	45–300 bps	Message switching
Voice band	Less than 4,800–7,200 bps	Time sharing remote; job entry
Switched	Up to 9,600 bps	Remote job entry;
Leased		computer-to-computer
Wideband	9600 bps and up	Computer-to-computer; remote job entry; tape-to-tape transmission; high-speed terminal to high-speed terminal
Digital		
Leased line	2.4, 4.8, 9.6, 56 kbps	Remote job entry; computer-to-computer; high-speed facsimile
Switched		
(proposed)	56,000 bps	Terminal-to-terminal; computer-to-computer; high-speed terminal to computer

speeds of 2,400, 4,800, 9,600, and 56,000 bps, as well as data transmission at 1.344 and 1.544 million bps between the servicing areas of a few digital cities.

A new high-speed digital switched communications service has been proposed by AT&T which will offer full-duplex, synchronous transmission over a common digital network at a transmission rate of 56,000 bps. In addition, several specialized communications carriers now offer or plan to offer digital service in selected areas of the United States and to overseas locations. Table 1.3 lists the main analog and digital facilities, the range of transmission speeds over those facilities, and the general use of such facilities.

1.9. Transmission Codes

Data within a computer is structured according to the architecture of the computer. The internal representation of data in a computer is seldom suitable for transmission to devices other than the peripheral units attached to the computer. In most cases, to effect data transmission, internal computer data must be reformatted or translated into a suitable transmission code. This transmission code creates a correspondence between the bit encoding of data for transmission or internal device representation and printed symbols. The end result of the translation is usually dictated by the character code that the remote terminal is built to accept. Frequently available terminal codes include Baudot, which is a 5-level (5 bits per character code), binary-coded decimal (BCD), which is a 6-level code, American Standard Code for Information Interchange (ASCII), which is normally a 7-level code, and the extended binary-coded decimal interchange code (EBCDIC), which is an 8-level code. In addition to information being encoded into a certain number of bits based upon the transmission code used, the unique configuration of those bits to represent certain control characters can be considered as a code that can be used to effect line discipline. These control characters may be used to indicate the acknowledgment of the receipt of a block of data without errors (ACK), the start of a message (SOH), or the end of a message (EXT), with the number of permissible control characters standardized according to the code employed. With the growth of computer-to-computer data transmission, a large amount of processing can be avoided by transferring the data in the format used by the computer for internal processing. Such transmission is known as binary mode transmission, transparent data transfer, code-independent transmission, or native mode transmission.

One of the most commonly known codes, the Morse code, is not practical for utilization in a computer communications environment. This code consists of a series of dots and dashes, which, while easy for the human ear to decode, are of unequal length and not practical for data transmission implementation. The 5-level Baudot code was devised by Emil Baudot to permit teletypewriters to operate faster and more accurately than relays used to transmit information via telegraph. Since the number of different characters which can be derived from a code having two different (binary) states is 2^m, where m is the number of positions in the code, the 5-level Baudot code permits 32 unique character bit combinations. Although 32 characters could be represented normally with such a code, the necessity of transmitting digits, letters of the alphabet, and punctuation marks made it necessary to devise a mechanism to extend the capacity of the code to include additional character representations. The extension mechanism was accomplished by the use of two "shift" characters: "letters shift" and "figures shift." The transmission of a shift character informs the receiver that the characters which follow the shift character should be interpreted as characters from a symbol and numeric set or from the alphabetic set of characters. The 5-level Baudot code is illustrated in Table 1.4 for one particular terminal pallet arrangement. A transmission of all ones in bit positions 1 through 5 indicates a letters shift, and the characters following the transmission of that character are interpreted as letters. Similarly, the transmission of ones in bit positions 1, 2, 4, and 5 would indicate a figures shift, and the following characters would be interpreted as numerals or symbols based upon their code structure.

Table 1.4.   5-Level Baudot Code

Letters	Figures	Bit Selection				
		1	**2**	**3**	**4**	**5**
Characters						
A	—	1	1			
B	?	1			1	1
C	:		1	1	1	
D	$	1			1	
E	3	1				
F	!	1		1	1	
G	&		1		1	1
H				1		1
I	8		1	1		
J	'	1	1		1	
K	(	1	1	1	1	
L	)		1			1
M	.			1	1	1
N	,			1	1	
O	9				1	1
P	Ø		1	1		1
Q	1	1	1	1		1
R	4		1		1	
S		1		1		
T	5				1	
U	7	1	1	1		
V	;		1	1	1	1
W	2	1	1			1
X	/	1		1	1	1
Y	6	1		1		1
Z	"	1				1
Functions						
Carriage return	<				1	
Line feed	=		1			
Space				1		
Letters shift		1	1	1	1	1
Figures shift		1	1		1	1

The development of computer systems required the implementation of coding systems to convert alphanumeric characters into binary notation and the binary notation of computers into alphanumeric characters. The BCD system was one of the earliest codes used to convert data to a computer-acceptable form. This coding technique permits decimal numeric information to be represented by 4 binary bits and permits an alphanumeric character set to be represented through the use of 6 bits of information. This code is illustrated in Table 1.5. An advantage of this code is that two-decimal digits can be stored in an 8-bit computer word and manipulated with appropriate computer instructions. Although only 36 characters are shown, a BCD code is capable of containing a set of 2^6 or 64 different characters.

In addition to transmitting letters, numerals, and punctuation marks, a considerable number of control characters may be required to promote

Table 1.5. Binary-Coded Decimal System

Bit Position						
b_6	b_5	b_4	b_3	b_2	b_1	Character
0	0	0	0	0	1	A
0	0	0	0	1	0	B
0	0	0	0	1	1	C
0	0	0	1	0	0	D
0	0	0	1	0	1	E
0	0	0	1	1	0	F
0	0	0	1	1	1	G
0	0	1	0	0	0	H
0	0	1	0	0	1	I
0	1	0	0	0	1	J
0	1	0	0	1	0	K
0	1	0	0	1	1	L
0	1	0	1	0	0	M
0	1	0	1	0	1	N
0	1	0	1	1	0	O
0	1	0	1	1	1	P
0	1	1	0	0	0	Q
0	1	1	0	0	1	R
1	0	0	0	1	0	S
1	0	0	0	1	1	T
1	0	0	1	0	0	U
1	0	0	1	0	1	V
1	0	0	1	1	0	W
1	0	0	1	1	1	X
1	0	1	0	0	0	Y
1	0	1	0	0	1	Z
1	1	0	0	0	0	0
1	1	0	0	0	1	1
1	1	0	0	1	0	2
1	1	0	0	1	1	3
1	1	0	1	0	0	4
1	1	0	1	0	1	5
1	1	0	1	1	0	6
1	1	0	1	1	1	7
1	1	1	0	0	0	8
1	1	1	0	0	1	9

line discipline. These control characters may be used to switch on and off devices which are connected to the communications line, control the actual transmission of data, manipulate message formats, and perform additional functions. Thus, an extended character set is usually required for data communications. One such character set is EBCDIC. This code is an extension of the BCD system and uses 8 bits for character representation. This code permits 2^8 or 256 unique characters to be represented, although currently a lesser number is assigned meanings. This code is primarily used for transmission by byte-oriented computers, where a byte is a grouping of eight consecutive binary digits operated on as a unit by the computer. The use of this code by computers may alleviate the necessity of the computer

Table 1.6.   EBCDIC Character Set[a]

4, 5, 6, 7[b] ↓	00				01			
	00	01	10	11	00	01	10	11
0000	NUL	DLE	DS		SP	&	-	
0001	SOH	DC1	SOS				/	
0010	STX	DC2	FS	SYN				
0011	ETX	TM						
0100	PF	RES	BYP	PN				
0101	HT	NL	LF	RS				
0110	LC	BS	ETB	UC				
0111	DEL	IL	ESC	EOT				
1000		CAN						
1001		EM						
1010	SMM	CC	SM		¢	!		:
1011	VT	CUT	CU2	CU3		$	,	#
1100	FF	IFS		DC4	<	*	%	@
1101	CR	IGS	ENQ	NAK	(	)	_	'
1110	SO	IRS	ACK		+	;	>	=
1111	SI	IUS	BEL	SUB	|	¬	?	"

[a] Control character representations: ACK—Acknowledge; BEL—Bell; BS—Backspace; BYP—Bypass; CAN—Cancel; CC—Cursor Control; CR—Carriage Return; CU1—Customer Use 1; CU2—Customer Use 2; CU3—Customer Use 3; DC1—Device Control 1; DC2—Device Control 2; DC4—Device Control 4; DEL—Delete; DLE—Data Link Escape; DS—Digit Select; EM—End of Medium; ENQ—Enquiry; EOT—End of Transmission; ESC—Escape; ETB—End of Transmission Block; ETX—End of Text; FF—Form Feed; FS—Field Separator; HT—Horizontal Tab; IFS—Interchange File Separator; IGS—Interchange Group Separator; IL—Idle; IRS—Interchange Record Separator; IUS—Interchange Unit Separator; LC—Lower Case; LF—Line Feed; NAK—Negative Acknowledge; NL—New Line; NUL—Null; PF—Punch Off; PN—Punch on; RES—Restore; RS—Reader Stop; SI—Shift In; SM—Set Mode; SMM—Start of Manual Message; SO—Shift Out; SOH—Start of

performing code conversion if the connected terminals operate with the same character set. Table 1.6 illustrates the EBCDIC character set.

Due to the proliferation of the number of data transmission codes, attempts to standardize codes for data transmission purposes have been made. One result of this quest for standardization was ASCII. This 7-level code is illustrated in Table 1.7 and is commonly employed as the character set used for teletype terminals.

A frequent problem in data communications is that of code conversion. Consider what must be done to enable a computer with an EBCDIC character set to transmit and receive information from a terminal with an ASCII character set. When that terminal transmits a character, that character is encoded according to the ASCII character code. Upon receipt of that character, the computer must convert the bits of information of the

	10				11		← 0, 1[b]		
00	01	10	11	00	01	10	11 ← 2, 3[b]		
								0	0000
a	j			A	J			1	0001
b	k	s		B	K	S		2	0010
c	l	t		C	L	T		3	0011
d	m	u		D	M	U		4	0100
e	n	v		E	N	V		5	0101
f	o	w		F	O	W		6	0110
g	p	x		G	P	X		7	0111
h	q	y		H	Q	Y		8	1000
i	r	z		I	R	Z		9	1001
									1010
									1011
									1100
									1101
									1110
									1111

Heading; SOS—Start of Significance; SP—Space; STX—Start of Text; SUB—Substitute; SYN—Synchronous Idle; TM—Tape Mark; UC—Upper Case; VT—Vertical Tab; Special graphic characters: ¢—Cent Sign; .—Period, Decimal Point; <—Less-than Sign; (—Left Parenthesis; +—Plus Sign; |—Logical OR; &—Ampersand; !—Exclamation Point; $—Dollar Sign; *—Asterisk;)—Right Parenthesis; ;—Semicolon; ¬—Logical NOT; -—Minus Sign, Hyphen; /—Slash; ,—Comma; %—Percent; ___—Underscore; >—Greater-than Sign; ?—Question Mark; :—Colon; #—Number Sign; @—At Sign; '—Prime, Apostrophe; =—Equal Sign; "—Quotation Mark
[b] Bit positions

ASCII character into an equivalent EBCDIC character. Conversely, when data is to be transmitted to the terminal, it must be converted from EBCDIC to ASCII so the terminal will be able to decode and act according to the information in the character that the terminal is built to interpret.

1.10. Protocols

Two types of protocol should be considered in a data communications environment: terminal protocols and data link protocols.

The data link protocol defines the control characteristics of the network and is a set of conventions that are followed which govern the transmission of data and control information. A terminal can have a predefined control character or set of control characters which are unique to the terminal and are not interpreted by the line protocol. This internal terminal protocol can include such control characters as the bell, line feed, and carriage return for teletype terminals, blink and cursor positioning

Table 1.7.   American Standard Code for Information Interchange*

B b₇ ───────▶	0	0	0	0	1	1	1	1
I b₆ ───────▶	0	0	1	1	0	0	1	1
T b₅ ───────▶	0	1	0	1	0	1	0	1

b₄ b₃ b₂ b₁								
0 0 0 0	NUL	DLE	SP	0	@	P	\	p
0 0 0 1	SOH	DC1	!	1	A	Q	a	q
0 0 1 0	STX	DC2	"	2	B	R	b	r
0 0 1 1	ETX	DC3	#	3	C	S	c	s
0 1 0 0	EOT	DC4	$	4	D	T	d	t
0 1 0 1	ENQ	NAK	%	5	E	U	e	u
0 1 1 0	ACK	SYN	&	6	F	V	f	v
0 1 1 1	BEL	ETB	/	7	G	W	g	w
1 0 0 0	BS	CAN	(	8	H	X	h	x
1 0 0 1	HT	EM	)	9	I	Y	i	y
1 0 1 0	LF	SS	*	:	J	Z	j	z
1 0 1 1	VT	ESC	+	;	K	[	k	{
1 1 0 0	FF	FS	,	<	L	\	l	|
1 1 0 1	CR	GS	-	=	M	]	m	}
1 1 1 0	SO	RS	.	>	N	^	n	~
1 1 1 1	SI	US	/	?	O	__	o	DEL

* *Note:* (CC)—Communication control; (FE)—Format effector; (IS)—Information separator.

Control characters: NUL—Null/Idle; SOH—Start of Heading (CC); STX—Start of Text (CC); ETX—End of Text (CC); EOT—End of Transmission (CC); ENQ—Enquiry (CC); ACK—Acknowledge (CC); BEL—Audible or attention signal; BS—Backspace (FE); HT—Horizontal Tabulation (punch card skip) (FE); LF—Line Feed; VT—Vertical Tabulation (FE); FF—Form Feed (FE); CR—Carriage Return (FE); SO—Shift Out; SI—Shift In; DLE—Data Link Escape (CC); DC1, DC2, DC3—Device Controls; DC4—Device Control (stop); NAK—Negative Acknowledge (CC); SYN—Synchronous Idle (CC); ETB—End of Transmission Block (CC); CAN—Cancel; EM—End of Medium; ESC—Escape; FS—File Separator (IS); GS—Group Separator (IS); RS—Record Separator (IS); US—Unit Separator (IS); DEL—Delete.

Special graphic characters: SP—Space; !—Exclamation Point; ∫—Logical OR; "—Quotation Mark; #—Number Sign; $—Dollar Sign; %—Percent; &—Ampersand; '—Apostrophe; (—Opening Parenthesis;)—Closing Parenthesis; *—Asterisk; + — Plus; ,—Comma; ·—Hyphen; .—Period; /—Slant; :—Colon; ;—Semicolon; <— Less Than; =—Equals; >—Greater Than; ?—Question Mark; @—Commercial At; [—Opening Bracket; \—Reverse Slant;]—Closing Bracket; ^—Circumflex; __—Underline; `—Grave Accent; {—Opening Brace; |—Vertical Line; }—Closing Brace; ~—Tilde

characters for a display terminal, and form control characters for a line printer.

Although poll and select is normally thought of as a type of line discipline or control, it is also a data link protocol. In general, the data link protocol enables the exchange of information according to an order or sequence by establishing a series of rules for the interpretation of control signals which will govern the exchange of information. The control signals govern the execution of a number of tasks which are essential in controlling

Table 1.8. Information Control Tasks

Connection establishment	Transmission sequence
Connection verification	Data sequence
Connection disengagement	Error control procedures

the exchange of information via a communications facility. Some of these information control tasks are listed in Table 1.8.

Although all of the tasks listed in Table 1.8 are important, not all are required for the transmission of data since the series of tasks required is a function of the total data communications environment. As an example, a single terminal connected directly to a computer by a leased line normally does not require the establishment and verification of the connection. However, several terminals connected to the computer on a multidrop or multipoint line would require the verification of the terminal's identification to insure that data transmitted from the computer would be received by the proper terminal. Similarly, when a terminal session is completed, this fact must be recognized so that the computer resources can be made available to other terminal users. Thus, connection disengagement on terminals other than those connected on a point-to-point leased line permits a port on the front-end processor to become available to service other users.

Another important task is the transmission sequence which is used to establish the precedence and order of transmission, to include both data and control information. As an example, this task defines the rules for when terminals on a multipoint circuit may transmit and receive information. In addition to the transmission of information following a sequence, the data itself may be sequenced. Data sequencing is normally employed in synchronous transmission where a long block is broken into smaller blocks for transmission, with the size of the blocks being a function of the terminal's buffer area and the error control procedure employed. By dividing a block into smaller blocks for transmission, the amount of data that must be retransmitted, in the event that an error in transmission is detected, is reduced. Although error-checking techniques currently employed are more efficient when short blocks of information are transmitted, the efficiency of transmission correspondingly decreases since an acknowledgment (negative or positive) is returned to the device transmitting after each block is received and checked. For communications between remote job entry terminals and computers, blocks of up to several thousand characters are typically used. However, block lengths from 80 to 512 characters are the most common sizes. Although some protocols specify block length, most protocols permit the user to set the size of the block.

Pertaining to error control procedures, the most commonly employed method to correct transmitted errors is to inform the transmitting device simply to retransmit a block. This procedure requires coordination between the sending and receiving devices, with the receiving device continuously informing the sending device of the status of each previously transmitted block. If the block previously transmitted contained no detected errors, the receiver will transmit a positive acknowledgment, and the sender will transmit the next block. If the receiver detects an error it will transmit a negative acknowledgment, and discard the block containing an error. The transmitting station will then retransmit the previously sent block. Depending upon the protocol employed, a number of retransmissions may be attempted. However, if a default limit is reached due to a bad circuit or other problems, then the computer may terminate the terminal's session, and the terminal operator will have to reestablish the connection.

Among currently used protocols, one of the most frequently used for synchronous transmission is International Business Machines' BISYNC (binary synchronous communications) protocol. This particular protocol provides a set of rules which effect the synchronous transmission of binary-coded data. This protocol can be used in a variety of transmission codes on a large number of medium- to high-speed equipment. Some of the limitations of this protocol are that it is limited to half-duplex transmission and that it requires the acknowledgment of the receipt of every block of data transmitted. A large number of protocols have been developed due to the success of the BISYNC protocol. Some of these protocols are bit oriented, whereas BISYNC is a character-oriented protocol, and some permit full-duplex transmission, whereas BISYNC is limited to half-duplex transmission.

1.11. Link Terminology

A circuit over which data is transmitted provides a link between those devices used to transmit and receive data. Thus, a circuit used to transmit data between two terminals is commonly referred to as a terminal-to-terminal link.

When data is transmitted from one terminal to a computer, the circuit may be called a computer-to-terminal link. When more than one terminal transmits data over a common circuit (multidrop circuit) to a computer, this line is called a multiterminal-to-computer link. Although terminals can communicate directly to a computer over individual computer-to-terminal links, economics may justify the utilization of a device to combine the data from many low-speed terminals onto one or more high-speed paths for retransmission to a computer. Such a device, that can be used to combine the data transmitted from many terminals, is called a concentrator. Circuits which connect the terminals to the concentrator are called concentrator-to-terminal links, while the high-speed lines that connect the concentrator to the computer or host processor are known as concentrator-to-host links. When one concentrator transmits data to another concentrator, this type of circuit is known as a concentrator-to-concentrator link. Finally, the transmission path from one computer to another computer is known as a host-to-host link. Such link terminology is illustrated in Fig. 1.14.

Fig. 1.14. Link Terminology

Link terminology defines the data path between communications
components, computers, and remote batch terminals.

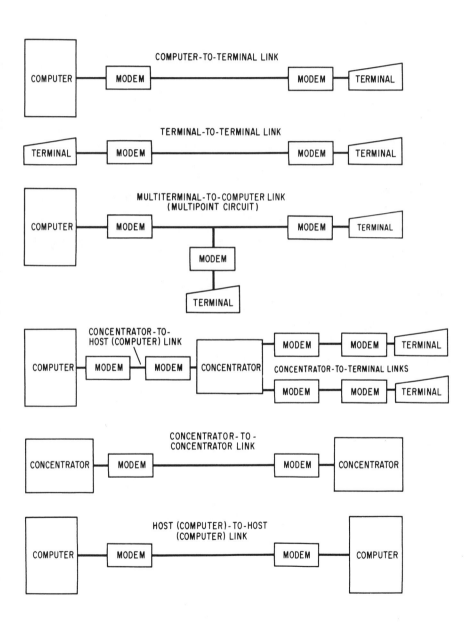

chapter 2
data transmission
equipment

One method of categorizing data communications components is by the function or group of functions they are designed to perform. In this chapter, the operation and utilization of components designed primarily to effect data transmission via a communications medium will be covered. Specific devices which will be explored in this chapter include a variety of couplers or devices that can be used to transmit data based upon the interrelationship of lines, terminals, and other data communications components which may be employed on a particular occasion. In addition, a device which permits the extension of parallel transmission from a computer to peripheral units located at a distance from the computational facility will also be covered.

2.1. Acoustic Couplers

Unlike conventional modems which may require a permanent or semi-permanent connection to a telephone line, an acoustic coupler is in essence a modem which permits data transmission through the utilization of the handset of an ordinary telephone. Similar in functioning to a modem, an acoustic coupler is a device which will accept a serial asynchronous data stream from data terminals, modulate that data stream into the audio spectrum, and then transmit the audio tones over a switched or dial-up telephone connection.

Acoustic couplers are equipped with built-in cradles or fittings into which a conventional telephone headset is placed. Through the process of acoustic coupling, the modulated tones produced by the acoustic coupler are directly picked up by the attached telephone handset. Likewise, the audible tones transmitted over a telephone line are picked up by the telephone earpiece and demodulated by the acoustic coupler into a serial data stream which is acceptable to the attached data terminal. Acoustic couplers use two distinct frequencies to transmit information, while two other frequencies are employed for data reception. A frequency from each pair is used to create a mark tone which represents an encoded binary one from the digital data stream, while another pair of frequencies generates a space tone which represents a binary zero. This utilization of frequencies permits full-duplex transmission to occur over the 2-wire switched telephone network.

Since acoustic couplers enable any conventional telephone to be used for data transmission purposes, the coupler does not have to be physically wired to the line and thus permits considerable flexibility in choosing a terminal working area which can be anywhere a telephone handset and standard electrical outlet are located. Acoustic couplers are manufactured both as separate units and as built-in units to data terminals, as shown in Fig. 2.1.

Since acoustic couplers are normally employed to permit portable terminals to communicate with data-processing facilities, and since a large portion of low-speed modems at such facilities are furnished by American Telephone and Telegraph Company (AT&T) operating companies, most manufacturers of acoustic couplers have designed them to be compatible with low-speed Bell System modems. Acoustic couplers that transmit and receive marks and spaces per the indicated frequencies shown in Table 2.1 are compatible with Bell System 103 and 113 type modems. Other acoustic couplers on the market transmit and receive data at speeds up to 1,200 bps and are compatible with Bell System 202 series data sets. For a discussion of Bell System data set compatibility, please refer to Sec. 2.1.

Operation

When a terminal is attached to or has a built-in acoustic coupler and the operator wishes to send data to a computer, he or she merely dials the computers' telephone access number and upon establishing the proper connection by hearing a high-pitched tone, places the telephone headset into

Fig. 2.1. Varying Coupler Connections
Left: Terminal with built-in coupler. Right: Terminal connected to coupler.

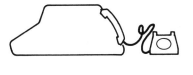

Table 2.1.   Acoustic Coupler Modem Compatability

Coupler frequency	Transmission speed	Bell System Modem Compatability
Transmit		
1,070 and 1,270 Hz (originate mode)	0–450 bps	103 and 113 type modems
2,025 and 2,225 Hz (answer mode)		(data sets)
Receive		
2,025 and 2,225 Hz (originate mode)		
1,070 and 1,270 (answer mode)		

the coupler. Although terminal usage varies by their numerous applications, the prevalent utilization of acoustic couplers is in obtaining access to time-sharing networks. In a time-sharing network, a group of dial-in computer telephone access numbers may be interfaced to a rotary which enables users to dial the low telephone number of the group and automatically "step" or bypass currently busy numbers. Each telephone line is then connected to a modem on a permanent basis, and the modem in turn is connected to a computer port or channel. An automatic answering device in each modem automatically answers the incoming call and in effect establishes a connection from the user who dialed the number to the computer port, as shown in Fig. 2.2.

In contrast with modems that are permanently connected to telephone lines, when not in the acoustic coupler the telephone can be used for conventional voice communications. To obtain the use of a line for voice communications when that line is connected to modems, a device known as a voice adapter must be installed.

Fig. 2.2. Network Access in a Time-sharing Environment
After dialing the computer access number the terminal user places the telephone headset into the cradle of the acoustic coupler.

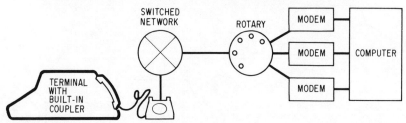

A disadvantage associated with the use of acoustic couplers is a reduction of transmission rates when compared to rates which can be obtained by using modems. Due to the properties of carbon microphones in telephone headsets, the frequency band that can be passed is not as wide as the band modems can pass. Although typical data rates of acoustic couplers vary between 110 and 300 bps, some units manufactured permit transmission at 450, 600, and 1,200 bps. For usage with slow-speed terminals, the acoustic coupler can be viewed as a low-cost alternative to a modem while increasing user transmission location flexibility.

Problems in Usage

A possible cause of errors in the transmission of data can occur from ambient noise leaking into the acoustic coupler. If the coupler is separate from the terminal, one should try to move it as far away from that device as possible to reduce noise levels. Similarly, if the terminal is not in use, one should remove the telephone from the coupler since the continuous placement of the headset in that device can cause crystallization of the speaker and receiver elements of the telephone to occur which will act to reduce the level of signal strength. Another item which may warrant user attention is the placement of a piece of cotton inside the earpiece behind the receiver of the telephone. Although the placement of cotton at this location is normally done by most telephone companies, this should be checked, since the cotton keeps speaker and receiver noise from interfering with each other and acts to prevent transmitted data interfering with received data.

An easily resolved problem is the placement of the telephone handset into the coupler. On many occasions users have hastily placed the handset only partially into the coupler, and this will act to reduce the level of signal strength necessary for error-free transmission.

2.2. Modems

Today, despite the introduction of a number of all-digital transmission facilities by several communications carriers, the analog telephone system remains the primary facility utilized for data communications. Since terminals and computers produce digital pulses, whereas telephone circuits are designed to transmit analog signals which fall within the audio spectrum used in human speech, a device to interface the digital data pulses of terminals and computers with the analog tones carried on telephone circuits becomes necessary when one wishes to transmit data over such circuits. Such a device is called a modem, which derives its meaning from a contraction of the two main functions of such a unit—modulation and demodulation. Although modem is the term most frequently used for such a device that performs modulation and demodulation, data set is another common term whose use is synonymous in meaning.

In its most basic form a modem consists of a power supply, a transmitter, and a receiver. The power supply provides the voltage necessary to operate the modem's circuitry. In the transmitter, a modulator, amplifier, and filtering, waveshaping, and signal level control circuitry converts digital direct current pulses, originated by a computer or terminal, into an analog, wave-shaped signal which can be transmitted over a telephone line. The receiver contains a demodulator and associated circuitry which reverse the process by converting the analog telephone signal back into a series of digital pulses that is acceptable to the computer or terminal device. This signal conversion is illustrated in Fig. 2.3.

Mode of Transmission

If the transmitter or the receiver of the modem is such that the modem can send or receive data in one direction only, the modem will function as a simplex modem. If the operations of the transmitter and the receiver are combined so that the modem may transmit and receive data alternately, the modem will function as a half-duplex modem. In the half-duplex mode of operation, the transmitter must be turned off at one location, and the transmitter of the modem at the other end of the line must be turned on before each change in transmission direction. The time interval required for this operation is referred to as turnaround time. If the transmitter and receiver operate simultaneously, the modem will function as a full-duplex

Fig. 2.3. Signal Conversion Performed by Modems

A modem converts a digital signal to an analog tone (modulation) and reconverts the analog tone (demodulation) into its original digital signal.

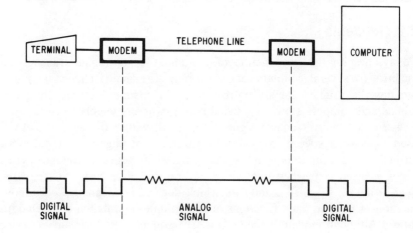

modem. This simultaneous transmission in both directions can be accomplished either by splitting the telephone line's bandwidth into two channels on a 2-wire circuit or by the utilization of two 2-wire circuits, such as obtained on a 4-wire leased line.

Transmission Technique

Modems are designed for asynchronous or synchronous data transmission. Asynchronous transmission is also referred to as start-stop transmission and is usually employed by unbuffered terminals where the time between character transmission occurs randomly. In asynchronous transmission, the character being transmitted is initialized by the character's start bit as a mark-to-space transition on the line and terminated by the character's stop bit which is converted to a "space/marking" signal on the line. The digital pulses between the start and stop bits are the encoded bits which determine the type of character which was transmitted. Between the stop bit of one character and the start bit of the next character, the asynchronous modem places the line in the "marking" condition. Upon receipt of the start bit of the next character the line is switched to a mark-to-space transition, and the modem at the other end of the line starts to sample the data. The marking and spacing conditions are audio tones produced by the modulator of the modem to denote the binary data levels. These tones are produced at predefined frequencies, and their transition between the two states as each bit of the character is transmitted defines the character. Asynchronous transmission is usually employed with low-speed, teletype-compatible terminals at data rates up to 1,800 bps.

Synchronous transmission permits more efficient line utilization since the bits of one character are immediately followed by the bits of the next character, with no start and stop bits required to delimit individual characters. In synchronous transmission, groups of characters are formed into data blocks, with the length of the block varying from a few characters to a thousand or more. Often, the block length is a function of the terminal's physical characteristics or its buffer size. As an example, for the transmission of data that represents punched card images, it may be convenient to transmit 80 characters of one card as a block, as there are that many characters if one constructed the card image from an 80-column card deck. If punched cards are being read by a computer for transmission, and data is such that every two cards contain information about one employee, the block size could be increased to 160 characters. In synchronous transmission, the individual characters within each block are identified based upon a transmitted timing signal which is usually provided by the modem and which places each character into a unique time period. This timing or clock signal is transmitted simultaneously with the data characters, as shown in Fig. 2.4.

Fig. 2.4. Synchronous Timing Signals

The timing signal is used to place each character into a unique time period.

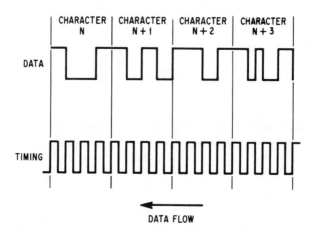

DATA FLOW

Modem Classification

Modems can be classified into many categories to include the mode of transmission and transmission technique as well as by the application features they contain and the type of lines they are built to service. Generally, modems can be classified into four line-servicing groups: subvoice or narrowband lines, voice-grade lines, wideband lines, and dedicated lines. Subvoice-band modems require only a portion of the voice-grade channel's available bandwidth and are commonly used with equipment operating at speeds up to 300 bps. On narrowband facilities, modems can operate in the full-duplex mode by using one-half of the available bandwidth for transmission in each direction and use an asynchronous transmission technique.

Modems designed to operate on voice-grade facilities may be asynchronous or synchronous, half-duplex or full-duplex. Asynchronous transmission is normally employed at speeds up to and including 1,800 bps. Although a leased, 4-wire line will permit full-duplex transmission at high speeds, transmission via the switched telephone network normally occurs in the full-duplex mode at data rates up to 1,200 bps.

Voice-grade modems currently transfer data at rates up to 9,600 bps, usually requiring leased facilities for transmission at speeds in excess of 7,200 bps. Wideband modems, which are also referred to as group-band modems since a wideband circuit is a grouping of lower speed lines, permit users to transmit synchronous data at speeds in excess of 9,600 bps. Although wideband modems are primarily used for computer-to-computer transmission applications, they are also used to service multiplexers which combine the transmission of many low- or medium-speed terminals to produce a composite higher transmission speed. The use of group-band modems and multiplexers is explained later in this book. Dedicated or limited distance modems, which are also known by such names as shorthaul modems and modem bypass units, operate on dedicated solid conductor twisted pair or coaxial cables, permitting data transmission at distances ranging up to 15 to 20 miles, depending upon the modem's operating speed and the resistance of the conductor.

Limited Distance Modems

Modems in this category can operate at speeds ranging up to approximately 1.5 million bps and are particularly well suited for in-plant usage where users desire to install their own communications lines between terminals and a computer located in the same facility or complex. Also, in comparison with voice-band and wideband modems, these modems are relatively inexpensive since they are designed to operate only for limited distances. In addition, by using this type of modem and stringing their own in-plant lines, users can eliminate a monthly telephone charge that would occur if the telephone company furnished the facilities. Limited distance modems are explained in greater detail in Sec. 2.5. In Table 2.2, the common application features of modems are denoted by the types of lines they can be connected to.

Line-type Operations

Most modems with a rated transmission speed of up to 4,800 bps and some modems which transmit data at 7,200 bps can operate over the switched, dial-up telephone network. Since a circuit obtained from a dial-up telephone connection is a 2-wire line, when this line is used to carry traffic in both directions, alternately, the line and the modem are said to operate in the half-duplex mode. In this mode, traffic can only flow in one direction at a time, and the line must be turned around to reverse the direction of the flow of traffic. Such turnaround time varies by device and can become a considerable overhead factor if short bursts of data are transmitted, with each burst requiring a short acknowledgment. To visualize some of the overhead problems associated with line turnaround, a short examination of an error control procedure for synchronous transmission follows.

A common error control procedure used in synchronous transmission is obtained by the use of an acknowledgment-negative acknowledgment (ACK-NAK) sequence, commonly referred to as PAR (positive acknowledgment retransmit) protocol. When this type of sequence is used, the terminal or computer transmits a block of data to the receiving station. Appended to the end of the block is a block check character which is computed based upon a predefined algorithm. At the receiving device, the block of data is examined, and a new block check character is developed using the same algorithm which is then compared to the transmitted block

Table 2.2. Common Modem Features

Features	Line type					
			Voice-grade			
	Subvoice (up to 300 bps)	Low, up to 1,800 bps	Medium, 2,000– 4,800 bps	High, 7,200– 9,600 bps	Wideband (19,200 bps and up)	Limited distance (up to 1.5 Mbps)
Asynchronous	✓	✓				✓
Synchronous	✓		✓✓✓	✓	✓	✓
Switched network	✓✓	✓✓✓	✓✓✓			
Leased only					✓	
Half duplex	✓✓	✓✓	✓✓✓	✓✓✓	✓	✓
Full duplex			✓✓✓	✓		✓✓
Fast turnaround for dial-up use			✓			
Reverse/secondary channel	✓	✓				
Manual equilization			✓✓✓	✓✓✓		✓
Automatic equilization	✓	✓	✓✓✓	✓✓✓		
Multiport capability			✓✓	✓✓		✓
Voice/data						✓✓

check character. If both block check characters are equal, the receiving device sends an ACK signal. If the block check characters do not match, then an error in transmission has occurred, and the receiving device transmits a NAK to signal the device which transmitted the block. This informs the transmitting device that the block should be retransmitted. This procedure is also referred to as automatic request for repeat (ARQ) and requires that the line upon which transmission occurs be turned around twice for each block. Returning to our 80-character punched card image block, transmitting this data as a 960-bit block with control characters appended, at 9,600 bps, would take 100 ms,* whereas if the modem turnaround time, 150 ms, 300 ms would be necessary to turn the line around. Although recently developed modem features have reduced modem turnaround time, this problem can be avoided or greatly eliminated by using a modem with a reverse channel or by establishing full-duplex transmission over a leased 4-wire circuit, depending upon the type of protocol employed for transmission.

Reverse and Secondary Channels

To eliminate turnaround time when transmission is over the 2-wire switched network or to relieve the primary channel of the burden of carrying acknowledgment signals on 4-wire dedicated lines, modem manufacturers have developed a reverse channel which is used to provide a path for the acknowledgment of transmitted data at a slower speed than the primary channel. This reverse channel can be used to provide a simultaneous transmission path for the acknowledgment of data blocks transmitted over the higher speed primary channel at up to 150 bps.

A secondary channel is similar to a reverse channel. However, it can be used in a variety of applications which includes providing a path for a high-speed terminal and a low-speed terminal. When a secondary channel is used as a reverse channel, it is held at one state until an error is detected in the high-speed data transmission and is then shifted to the other state as a signal for retransmission. Another application where a secondary channel can be utilized is when a location contains a high-speed, synchronous terminal and a slow-speed, asynchronous terminal, such as a Teletype. If both devices are required to communicate with a similar distant location, one way to alleviate dual line requirements as well as the cost of extra modems to service both devices is by using a pair of modems that have secondary channel capacity, as shown in Fig. 2.5. Although a reverse channel is usable on both 2-wire and 4-wire telephone lines, the secondary channel technique is usable only on a 4-wire circuit. A secondary channel modem derives two channels from the same line, a wide one to carry synchronous data at speeds of 2,000, 2,400, 3,600, or 4,800 bps and a narrow channel to carry

---

* ms = millisecond

Fig. 2.5. Secondary Channel Operation

Two terminals can communicate with a distant location by sharing a common line through the use of a modem with a secondary channel.

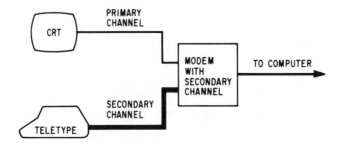

asynchronous teletype-like data. Some modems with the secondary channel option can actually provide two slow-speed channels as well as one high-speed channel, with the two slow-speed channels being capable of transmitting asynchronous data up to a composite speed of 150 bps.

Equalization

Due to the inconsistencies inherent in a transmission medium that was designed for voice rather than data transmission, modem manufacturers build equalizers into a modem to compensate for those inconsistencies produced by the telephone circuit, amplifiers, switches, and relays, as well as other equipment that data may be transmitted across in establishing a data link between two or more points. An equalizer is basically an inverse filter which is used to correct amplitude and delay distortion, which if uncorrected could lead to intersymbol interference during transmission. A well-designed equalizer matches line conditions by maintaining certain of the modem's electrical parameters at the widest range of marginal limits in order to take advantage of the data rate capability of the line while eliminating intersymbol interference. The design of the equalizer is critical, since if the modem operates too near or outside these marginal limits, the transmission error rate will increase. There are three basic methods for achieving equalization. The first method, the utilization of fixed equalizers, is typically accomplished by using manually adjustable high-Q filter sections. Modems with transversal filters use a tapped delay line with manually adjustable variable tap gains, while automatic equalization is usually accomplished by a digital transversal filter with automatic tap gain adjustments. The faster the modem's speed, the greater the need for equalization and the more complex the equalizer. Most modems with rated speeds up to 4,800 bps incorporate nonadjustable, fixed equalizers which have been designed to match the average line conditions that have been found to occur on the dial-up network. Thus, most modems with fixed or nonadjustable equalizers are designed for a normal, randomly routed call between two locations over the dial-up network. If the modem is equipped with a signal-quality light which indicates an error rate that is unacceptable, or if the operator encounters difficulty with the connection, the problem can be alleviated by simply disconnecting the call and dialing a new call, which should reroute the connection through different points on the dial-up network.

Manually adjustable equalization is employed on some 4,800-bps modems used for transmission over leased lines, with the parameters being tuned or preset at installation time, and reequalization usually not required unless the lines are reconfigured. One modem manufacturer uses an 8-level (4-phase, 2-amplitude) modulation technique and has eight equalizer controls on the front panel of the modem for transmission and eight additional controls for reception. Using this type of modem, equalization may be performed from a single end of a point-to-point network without assistance from the opposite end. Primarily designed to operate over unconditioned leased telephone lines, manually equalized modems allow the user to eliminate the monthly expense associated with line conditioning.

Automatic equalization is used on some 4,800-bps modems designed for operation over the switched telephone network and all 7,200- and 9,600-bps modems which are primarily designed to operate over dedicated lines but which can operate over the switched network in a fallback operational mode. With automatic equalization, a certain initialization time is required to adapt the modem to existing line conditions. This initialization time becomes important during and after line outages, since long initial equalization times can extend otherwise short dropouts unnecessarily. Recent modem developments have shortened the initial equalization time to between 25 and 50 ms, whereas only a few years ago a much longer time was commonly required. After the initial equalization, the modem continuously monitors and compensates for changing line conditions by an adaptive process. This process allows the equalizer to "track" the frequently occurring line variations that occur during data transmission without interrupting the traffic flow. On one 9,600-bps modem, this adaptive process occurs 2,400 times a second, permitting the recognition of variations as they occur.

Synchronization

For synchronous communications, generally in speeds exceeding 1,800 bps, the start-stop bits characteristic of asynchronous communications can be eliminated. Bit synchronization is necessary so that the receiving modem samples the link at the exact moment that a bit occurs. The receiver clock is supplied by the modem in phase coherence with the incoming data bit stream, or more simply stated, tuned to the exact speed of the transmitting clock. The transmitting clock can be supplied by either the modem (internal) or the terminal (external).

The transmission of synchronous data is generally under the control of a master clock which is the fastest clock in the system. Any slower data clock rates required are derived from the master clock by digital division logic, and those clocks are referred to as slave clocks. For instance, a master clock oscillating at a frequency of 96 Hz could be used to derive 9.6-kbps ($\frac{1}{10}$), 4.8-kbps ($\frac{1}{20}$), and 2.4-kbps ($\frac{1}{40}$) clock speeds.

Multiport Capability

Modems with a multiport capability offer a function similar to that provided by a multiplexer. In fact, multiport modems contain a limited function time division multiplexer (TDM) which provides the user with the capability of transmitting more than one synchronous data stream over a single transmission line, as shown in Fig. 2.6.

In contrast with typical multiplexers, the limited function multiplexer used in a multiport modem combines only a few high-speed synchronous data streams, whereas multiplexers can normally concentrate a mixture of asynchronous and synchronous, high- and low-speed data streams. A further description, as well as application examples, will be found in Sec. 2.3.

Multiple Speed Selection Capability

For data communication systems which require the full-time service of dedicated lines but need to access the switched network if the dedicated line should fail or degrade to the point where it cannot be used, dial backup capability for the modems used is necessary. Since transmission over dedicated lines usually occurs at a higher speed than one can obtain

Fig. 2.6. Multiport Modem

Containing a limited function time division multiplexer, a multiport modem combines the input of a few synchronous input data streams for transmission.

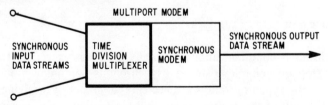

over the switched network, one method of facilitating dial backup is through switching down the speed of the modem. Thus, a multiple speed modem which is designed to operate at 9,600 bps over dedicated lines may be switched down to 7,200 or 4,800 bps for operation over the dial-up network until the dedicated lines are restored.

Voice/Data Capability

Many modems can now be obtained with a voice/data option which permits a specially designed telephone set commonly called a voice adapter to be used to provide the user with a voice communication capability over the same line which is used for data transmission. Depending upon the modem, this voice capability can be either alternate voice/data or simultaneous voice/data. Thus, the user may communicate with a distant location at the same time data transmission is occurring, or the user may transmit data during certain times of the day and use the line for voice communications at other times. Voice/data capability can also be used to minimize normal telephone charges when data transmission sequences require voice coordination. Voice adapters are examined in more detail in Chapter 6, Sec. 6.4.

Bell System Compatibility

Many modem manufacturers describe their equipment in terms of compatibility or equivalency with modems manufactured by Western Electric for the Bell System. Table 2.3 contains a reference list of Bell System data sets by model numbers, their maximum transmission speeds, transmission technique, transmission mode, compatibility with other Bell System modems, transmitter receiver usage, line usage, and the principal application of the modem. Numerous modem manufacturers produce devices compatible with Bell System data sets that operate at speeds up to 2,400 bps, and a few vendors manufacture equipment compatible with Bell System data sets which transmit at speeds up to 4,800 bps.

Bell System 103/113 Series Modems

Although they operate in the lowest speed category, the terminology used to describe the functions of Bell System 103 and 113 series compatible modems can lead to confusion. This confusion is a result of the terminology used in the designation of ORIGINATE and ANSWER ONLY operations of the modems. In this case, the terminology should not be confused with simplex operation, since both the ORIGINATE ONLY and ANSWER ONLY modems each have and utilize both a transmitter and receiver. This designation is used to describe the reversing of the transmit and receive

Table 2.3.   Bell System Data Set Compatibility Guide

Bell System model number	Maximum speed (bps)	Transmission technique	Transmission mode	Compatible with	Transmitter (T); receiver (R)	Line use	Principal application
103A	300	Asynchronous	Half-duplex or full-duplex on 2-wire facilities	103 and 113 modems	T-R	Switched; leased	Low-speed teletype-compatible terminals
103E	300	Asynchronous	Half-duplex or full-duplex on 2-wire	103 and 113 modems	T-R	Switched; leased	Provides a multiple arrangement cabinet mounting for up to 40 modems; used for low-speed computer ports that provide teletype compatible terminal access
103F	300	Asynchronous	Half-duplex or full-duplex on 2-wire	103F	T-R	Leased	Low-speed teletype-compatible terminals
103J	300	Asynchronous	Full-duplex on 2-wire	103 and 113	T-R	Switched	Low-speed teletype-compatible terminals
108D	300	Asynchronous	Half-duplex on 2-wire; full-duplex on 4-wire	108D, E	T-R	Leased	Low-speed teletype-compatible terminals
108E	300	Asynchronous	Half-duplex, 2-wire; full-duplex, 4-wire	108D, E	T-R	Leased	Low-speed teletype-compatible terminals
109B, C, D, E, F, G, H	300	Asynchronous	Half-duplex, 2-wire; full-duplex, 2-wire	any 109 HDX set	T-R	Leased	Private line telegraph systems

	Speed	Mode	Duplex	Compatible modems	T-R	Line	Application
113A	300	Asynchronous	Half-duplex or full-duplex on 2-wire	103 and 113 type modems	T-R Originate call only	Switched	Low-speed teletype-compatible devices
113B	300	Asynchronous	Half-duplex or full-duplex on 2-wire	103 and 113 type modems	T-R Answer call only	Switched	Low-speed teletype-compatible devices
113C	300	Asynchronous	Full-duplex on 2-wire	103 and 113B, 113D	T-R Originate call only	Switched	Low-speed teletype-compatible devices
113D	300	Asynchronous	Full-duplex on 2-wire	103 and 113A	T-R	Switched	Low-speed teletype-compatible devices
201A	2,000	Synchronous	Half-duplex, 2-wire; full-duplex, 4-wire	201A modems	T-R	Switched; leased	Medium-speed synchronous devices
201B	2,400	Synchronous	Half-duplex, 2-wire; full-duplex, 4-wire	201B, 201C	T-R	Leased	Medium-speed devices connected on multipoint circuits
201C	2,400	Synchronous	Half-duplex, 2-wire; full-duplex, 4-wire	201B, 201C, 209	T-R	Switched; leased	Medium-speed synchronous devices
202B	1,800	Asynchronous	Half-duplex, 2-wire; full-duplex, 4-wire	202	T-R	Switched	Medium-speed asynchronous devices
202C	1,200 on switched network, 1,800 on leased line	Asynchronous	Half-duplex, 2-wire; full-duplex, 4-wire	202A, 202C, 202D, 202E, 202R	T-R	Switched; leased	Medium-speed asynchronous devices

Table 2.3. Bell System Data Set Compatibility Guide (Continued)

Bell System model number	Maximum speed (bps)	Transmission technique	Transmission mode	Compatible with	Transmitter (T); receiver (R)	Line use	Principal application
202D	1,200 on switched network, 1,800 on leased line	Asynchronous	Half-duplex, 2-wire; full-duplex, 4-wire	202A, 202C, 202D, 202E, 202R	T-R	Switched; leased	Medium-speed asynchronous devices connected to multipoint lines
202E	1,200 on switched network, 1,800 on leased line	Asynchronous	Half-duplex, 2-wire	202A, 202C, 202D, 202R	T	Switched; leased	Medium-speed asynchronous transmitting devices
202R	1,200 on switched network, 1,800 on leased line	Asynchronous	Half-duplex, 2-wire; full-duplex, 4-wire	202A, 202C, 202D, 202E, 202R, 202S	T-R	Switched; leased	Medium-speed asynchronous devices connected to multipoint lines
202S	1,200	Asynchronous	Half-duplex, 2-wire	202C, 202E, 202D, 202R	T-R	Switched	Medium-speed asynchronous devices
202T	1,800	Asynchronous	Half-duplex, 2-wire; full-duplex, 4-wire	202D, R, T,	T-R	Leased	Medium-speed asynchronous devices
203A,B,C	1,800–10,800	Synchronous	Half-duplex, 2-wire; full-duplex, 4-wire	203 modems	203A T-R 203B T 203C R	Switched; leased	Medium-speed synchronous devices

					T-R		
208A	4,800	Synchronous	Half-duplex, 2-wire; full-duplex, 4-wire	208A 209	T-R	Leased	Medium-speed synchronous devices
208B	4,800	Synchronous	Half-duplex, 2-wire	208B	T-R	Switched	Medium-speed synchronous devices
209A	9,600	Synchronous	Full-duplex, 4-wire	209A	T-R	Leased	Medium-speed synchronous devices
212A	300, 1,200	300 asynchronous, 1,200 asynchronous or synchronous	Full-duplex	Most bell 100 series, 212A	T-R	Switched	Low-speed teletype-compatible devices
303B,C,D	B–19,200 C–50,000 D–230,400	Synchronous	Half-duplex, 4-wire; full-duplex, 4-wire	B with B C with C D with D	T-R	Leased; wideband	High-speed asynchronous (303B) or synchronous (303B,C,D,) devices

functions between two channels at opposite ends of the telephone line. This reversal of the transmit and receive functions is accomplished within the 3,000-Hz bandwidth of the telephone circuit by assigning the two channels used to different frequencies, providing filtering circuitry in the modems to separate these channels into discrete bands, and establishing a design criteria so that a modem that transmits in one band and receives in a second band is designated as an originate modem or an answer modem, depending upon the bands used.

Bell System 103 and 113 series modems are designed so that one channel is assigned to the 1,070- to 1,270-Hz frequency band while the second channel is assigned to the 2,025- to 2,225-Hz frequency band. Modems that transmit in the 1,070- to 1,270-Hz band but receive in the 2,025- to 2,225-Hz band are designated as originate modems, while a modem which transmits in the 2,025- to 2,225-Hz band but receives in the 1,070- to 1,270-Hz band is designated as an answer modem. When using such modems, their correct pairing is important, since two originate modems cannot communicate with each other. Bell System 113A modems are originate only devices that should normally be used when calls are to be placed in one direction. This type of modem is mainly used to enable teletype-compatible terminals to communicate with time-sharing systems where such terminals only originate calls. Bell System 113B modems are answer only and are primarily used at computer sites where users dial in to establish communications. Since these modems are designed to transmit and receive on a single set of frequencies, their circuitry requirements are less than other modems and their costs are thus more economical. Table 2.4 shows the frequency assignment for modems in this series.

Modems in the 103 series, which includes the 103A, E, F, G, and J modems, can transmit and receive in either the low or the high band. This ability to switch modes is denoted as "originate and answer," in comparison to the Bell 113A which operates only in the originate mode and the Bell 113B which operates only in the answer mode.

Bell System 201 Series Modems

The Bell 201 series modems are designed for synchronous bit serial transmission at data rates of 2,000 and 2,400 bps. The 201A modem is an obsolete device which is being phased out of use. The 201A is designed to operate over the switched network at 2,000 bps. The 201B modem is designed for 2,400-bps transmission over leased lines. The 201C modem is designed to operate at 2,400 bps over the switched network or leased lines, and its introduction made both the 201A and 201B obsolete since it provides increased data transfer rates over the 201A and can operate on either switched or leased lines, whereas the prior models did not have this flexibility.

Table 2.4.   Frequency Assignment of Bell System
103/113 Modems

	Originating end	Answering end
Transmit	1070-Hz space	2025-Hz space
	1270-Hz mark	2225-Hz mark
Receive	2025-Hz space	1070-Hz space
	2225-Hz mark	1270-Hz mark

Bell System 202 Series Modems

Bell System 202 series modems are designed for speeds up to 1,200 or 1,800 bps. The 202C modem can operate on either the switched network or on leased lines, in the half-duplex mode on the former and the full-duplex mode on the latter. The 202C modem can operate half-duplex or full-duplex on leased lines. This series of modems uses frequency-shift keyed (FSK) modulation, and the frequency assignments are such that a mark is at 1,200 Hz and a space at 2,200 Hz. When either modem is used for transmission over a leased 4-wire circuit in the full-duplex mode, modem control is identical to the 103 series modem in that both transmitters can be strapped on continuously which alleviates the necessity of line turnarounds.

Since the 202 series modems do not have separate bands, on switched network utilization half-duplex operation is required. This means that both transmitters (one on each modem) must be alternately turned on and off to provide two-way communications.

The Bell 202 series modems have a 5-bps reverse channel for switched network use. Due to the slowness of this reverse channel, its use is limited to status and control function transmission. Status information such as "ready to receive data" or "device out of paper" can be transmitted on this channel. Due to the slow transmission rate, error detection of received messages and an associated NAK and request for retransmission is normally accomplished by the regular turnaround which can be completed at almost the same rate one obtains in using the reverse channel for that purpose. Non-Bell 202-equivalent modems produced by many manufacturers provide reverse channels of 75 to 150 bps which can be utilized to enhance overall system performance. Reverse keyboard-entered data as well as error detection information can be practically transmitted over such a channel.

While a data rate of up to 1,800 bps can be obtained with the 202D modem, transmission at this speed requires that the leased line be conditioned for transmission by the telephone company. The 202S and 202T modems are recent additions to the 202 series and are designed for transmission at 1,200 and 1,800 bps over the switched network and leased lines, respectively. At speeds in excess of 1,400 bps, the 202T requires line conditioning when interfaced to either 2- or 4-wire circuits, whereas for a 2-wire circuit, conditioning is required at speeds in excess of 1,200 bps when an optional reverse channel is used.

Bell System 203 Series Modems

This series of obsolete modems permits transmission of data at up to 3,600 bps on the switched network and up to 10,800 bps when leased lines are used. This series of modems was obsoleted by the introduction of the 208 and 209 Bell modems.

Bell System 208 Series Modems

The Bell System 208 Series modems are of recent design and use a quadrature amplitude modulation technique. The 208A modem is designed for either half-duplex or full-duplex operation at 4,800 bps over leased lines. The 208B modem is designed for half-duplex operation at 4,800 bps on the switched network.

Bell System 209 Series Modem

Currently, the 209A modem is the only product offered in this series. This modem is designed for single-channel transmission at 9,600 bps over leased lines or for selective data rates, depending upon the number of channels of data in increments of 2,400 bps one wishes to transmit. The 209A modem has a built-in synchronous multiplexer which will combine up to four data rate combinations for transmission at 9,600 bps. The multiplexer combinations are shown in Table 2.5. The use of a multiplexer incorporated into a modem is discussed more thoroughly in Sec. 2.3.

Bell System 212A Modem

This dual-speed modem permits either asynchronous or synchronous transmission over the switched network. The 212A contains a 103-type modem for asynchronous transmission at speeds up to 300 bps. FSK modulation is

Table 2.5. Bell 209A Multiplexer Combinations

2,400–2,400–2,400–2,400 bps
4,800–2,400–2,400 bps
4,800–4,800 bps
7,200–2,400 bps
9,600 bps

used for 300-bps transmission, and Dibit-phased shift keyed modulation is used for 1,200-bps transmission which permits the modem to operate either asynchronously or synchronously at this speed. The key advantage in the use of this modem is that it permits the reception of transmission from terminals of two different transmission speeds. Before the operator initiates a call, he or she selects the operating speed at the originating set. When the call is made, the answering 212A modem automatically switches to that operating speed. During data transmission, both modems remain in the same speed mode until the call is terminated, when the answering 212A can be set to the other speed by a new call. The dual-speed 212A permits both terminals connected to Bell System 100 series data sets operating at up to 300 bps or terminals connected to other 212A modems operating at 1,200 bps to share the use of one modem at a computer site and thus can reduce central computer site equipment requirements.

Modem Handshaking

Modem handshaking is the exchange of control signals necessary to establish a connection between two data sets. These signals are required to set up and terminate calls, and the type of signaling used is predetermined according to the Electronics Industry Association (EIA) standard RS-232C. The control signals used by the 103 and 201 series modems are illustrated in Table 2.6A, while the handshake sequence is illustrated in Table 2.6B.

The handshaking routine commences when an operator at a remote terminal dials the telephone number of the computer. At the computer site, a ring indicator (RI) signal at the answering modem is set and passed to the computer. The computer then sends a data terminal ready (DTR)

Table 2.6A.   Modem Handshaking Signals and Their Function

Control signal	Function
Transmit data	Serial data sent from device to modem
Receive data	Serial data received by device
Request to send	Set by device when user program wishes to transmit
Clear to send	Set by modem when transmission may commence
Data set ready	Set by modem when it is powered on and ready to transfer data; set in response to data terminal ready
Carrier detect	Set by modem when signal present
Data terminal ready	Set by device to enable modem to answer an incoming call on a switched line; reset by adapter disconnect call
Ring indicator	Set by modem when telephone rings

Table 2.6B.   Handshake Sequence

Remote terminal	Line	Computer
Operator raises		← Data terminal ready
handset and dials	Connect call	↗ Ring indicator
		↗ Data set ready
Tone ┌Data carrier detect ←	2,225 Hz ──	Request to send
heard └→(couple)	1,270 Hz	Data carrier detect ┐
Delay		
Data set ready ←		Transmit data ──┘
Clear to send ←		
┌Receive data ←		
└Transmit data ────────────		→ Receive data

signal to its modem, which then transmits a tone signal to the modem connected to the terminal. Upon hearing this tone, the terminal operator presses the data pushbutton on the modem. Upon depression of the data button, the originating modem sends a data set ready (DSR) signal to the terminal, and the answering modem sends the same signal to the computer. At this point in time both modems are placed in the data mode of operation. In a time-sharing environment the computer normally transmits a request for identification to the terminal. To do this the computer sets request to send (RTS) which informs the terminal's modem that it wishes to transmit data. The terminal's modem will respond with the clear to send (CTS) signal and will transmit a carrier signal. The computer's modem detects the clear to send and carrier on signals and begins its data transmission to the terminal. When the computer completes its transmission it drops the RTS, and the terminal's modem then terminates its carrier signal. Depending upon the type of circuit transmission occurs over, some of these signals may not be required. For example, on a switched 2-wire telephone line, the RTS signal determines whether a terminal is to send or receive data, whereas on a leased 4-wire circuit RTS can be permanently raised. For further information the reader should refer to specific vendor literature or appropriate Bell System technical reference publications.

Applying Modems to Communications Requirements

For a point-to-point data communications system, two modems, one at each end of the line, are necessary, as shown in Fig. 2.7. Depending upon the manufacturer of the modem (Bell System or non-Bell System), and the type of circuit (switched or leased) that the modem is used on, a device known as a data access arrangement (DAA) may be required to act as a protective interface between the modem and the telephone circuit. Internal to Bell System modems used for transmission over the switched network is a line coupling unit that performs several functions to include ring detection, dc isolation, and surge protection which protects the transmission line from being disturbed by a modem malfunction. In 1969 the Federal Com-

Fig. 2.7. Modems Used on a Point-to-point Data Communications System

On a point-to-point line, two modems are required to modulate and demodulate the transmission.

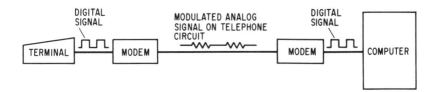

munications Commission (FCC) reached the Carterphone decision which permitted the connection of non-Bell System modems to the switched network. This connection of non-Bell modems was permitted as long as a network-protecting device known as a DAA was connected between the non-Bell modem and the telephone line. A further revision in FCC regulations now permits non-Bell modems to be directly connected to the telephone line without a Bell DAA under the following conditions:

1. The modem is certified for use by a state regulatory commission: in this case the modem is connected to the telephone line via a telephone company provided data jack.
2. The modem manufacturer provides a built-in line-coupling unit in the modem.
3. The modem manufacturer provides an external line-coupling unit.

There are three types of DAA in use today, and their characteristics and use are examined in more detail in Chapter 6, Sec. 6.3. The telephone company leases this device to the user, with the cost dependent upon the type of DAA required and the tariff schedule of the particular telephone company. A number of independent manufacturers now offer these devices for purchase as well as on a rental basis. The utilization of DAA when non-Bell modems are used on the switched network is examined in Sec. 6.3.

Self-testing Features

Many low-speed and most high-speed modems have a series of pushbutton test switches which may be used for local and remote testing of the data set and line facilities.

In the local or analog test mode, the transmitter output of the modem is connected to the receiver input, disconnecting the customer interface from the modem. A built-in word generator is used to produce a stream of bits which are checked for accuracy by a word comparator circuit, and

Fig. 2.8. Local (Analog) Testing

In local testing the transmitter is connected to the receiver, and the bit stream produced by the word generator is checked by the word comparator.

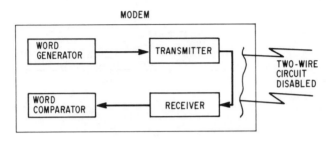

errors are displayed on an error lamp as they occur. The local test is illustrated in Fig. 2.8.

To check the data sets at both ends as well as the transmission medium, a digital loop-back self-test may be employed. To conduct this test, personnel must normally be at each data set to push the appropriate test buttons, although a number of vendors have introduced modems that can be automatically placed into the test mode at the distant end when the central site modem is switched. In the digital loop-back test, the modem at the distant end has its receiver connected to its transmitter, as shown in Fig. 2.9. At the other end, the local modem transmits a test bit stream from its word generator, and this bit stream is looped back from the distant end to the receiver of the central site modem where it is checked by the comparator circuitry. Again, an error lamp indicates abnormal results and indicates that either the modems or the line may be at fault.

The analog loop-back self-test should normally be used to verify the internal operation of the modem, while the digital loop-back test will check both modems and the carrier. While analog and digital tests are the main

Fig. 2.9. Digital Loop-back Self-test

In the digital loop-back test both the modems and the transmission facility are tested.

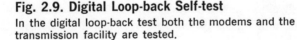

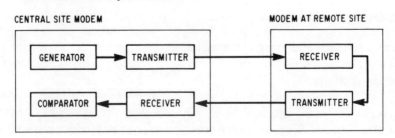

self-tests built into modems, several vendors offer additional diagnostic capabilities that may warrant attention.

2.3. Multiport Modems

The integration of modems and limited-function multiplexers into a device known as a multiport modem offers significant benefits to data communications users who require the multiplexing of only a few channels of data. Until recently, users who desired to multiplex a few high-speed data channels were required to obtain both multiplexers and modems as individual units which were then connected to each other to provide the multiplexer and data transmission requirements of the user. Since multiplexers are normally designed to support both asynchronous and synchronous data channels, the cost of the extra circuitry and the additional equipment capacity was an excess burden for many user applications.

The recognition by users and vendors that a more cost-effective, less wasteful method of multiplexing and transmitting a small number of synchronous channels for particular applications lead to the development of multiport modems. By the combination of the functions of a TDM with the functions of a synchronous modem, substantial economies over past data transmission methods can be achieved for certain applications.

Operation

A multiport modem is basically a high-speed synchronous modem with a built-in TDM that uses the modem's clock for data synchronization, rather than requiring one of its own, as would be necessary when separate modems and multiplexers are combined. In contrast with most traditional TDMs, a multiport modem multiplexes only synchronous data streams, instead of both synchronous and asynchronous data streams. An advantage of the built-in, limited function multiplexer is that it is less complex and expensive, containing only the logic necessary to combine into one data stream information transmitted from as few as two synchronous data channels rather than the minimum capacity of four or eight channels associated with most separate multiplexers. The data channels in a multiport modem are normally comprised of a number of 2,400-bps data streams, with the number of channels available being a function of the channel speed as well as the aggregate throughput of the multiport modem selected by the user.

Selection Criteria

When investigating the potential use of multiport modems for a particular application, the user should determine the speed combinations and the number of selectable channels available, as well as the ability to control the

Fig. 2.10. 9,600 Multiport Modem Schematic Utilization Diagram

Multiport modem with six modes of operation is schematized here to show all possible data rate combinations for networking flexibility.

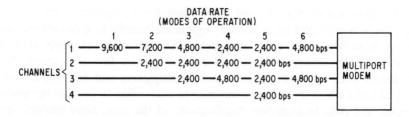

carrier function (mode of operation) independently for each of the channels. One 9,600-bps multiport modem now being marketed can have as many as six different modes of operation; however, only one mode can be functioning at any given time. As illustrated in Fig. 2.10, operating speeds can range in combination from a single channel at 9,600 bps through four 2,400-bps channels.

Application Example

Using the fifth mode of operation shown in Fig. 2.10, with four channels at 2,400 bps, a typical application of a 9,600-bps multiport modem is illustrated in Fig. 2.11. This example shows a pair of four-channel, 9,600-bps multiport modems servicing two interactive synchronous cathode ray tube (CRT) terminals, a synchronous printer operating at up to 300 characters

Fig. 2.11. Multiport Modem Application Example

A pair of 4-channel multiport modems services two CRT, a 300-cps printer, and eight teletypewriter terminals over a single transmission line.

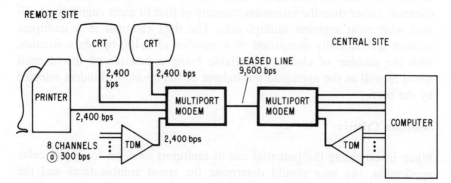

per second, and eight low-speed asynchronous teletypewriter terminals connected by a traditional TDM. The output of the eight-channel TDM is a 2,400-bps synchronous data stream, which is in turn multiplexed by the multiport modem. Here, the multiport modem's multiplexer combines the eight asynchronous multiplexed 300-bps channels with the three synchronous unmultiplexed 2,400-bps channels into a single multiplexed synchronous data stream. At the central site where the computer is located, the multiport modem at that end splits the 9,600-bps stream into four 2,400-bps data streams, one of which is channeled through another eight-channel, traditional TDM, whose eight output data streams in turn are connected to the computer. The eight-channel TDM takes the 2,400-bps synchronous data stream from the multiport modem and demultiplexes it into eight 300-bps asynchronous data streams, which are passed to the appropriate computer ports. The remaining data streams produced by the demultiplexer in the multiport modem are connected to three additional computer ports. As this example demonstrates, the high-speed multiport modem's utilization in conjunction with other communications components permits a wide degree of flexibility in the design of a data communications network. Additional multiport modem and channel combinations available to the user are listed in Table 2.7.

Although most manufacturers of multiport modems produce equipment that appears to be functionally equivalent, the system designer should exercise care in selecting equipment due to the differences that exist between modems but are hard to ascertain from vendor literature.

For modem aggregate throughput above 4,800 bps, the modes of operation available for utilization by the system designer are quite similar

Table 2.7.   Multiport Modem Channel Combinations*

Modem aggregate throughput	Modems available	Channels available	Data rates (bps)
9,600	1	1	9,600
	2	1, 4	7,200/2,400
	3	1, 3, 4	4,800/2,400/2,400
	4	1, 2, 3	2,400/2,400/4,800
	5	1, 2, 3, 4	2,400/2,400/2,400/2,400
	6	1, 3	4,800/4,800
7,200	1	1	7,200
	2	1, 3	4,800/2,400
	3	1, 2, 3	2,400/2,400/2,400
4,800	1	1	4,800
	2	1, 2	2,400/2,400

* The wide degree of flexibility that can be provided by multiport modems in a network configuration is a function of several factors: throughput, available modes and channels, and data rates.

regardless of manufacturer. However, at 4,800 bps, wide variances exist between equipment manufactured by different vendors. While most multi-port modem manufacturers offer two-mode capability (one 4,800-bps channel or two 2,400-bps channels), some manufacturers have a built-in TDM which has the capability of servicing 1,200-bps data streams. When multiport modems are equipped with this type of multiplexer, the number of modes of operation available to the user is increased to five, as shown in Table 2.7. By using multiport modems that permit an independently controlled carrier signal for each channel, data communications users can combine several polled circuits and further reduce leased line charges.

Standard and Optional Features

A wide range of standard and optional data communications features are available for users of multiport modems, including almost all of the features available in regular nonmultiplexing modems, as well as such unique multiport modem features as multiport configuration selection, individual port testing, individual port display, and a data communications equipment (DCE) interface.

The multiport selector feature permits the user to alter the multiport configuration simply by throwing a switch into a new position. This feature can be especially useful for an installation such as the one shown in Fig. 2.12 (top), where daytime operations require the servicing of a large number of time-sharing users, and operations at night (Fig. 2.12, bottom) require the servicing of only two high-speed remote batch terminals. During daytime operations, 16 low-speed asynchronous, 300-bps, time-sharing terminals with a composite speed of 4,800 bps are serviced at this installation by one channel of the multiport modem. One remote batch terminal and a CRT are serviced by two additional channels, each of which operates at 2,400 bps. Because of daytime load requirements, the second batch terminal cannot be operated since the modem's maximum aggregate speed of 9,600 bps has been reached. On the assumption that the installation does not require the servicing of time-sharing users at night, one possible reconfiguration is shown in Fig. 2.12 (bottom). The multiport selector permits both remote batch terminals to be serviced until the start of the next business day by two 4,800-bps channels while everything else in this network is shut down.

Numerous multiport modems contain a built-in test pattern generator and an error detector which permit users of such modems to determine if the device is faulty without the need of an external bit error rate tester. The use of this feature normally permits the individual ports of the modem to be tested.

Another option offered by some multiport modem manufacturers is a data communications equipment (DCE) interface. This option can be used to integrate remotely located terminals into a multiport modem network.

Fig. 2.12. Using Multiport Selector Switches

Day (top) and night (bottom) configurations for networks with multiport modems can be varied according to the requirements of different operations.

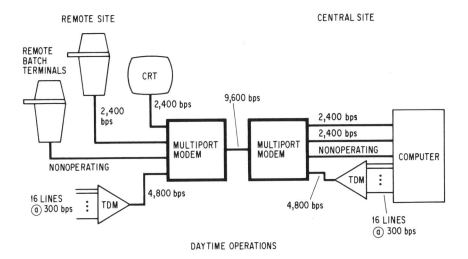

DAYTIME OPERATIONS

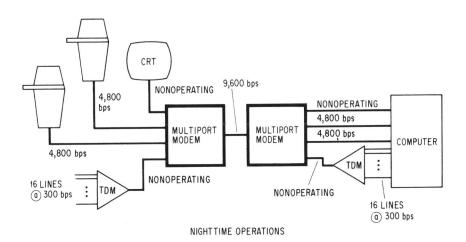

NIGHTTIME OPERATIONS

Whereas the standard data terminal equipment (DTE) interface may require data sources to be colocated and within a 50-ft radius of the multiport modem, the DCE interface permits one or more data sources to be remotely located from the multiport modem. Installation of a multiport modem with a DCE option on one port permits that modem's port to be interfaced with another modem. This low-speed conventional modem can

Fig. 2.13. Multiport Modem Data Communications Equipment Option

Using a data communications equipment (DCE) interface on port 3 of the multiport modem permits a second remote site to share the communications line from the first site to the computer.

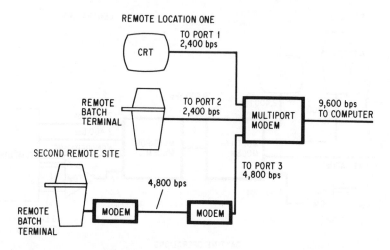

be used to provide a new link between the multiport modem's location and terminals located at different sites. As shown in Fig. 2.13, the installation of a multiport modem with a DCE option on port 3 permits the port on that modem to be interfaced with another modem. This new modem can then be used to provide a new link between the multiport modem at location 1 and an additional remote batch terminal which is located at a second site.

In Table 2.8 the reader will find a list of vendors and their typical multiport modem offerings. Specific addresses for these vendors are located in Chapter 8.

2.4. Multipoint Modems

To alleviate substantial confusion, it should be noted that a multiport modem contains a built-in multiplexer which enables two or more separate data streams to be combined for transmission over a single circuit. In contrast, a multipoint modem is basically a modem designed to achieve fast polling acquisition times on multipoint lines.

Multipoint, or multidrop lines as they are also referred to, usually are installed for applications that require interactive terminal access from a number of geographically dispersed locations into a central computer facility. This type of line may link a number of CRTs used for programming, debugging, and executing time-sharing jobs, or they may be installed to

Table 2.8. Typical Multiport Modem Offerings

Vendor	Speed (kbps)	Ports	Available channel speed combinations
AT&T	9.6	4	[9.6] or [7.2 + 2.4] or [4.8 + 4.8] or [4.8 + 2 × 2.4] or [4 × 2.4]
Codex	9.6	4	[9.6] or [7.2 + 2.4] or [4.8 + 2 × 2.4] or [2 × 2.4 + 4.8] or [4 × 2.4] or [2 × 4.8]
	7.2	3	[7.2] or [4.8 + 2.4] or [3 × 2.4]
	4.8	4	[4.8] or [2 × 2.4]
General Data Communica- tions	9.6	4	[9.6] or [7.2 + 2.4] or [4.8 + 4.8] or [4.8 + 2 × 2.4] or [4 × 2.4]
	7.2	3	[7.2] or [4.8 + 2.4] or [3 × 2.4]
	4.8	2	[4.8] or [2 × 2.4]
Intertel	9.6	4	[9.6] or [4 × 2.4] or [4.8 + 2 × 2.4] or [2 × 4.8] or [7.2 + 2.4]
Paradyne	9.6	4	[9.6] or [7.2 + 2.4] or [4.8 + 4.8] or [4.8 + 2 × 2.4]
	7.2	4	[7.2] or [4.8 + 2.4] or [3 × 2.4]
	4.8	2	[4.8] or [2 × 2.4]
Ralcal-Milgo	9.6	4	[9.6] or [7.2 + 2.4] or [2 × 4.8] or [4 × 2.4]
	7.2	4	[7.2] or [4.8 + 2.4] or [3 × 2.4]
	4.8	2	[4.8] or [2 × 2.4]

provide remote terminal access to a centralized data base for one particular application. An airline reservation system in which dispersed terminals randomly access the computer's data base to determine flight information and seat availability is a representative application that uses multipoint lines. Another example would be an inventory control system where terminals are located at many warehouses and are used to report shippings and arrivals so that company inventories are continuously updated. For either application, the key item of interest is that each terminal only uses a small fraction of the total time available to all terminals connected to the line to complete a transaction, and the terminal is addressable and can recognize messages for which it is a recipient. Although most terminals connected to multipoint circuits contain a buffer, this buffer primarily serves to enhance data throughput and is not a necessity. For example, consider the situation where an operator is entering data on the screen of a CRT through an attached keyboard. If the CRT does not have a buffer, the time it takes to transmit the data depends upon the operator's speed in typing it. During that time communications with all other terminals on the line are suspended. If the terminal has a buffer, the transmission speed from the terminal to the computer can be at a much higher rate than the operator's typing rate. Thus, once the operator has filled the CRT screen with data, the depression of a transmit key will permit the computer to select and receive the data from the terminal at a higher transfer speed and in a shorter time interval. During the time the operator is entering

Fig. 2.14. Typical Multipoint Circuit

On a multipoint circuit many polled terminals share the use of common communications facilities.

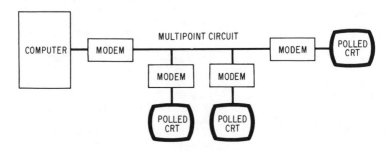

data the computer is free to select other terminals. Therefore, the wait time per terminal on the common line is reduced. Since a slow operator on a multidrop line without buffered terminals could obtain an unjustified proportion of the total transmission time, some multidrop systems incorporating unbuffered terminals have a built-in time out feature. This time out feature permits another operator to gain control of the line if the first operator pauses for a time greater than the time out feature permits. When either type of terminal is used in the previously described working environment, then many terminals can share the same communications circuit on an interleaved basis. The polling and selecting protocol used will make it appear to each terminal operator as if a private connection existed for his or her exclusive use for transmitting and receiving data from the computer. A typical multipoint circuit used to connect four terminals is illustrated in Fig. 2.14.

Factors That Affect Multipoint Circuits

When investigating the applicability of a multipoint circuit, several parameters warrant careful investigation; two such parameters are the response time and the transaction rate of the terminals.

From a broad viewpoint, response time is the time interval from when an operator presses a transmit key at the terminal until the first character of the response appears back at that terminal. This response time consists of the many delay times associated with the components on the circuit, the time required for the message to travel down the circuit to the computer and back to the terminal, as well as the processing time required by the computer.

The transaction rate is a term used to denote the volume of inquiries and responses that must be carried by the circuit during a specific period of time. This rate is normally expressed in terms of a daily average and as a peak for a specific period of the day.

Additional factors that affect the data transfer rates on multipoint circuits include the line protocol used and its efficiency, the transmission rate of the modems, and the turnaround time of the line. While there are many factors that contribute to multipoint line efficiency utilization, the focus of this section will be on multipoint modem characteristics which should be investigated to obtain a more efficient transmission process on such circuits.

Delay Factors

When a terminal connected to a computer via a multipoint circuit is polled, several factors, which by themselves may appear insignificant, accumulate to degrade response time.

In the transmission of a message or poll from the computer to a terminal on the multipoint line, the first delay encountered is caused by the modems internal delay time (D_m). This is the delay that would be seen if the time between the first bit entering the modem and the first modulated tone put on the circuit were measured. For a poll transmitted from the computer to a terminal or a response transmitted from the terminal to the computer, total modem delay time is equal to two times the modem's internal delay time ($2D_m$), since the poll or message is transmitted through two modems. In this case, the internal delay time of the modems is equivalent to the delay one would measure if the modems were placed back to back and the time between the first bit entering the first modem and the first bit demodulated by the second modem were compared. This is shown in Fig. 2.15. Depending upon the type of modem used, this internal delay time can vary from a few milliseconds to 20 ms or more.

The second delay time on a multipoint circuit is a function of the distance between the computer and the terminal it is communicating with. This delay time is called transmission delay and represents the time it takes for the signal to propagate down the line to the receiving location; hence, it is also referred to as propagation delay time (D_p). Although this delay time is insignificant for short transmission distances, coast-to-coast transmission can result in a transmission delay of approximately 30 ms.

When a response to a transmitted poll or message is returned from

Fig. 2.15. Internal Modem Delay Time
Time difference from first bit transmitted (1) to first bit received (2) is denoted as total internal modem delay time ($2D_m$).

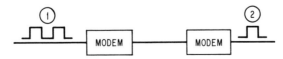

the remote terminal, several additional delay factors are encountered. First, the terminal itself causes a delay, since some time is required for the terminal to recognize the poll and initiate a response. This terminal delay (D_T) is usually a few milliseconds, but can be considerably longer, depending upon the design of the terminal and the software protocol used.

Since every modem on the multipoint line shares the use of this common circuit, only one modem at any point in time may have its carrier on. The carrier of each modem is turned on in response to the connected terminal or computer raising its request to send (RTS) signal, which indicates that a message is to be transmitted. The modem at the opposite end of the transmission path will then require some time interval to recognize this signal and adjust its internal timing. If the modems have automatic and adaptive equalization, additional time is spent adapting the modem to the incoming signal's characteristics. Once these functions are completed, the modem located at the opposite end of the transmission path will raise its clear to send (CTS) signal which is required in response to the RTS signal if a return message is to be transmitted. This delay time is referred to as the request to send/clear to send delay time (RTS/CTS) and is usually denoted as $D_{R/S}$. Since the RTS/CTS delay time occurs twice in responding to a poll, the total RTS/CTS turnaround delay is $2D_{R/C}$. Disregarding terminal, propagation, and processing delays, the total turnaround delay attributable to the modems is M_D, where:

$$M_D = 2(D_{R/C} + D_m)$$

Although the RTS/CTS delay varies by the type of modem used, delays can range from about 5 to 100 ms or more and normally cause most of the line's turnaround delay.

When multipoint networks were initially implemented, modem operating rates were at speeds of 2,400 bps or lower. These modems were normally equalized and were adjusted and set at installation time. For this category of modems, the RTS/CTS delay ranges from about 7 to 15 ms, depending upon manufacturer. Due to the advancement in modem transmission rates as well as new applications which required higher traffic rates and shorter response times, multipoint networks with 4,800-bps modems were implemented. At this data rate, two types of modem equilization are used, the manual type previously discussed and that which is automatically equalized. In comparison to the static nature of manual equilization, automatic equilization permits the modem to continuously monitor and compensate for changing line conditions. However, an initial period of time is required for the modem to "train" on the signal each time the transmission direction reverses. For manually equalized modems, the RTS/CTS delay time is normally between 10 and 20 ms, since they are static in nature. For automatically equalized modems, the training time necessary for the modem to adapt to the incoming signal adds significantly to the RTS/CTS delay time, with such delays increased to 50 ms or more.

Recent Developments

Until the early 1970s, users were forced to trade off the benefits derived from automatic equalization with the longer RTS/CTS delay time that was obtained through the use of a modem equipped with this feature. Recently, several modem manufacturers have incorporated proprietary techniques that reduce the RTS/CTS delay time while permitting automatic equalization.

One manufacturer uses a so-called "gearshift" technique where data transmission begins at a rate of 2,400 bps, using a modulation technique that does not require extensive equalization. This reduced the RTS/CTS delay to a level of about 9 ms, which is the delay time normally associated with manually equalized modems transmitting at 2,400 bps. Next, as transmission proceeds at 2,400 bps, the receiving modem automatically equalizes on the incoming signal. After an initial transmission of 64 bits of data is received at the 2,400-bps data rate, the training cycle is completed and both the sending and receiving modems "gearshift" up to the faster 4,800-bps data rate to continue transmission. While this technique will reduce the RTS/CTS delay time, the actual number of data bits transmitted during an interval of time will depend upon the size of the message transmitted. This is because the first 64 bits of data of each message are transmitted at 2,400 bps prior to the modem gearshifting to the 4,800-bps data rate.

A new technique used to increase the number of bits of information transmitted has been obtained by incorporating a 12-bit microprocessor into a modem. This microprocessor is used to perform equalization and provides a very fast polling feature which increases the data traffic transmitted during a period of time when compared to the standard Bell System equivalent 4,800-bps modems or the gearshift-type modem. This comparison is illustrated in Table 2.9.

Table 2.9. Comparison of Data Traffic Transmitted by 4,800-bps Multipoint Modems

	Data bits		
Time (ms)	Modem with microprocessor	Modem using "gearshift" technique	Bell System equivalent
9	0	0	0
20	24	24	0
26	58	41	0
36	106	65	48
50	173	133	115

2.5. Limited Distance Modems

Limited distance modems are being employed more frequently in data communications networks. This increase in usage is the result of a number of factors, of which the cost of the device is a major consideration. As the name implies, limited distance modems are designed for data transmission over relatively short distances when compared to traditional modems. The utilization of such devices can result in dramatic cost savings in contrast to the cost of using conventional modems for the transmission of data over short distances. Currently, more than a dozen manufacturers produce these devices, with purchase prices ranging from several hundred to several thousand dollars. These devices have operating rates ranging from 110 bps to over 1 million bps for distances ranging from 1 to 20 miles or more. The names given to these devices include not only limited distance modems but such descriptive terms as modem bypass units, short-range data sets, short-haul modems, and wire line modems.

Contrasting Devices

In contrast to line drivers where one or more such devices are used to regenerate digital data and extend transmission ranges, limited distance modems require two matching components, one at each end of the circuit. In most cases, limited distance modems convert digital data into analog signals for transmission. However, some devices on the market convert the terminal's serial binary bits into bipolar return to zero signals to maintain transmission entirely in digital form. The utilization of this type of device can provide one with a direct limited distance digital extension to a DATA-PHONE® digital service channel service unit (CSU).

Transmission Mediums

In Fig. 2.16, some of the distances that can be achieved with limited distance modems are illustrated when transmission is over unloaded, twisted-pair metallic wire cables. The representative transmission distances illustrated represent a refined composite derived from manufacturers' data sheets and should be used as a guide due to the variations in methods of signaling and sensitivity in receiving levels between devices. As discussed in Sec. 2.6, the smaller the wire gauge the greater the diameter of the wire and the lower the resistance of the wire to passage of current. The 4-wire gauges selected for illustration in Fig. 2.16 were used because they correspond to the common wire sizes used in the U.S. telephone systems, and many users prefer to utilize the existing common carrier cables in lieu of routing their own private cables. Of course, there is no gauge restriction in

Fig. 2.16. Representative Transmission Distance
Miles per twin pair wire gauges (unloaded).

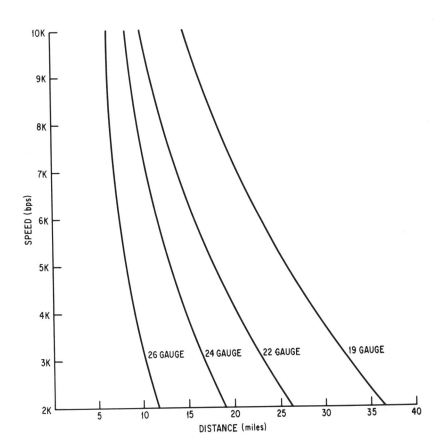

routing a private cable, and in light of the differences shown in Fig. 2.16 between 19- and 26-gauge cable, many users will install a lower gauge cable even when transmitting at a nominal data rate to alleviate the necessity of recabling if the data transmission rate should increase at a later date.

In Table 2.10, common telephone wire sizes and associated measured resistance are listed. In this table, a loop mile is a term which is used to describe two wires connecting two points which are physically located 1 mile apart, an important measurement when one considers using carrier facilities for supporting their limited distance transmission requirements.

If the use of existing carrier facilities is being contemplated, a close liaison with the local telephone company should be established. Common carriers and their operating companies in some areas may not be completely familiar with this particular type of hardware or the tariff structure for the service to support limited distance transmission. It is also important

Table 2.10. Telephone Wire Sizes and Resistances

Circuit type	Gauge (AWG)	Diameter (mm)	Resistance (Ω) 1000 ft	Resistance (Ω) loop mile
Station wire	22	1.00	16	
Station wire	24	0.79	25	
Station wire	26	0.625	40	
Toll wire	19	1.42	8	
Interoffice wire	19	1.42	8	
Open wire lines				
Copper	10	4.00		6.7
Copper	12	3.00		10.2
Copper-clad steel	12	3.00		25
Copper-clad steel	14	2.00		44

that the proposed limited distance modem conform to the specifications set forth in the Bell System publication 43401 entitled "Transmission Specifications for Private Line Metallic Circuits." This publication describes the signal level criteria objectives for private line metallic circuits (cable pairs without signal battery or amplification devices). In addition, the publication notes that the telephone companies have no obligation to provide private line channels on a metallic basis.

Most manufacturers of limited distance modems clearly specify that their equipment operate in accordance with the previously mentioned publication. If it is not explicitly stated, one may encounter delays and additional cost to insure that the transmitter of the device is modified to comply with the specifications.

Operational Features

Most limited distance modems utilize a differential diphase modulation scheme and permit internal transmit timing or externally derived timing from the associated data terminal. These devices act similarly to a line driver, and most will accommodate 4-wire half/full duplex and 2-wire half-duplex/simplex data transmission. Data rate switches on some asynchronous units provide selectable data rates ranging from 110 through 1,800 bps, while the selectable rates of most synchronous units include 2,400, 4,800, 7,200, 9,600, and 19,200 bps. Since users often select a transmission speed only to realize that by that time the equipment is installed changing requirements may dictate a different speed, the ease of adjustment of the unit should be investigated. This is especially true when an installation goes operational for the first time and the user starts operation with leased terminals which may be replaced at a later date.

Some manufacturers state that their limited distance modems can be inserted into a transmission line to serve as a repeater, as illustrated in Fig. 2.17, to further extend the transmission distance. An obvious limita-

Fig. 2.17. Typical Point-to-point Applications

If a limited distance modem is planned to be used as a repeater, care should be taken to insure that shelter, a power source, and access for diagnostic testing and maintenance is available.

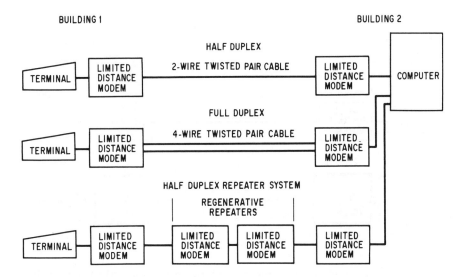

tion to inserting such devices to serve as repeaters, or data regenerators, is the fact that they must be sheltered, have an available power source, and be readily accessible for diagnostics and maintenance. Since these combinations are difficult to achieve at locations between buildings, normal utilization of limited distance modems has their locations fixed at each end of a transmission medium.

A very desirable feature that is offered on some units is a multiport or split stream feature. This feature permits several colocated terminals to utilize a single limited distance transmission link at a considerable cost savings over the less expensive but more limited capability single-channel device. The key advantage to the employment of a multiport limited distance modem is that only one cable instead of many cables can be used to service the transmission requirements of multiple terminals, as illustrated in Fig. 2.18. For additional information on the advantages of multiport operations, the reader is referred to Sec. 2.4.

Diagnostics

Diagnostic capabilities vary both by the model produced by a manufacturer and between manufacturers of these units. Some limited distance modems have self-testing circuitry which permits the user to easily determine if the unit is operating correctly, or, if it is defective, by notifying the user of the operational status of the unit through the display of one or more lights

Fig. 2.18. Multiport Operation Reduces Cabling Requirements

Using a limited distance modem with a multiport feature, one cable may be utilized to provide access to a computer from several terminals.

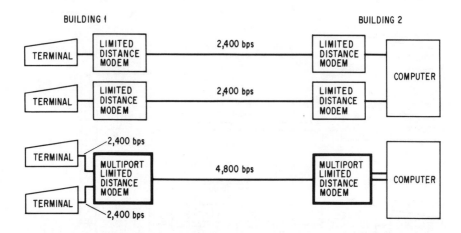

which indicate equipment status and alarm conditions. Most self-testing features available with limited distance modems involve some form of loop-back testing. In such a test, the transmitter output of the modem is looped back or returned to the receiver of the same unit so that the transmitter signal can be checked for errors. Other tests which are available on some models include dc busback, in which the received data and clocking is transmitted back to the limited distance modem at the opposite end of the line to provide an end-to-end test and a remote loop-back test which can be used to trigger a dc busback at a remote location.

2.6. Line Drivers

If one concentrates on conventional data transmission methods, eliminating such unconventional techniques as laser transmission through fiber optic bundles, four basic means of providing a data link between a terminal and a computer can be considered. These methods are listed in Table 2.11. It is

Table 2.11.   Terminal-to-Computer Circuit Connections

Direct connection of terminals through the use of wire conductors
Connection of terminals through the utilization of line drivers
Connection of terminals through the utilization of limited distance modems
Connection of terminals through the utilization of modems or digital service units

interesting to observe that each of the methods listed in Table 2.11 provides for progressively greater distances of data transmission while incurring progressively greater costs to the users. In this chapter the limitations and cost advantages of the first two methods will be examined in detail.

Direct Connection

The first and most economical method of providing a data circuit is to connect the terminal directly to a computer through the utilization of a wire conductor. Surprisingly, many installations limit such direct connections to 50 ft in accordance with terminal and computer manufacturers specifications, specifications which are based upon EIA standards. If the maximum 50-ft standard is exceeded, manufacturers may not support the interface, yet teletype terminals have been operated in a reliable manner at distances in excess of 1,000 ft from a computer over standard EIA data cables. This contradiction between operational demonstrations and usage and standard limitations is easily explained.

If one examines both the EIA RS-232-C and CIITT V.24 standards, such standards limit direct connections to 50 ft of cable for data rates up to and including 20 kbps. Since the data rate is inversely proportional to the length of the cable, taking capacitance and resistance into account, it stands to reason that slower terminals can be located further away than 50 ft from the computer without incurring any appreciable loss in signal quality. Simply stated, the longer the cable length the weaker the transmitted signal at its reception point and the slower the pulse rise time. As transmission speed is increased, the time between pulses is shortened until the original pulse may no longer be recognized at its destination. This becomes more obvious when one considers that a set amount of distortion will effect a smaller (less wide) pulse than a wider pulse. In Fig. 2.19, the relationship between transmission speed and cable length is illustrated for distances up to approximately 3,400 ft and speeds up to 50,000 bps. This figure portrays the theoretical limits of data transfer speeds over an unloaded length of 22 American wire gauge (AWG) cable. Many factors can have an effect on the relationship between transmission speed and distance, including noise, distortion introduced due to the routing of the cable, and the temperature of the surrounding area where the cable is installed. The ballast of a fluorescent fixture, for instance, can cause considerable distortion of a signal transmitted over a relatively short distance.

The diameter of the wire itself will affect total signal loss. If the crosssectional area of a given length of wire is increased, the resistance of the wire to current flow is reduced. Table 2.12 shows the relationship between the dimensions and resistances of several types of commercially available copper wire denoted by gauge numbers. By increasing the gauge from 22 to 19, the resistance of the wire is reduced by approximately one-half.

Fig. 2.19. Speed and Cable Length Relationship

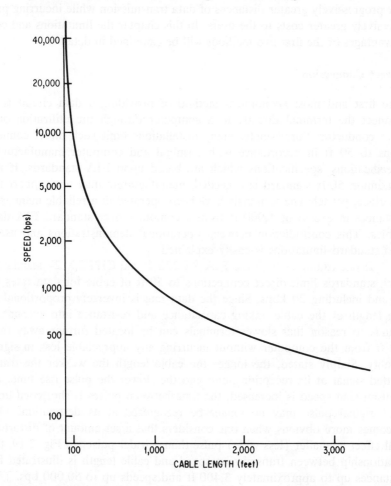

Another method which can be utilized to extend the length of a direct wire connection is limiting the number of signals transmitted over the data link. After the connect sequence, or handshaking, is accomplished, only two signal leads are required for data transfer: the transmitted data and receive data leads. With some minor engineering at both ends of the data link and an available dc voltage source, the remaining signals can be held continuously high, permitting the use of a simple paired cable to complete the data link.

Cable length can be further extended by the use of commercially available low-capacitance shielded cable. The shield consists of a thin wrapping of lead foil around the insulated wires and is quite effective in reducing the overall capacitance of the data cable with a very modest increase in price over standard unshielded cables. The use of low-capacitance

Table 2.12. Relationship Between Wire Diameter and Resistance

Gauge number	Diameter (in.)	Ohms/1000 ft. at 70°F
10	0.102	1.02
11	0.091	1.29
12	0.081	1.62
13	0.072	2.04
14	0.064	2.57
15	0.057	3.24
16	0.051	4.10
17	0.045	5.15
18	0.040	6.51
19	0.036	8.21
20	0.032	10.30
21	0.028	13.00
22	0.025	16.50
23	0.024	20.70
24	0.020	26.20
25	0.018	33.00
26	0.016	41.80
27	0.014	52.40
28	0.013	66.60
29	0.011	82.80

shielded cables is strongly recommended when several cables must be routed through the same limited diameter conduit. Once the practical limitation of cable length has been reached, signal attenuation and line distortion can become significant, and either reduce the quality of data transmission or prevent its occurrence. One method of further extending the direct interface distance between terminals and a computer is by incorporating a line driver into the cable connection.

Line Drivers

As the name implies, a line driver is a device which performs the function of extending the distance a signal can be transmitted down a line. A single line driver, depending upon manufacturer and transmission speed, can adequately drive signals over distances ranging from hundreds of feet up to a mile. One manufacturer has introduced a line driver capable of transferring signals at a speed of 100 kbps at a distance of 5,000 ft and a 1 Mbps signal over a distance of 500 ft using a typical multipair RS-232 cable.

A multitude of names have been given to the various brands of line drivers to include local data distribution units and modem eliminator drivers. For the purpose of this discussion a line driver is a standalone device inserted into a digital transmission line in order to extend the signal distance.

In Fig. 2.20, the distinction between single and multiple line drivers is illustrated and contrasted to limited distance modems which were explored in Sec. 2.5. The primary distinction between line drivers and limited distance modems is that two identical units must be used as limited distance modems to pass data in analog form over a conductor, whereas a line driver serves as a repeater to amplify and reshape digital signals.

Although some models of line drivers can theoretically have an infinite number of repeaters installed along a digital path, the cost of the additional units as well as the extra cabling and power requirements must be considered. Generally, the use of more than two line drivers in a single digital circuit makes the use of limited distance modems a more attractive alternative.

Applications

The characteristics of line drivers become important when one considers their incorporation into a data link. If the EIA RS-232 signals are accepted, amplified, regenerated, and passed over the same leads, they can be used

Fig. 2.20. Line Drivers and Limited Distance Modems

When line drivers are used, the signal remains in its digital form for the entire transmission. Distances can be extended by the addition of one or more line drivers which serve as digital repeaters. For longer distances, limited distance modems can be utilized where the transmitted data is converted into an analog signal and then reconverted back into its digital signal by the modem.

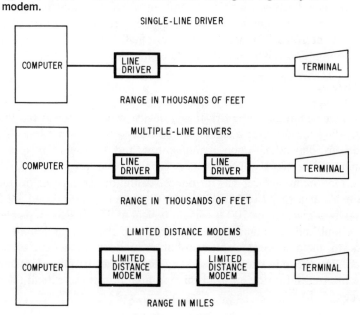

as repeaters. If, however, the line driver also serves as a modem eliminator by providing a synchronous clock, inserting RTS/CTS delays and reversing transmit and receive signals, care should be taken when attempting to use them as repeaters. If this type of line driver is used, and strapping options are provided for the RTS/CTS delay and such desirable features as internal/external clock, it is a simple matter to convert it to a repeater by setting the delay to zero, setting the clock to external, and using a short pigtail cable to reverse the signals. One manufacturer offers a single stand-alone device that performs the function of a pair of two synchronous modems along with a less expensive remote cable extender option which serves as a matching line driver similar to that previously described.

In Fig. 2.21, a typical application where line drivers would be installed is illustrated. In this office building the computer system is located in the basement. The three remote terminals to be connected to the computer are located on different floors of the building. A remote terminal located on the second floor of the building is only 100 ft from the computer and is directly connected by the use of a low-capacitance shielded cable. The second terminal is located on the eighth floor, approximately 500 ft from the computer and is connected by the use of line drivers to extend the

Fig. 2.21. A Variety of Methods Can Be Used to Connect a Terminal to a Computer Located in the Same Building

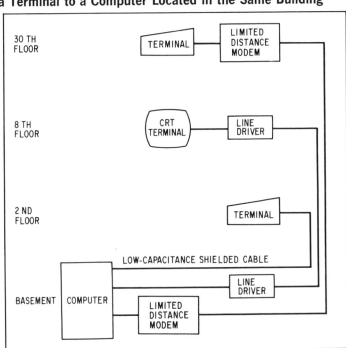

signal transmission range. A third terminal, located on the 30th floor, uses a pair of limited distance modems for transmission since a large number of line drivers would be cost prohibitive.

2.7. Digital Service Units

In the early part of this decade carriers began offering communication systems designed exclusively for the transmission of digital data. Specialized carriers, including the now-defunct DATRAN, performed a considerable service to the information-processing community through their pioneering efforts in developing digital networks. Without their advancements, major communications carriers may have delayed the introduction of an all-digital service.

In December, 1974, the FCC approved the Bell System's DATA-PHONE® digital service (DDS), which was shortly thereafter established between five major cities. Since then the service has been rapidly expanded to the point where, at the beginning of 1978, more than 100 cities had been added to the DDS network. Western Union International set another milestone in February, 1975, by applying to the FCC for authority to offer their International Digital Data Service (IDDS) from New York to Austria, France, Italy, and Spain. Digital data transmission by major carriers had become a reality.

Comparison of Facilities

When analog, or voice-grade, transmission facilities are utilized, the data stream is modulated into two distinct frequencies representing marks and spaces, or binary ones and zeros, respectively, as illustrated in the center of Fig. 2.22. In so-called "voice-grade" telephone circuits, the usable bandwidth extends from 300 Hz to 3,000 Hz, and the power transmitted at the higher frequency is significantly lower than the lower frequency. This bandwidth limitation not only causes a loss of distinction between the vocal "S" and "F" sounds, but limits the amount of information which can be transmitted via modulated digital forms.

In the case of the switched telephone network, the characteristics of a data link cannot be exactly determined because each new call may take a different path. Over long distances, multiple voice-grade lines are often combined into 3,600 channels of 4,000 Hz each and sent by microwave transmission. In the combining, or multiplexing process, an original 2,225-Hz signal may be shifted to 19,225 Hz for transmission and end up as a 2,220-Hz or 2,230-Hz signal at the receiver. This transmission over the switched network normally occurs at data rates up to 4,800 bps. By obtaining a leased line, employing automatic equalization, and conditioning the line, data rates of 9,600 bps can be achieved.

Fig. 2.22. Modulated Analog Signal

When data is transmitted over an analog medium, the digital data is first modulated at the source and then demodulated at the destination back into its digital form. On a digital network the digital data is transmitted as a digital bipolar signal.

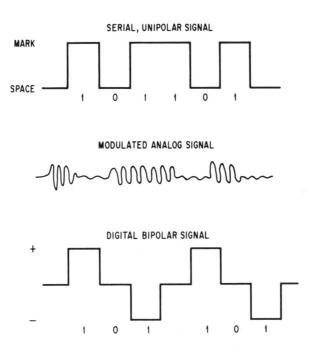

With the voice-grade type of analog transmission, the data travels in a continuous manner, and although it is easily amplified, any noise or distortion along the link is also amplified. In addition, the data signals become highly attenuated, or weakened, by the telephone characteristics originally geared to voice transmission. For the analog transmission of data, expensive and complex modems must be employed at both ends of the link to shape (modulate) and reconstruct (demodulate) the digital signals.

When digital transmission facilities are used, the data travels from end to end in its original form with the digital pulses regenerated at regular intervals as simple values of one and zero. Inexpensive digital service units are employed at both ends of the link to condition the digital signals for digital transmission.

The Bell System DDS is strictly a synchronous facility providing full-duplex, point-to-point, and multipoint service limited to speeds of 2.4, 4.8, 9.6, and 56 kbps. Terminal access to the DDS network is accomplished by means of a digital service unit which alters serial unipolar signals into a form of modified bipolar signals for transmission and returns them to serial unipolar signals at the receiving end. The various types of service units will be discussed in detail later in this section.

Digital Signaling

It is important to understand what modified bipolar signaling is and why it is necessary, since this form of signaling is the cornerstone of digital transmission. Figure 2.22 shows a comparison of how a serial unipolar signal from a teletype is transmitted as a modulated analog "voice" signal and as a digital bipolar signal. In normal return to zero bipolar signaling, a binary zero is transmitted as zero volts and binary ones are alternately transmitted as positive and negative pulses. Since DDS incorporates its own network codes (to include zero suppression, idle, and out-of-service) the original digital format is "violated" in that two successive binary ones could have the same polarity. To avoid any highly undesirable dc build-up in the line, each "violation" is in turn given an alternating polarity which will again return the voltage sum to zero.

An interesting aspect of the network control codes inserted, which modify and violate the bipolar signal, is the use of a zero-suppression code. Since a long succession of binary zeros would not provide the necessary transitions to maintain proper timing recovery, strings of more than six zeros are replaced with zero suppression codes to maintain synchronization. Figure 2.23 shows how a bipolar signal undergoes violation insertion. In this example, a zero-suppression sequence is inserted into the binary channel signal. The resultant signal, as shown, returns the voltage sum to zero.

Fig. 2.23. Modified Bipolar Signaling

Top: Original bipolar signal. Bottom: Modified bipolar signal "violated" by zero-suppression codes. Since a long succession of binary zeros does not provide the necessary translations to maintain proper timing recovery, strings of zeros are replaced with zero suppression codes to maintain synchronization.

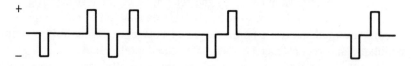

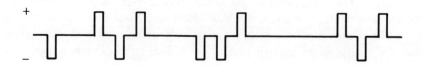

For digital transmission, precise synchronization is the key to success of an all-digital network. It is essential that the data bits be generated at precise intervals, interleaved in time, and read out at the receiving end at the same interval to prevent loss or garbling of data sequences. To accomplish the necessary clock synchronization on the Bell digital network, a master reference clock is used to supply a hierarchy of timing in the network. Should a link to the master clock fail, the nodal timing supplies can operate independently for up to 2 weeks without excessive slippage during outages. In Fig. 2.24, the hierarchy of timing supplies as linked to the Bell System's master reference clock is illustrated. As shown, the subsystem is a treelike network containing no closed loops.

Service Units and Network Integration

In discussing the characteristics of service units which interface terminals to digital networks, it is important to understand the functional differences between channel service units (CSU) and data service units (DSU). Figure 2.25 illustrates a simplified schematic diagram of the Bell System 500A-type DSU compared to their 550A-type CSU. When a CSU is installed, the customer must supply all of the transmit logic, receive logic, and timing recovery in order to use that device, whereas the DSU performs these functions.

Fig. 2.24. DDS Timing Subsystem

In the Bell System DATAPHONE® digital service network a hierarchy of timing is provided to effect network synchronization.

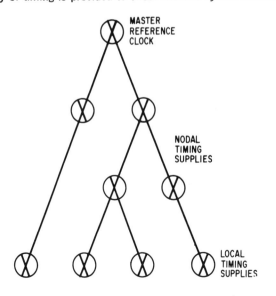

MASTER
REFERENCE
CLOCK

NODAL
TIMING
SUPPLIES

LOCAL
TIMING
SUPPLIES

Fig. 2.25. Service Units for Digital Transmission

The DSU contains all of the circuitry necessary to make the device plug compatible with existing modems and terminals. When using a CSU, the customer must provide timing recovery and detect or generate DDS network control codes.

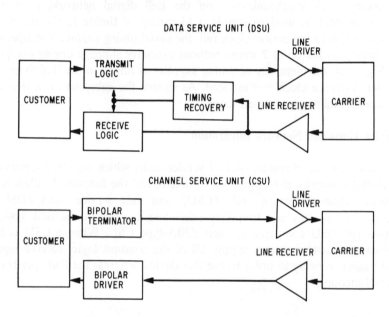

The CSU is devoid of circuitry necessary to provide timing recovery and detect or generate DDS network control codes, which becomes the customer's responsibility when this device is used. Nominal 50 percent duty cycle bipolar pulses are accepted from the customer on the transmit and receive data leads. The pulses, synchronized with the DDS, are amplified, filtered, and passed on to the 2-wire metallic pair telephone company cable. The signals on the receive pair are amplified, equalized, and sliced by the line receiver. The resultant bipolar pulses are then passed to the customer, who must recover the synchronous clock used for timing the transmitted data and sampling the received data. The customer must further detect the DDS network codes, enter appropriate control states, and remove bipolar "violations" from the data stream.

CSU interfacing is accomplished by use of a 15-pin female connector which utilizes the first 6 pins: the four previously described plus a status indicator and a ground lead. In addition to the communications carriers, several independent vendors offer compatible CSU for customer interconnection to digital networks.

In comparison to CSUs, DSUs incorporate all the circuitry necessary to make the device plug compatible with existing modems and terminals. The unit incorporates an analog circuit similar to that described in the CSU

Table 2.13. Dataphone Digital Service Interface Units*

	Speed (kbps)	List code
Bell 500A-type DSU	2.4	500A-L1/2
	4.8	500A-L1/3
	9.6	500A-L1/4
	56	500A-L1/5
Bell 550A-type CSU	2.4	550A-L1/2
	4.8	550A-L1/3
	9.6	550A-L1/4
	56	550A-L1/5

* The 2.4- through 9.6-kbps service units are categorized as those operating at subrated speeds.

plus a digital circuit which handles all timing recovery and network control codes.

DSU interfacing is accomplished by use of a standard 25-pin EIA RS-232 female connector on the 2.4 through 9.6 kbps units, using 10 pins for signaling. The wideband, 56 kbps device utilizes a 34-pin CCITT, V.35 (Winchester-type) connector using 14 pins for signaling. Several independent suppliers also manufacture DSU-type units which offer even more flexibility in the form of multiport options. Current Bell System 550A CSU and 500A-type DSU are listed in Table 2.13. Both the DSU and CSU incorporate properly balanced and equalized terminations for the 4-wire loop as well as circuitry to permit rapid, remote testing of the channel. The signals on the 4-wire loop are the same for both devices and are terminated in the servicing central office of the communications carrier into a complimentary unit called an office channel unit (OCU). From here, the time division multiplexing hierarchy begins as illustrated in Fig. 2.26.

Signals from the OCU are fed into the first stage of multiplexing, which combines up to twenty 2.4, ten 4.8, or five 9.6 kbps signals into a single 64-kbps channel which is the digital capacity of a voice channel in the T1 digital transmission system. A second stage of multiplexing takes the 64-kbps bit streams and efficiently packs them into a T1-bit stream operating at 1.544 Mbps, which may carry voice as well as data signals over existing long-line facilities. Using this scheme, future expansion of DDS may be accomplished at a very rapid pace which could at a later date relegate analog transmission of data to history. In the early 1970s, the Bell System was expanding their T1 system by as much as 10,000 channel miles per day. However, this expansion rate decreased after their initial network was established.

Analog Extensions to DDS

The Bell System provides an 831A data auxiliary set which allows analog access to DDS for customers located outside the DDS servicing areas. The 831A connects the EIA RS-232 interfaces between a data service unit

Fig. 2.26. DDS Multiplexing Arrangement

Signals from a DSU are terminated into a complementary office channel unit in the serving central office. From there they enter into a multiplexing hierarchy which may carry voice as well as data signals.

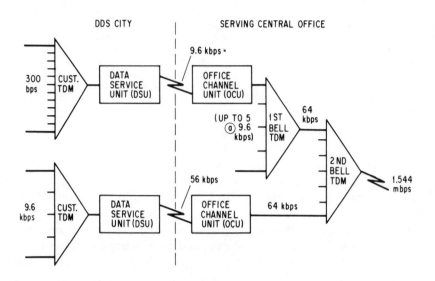

(500A type) and a voice-band data set. The 831A contains an 8-bit elastic store, control, timing, and test circuits which allow loop-back tests toward the digital network. Figure 2.27 illustrates a typical analog extension to a DDS servicing area.

Applications

As discussed in previous sections, the requirement for expensive modems in an off-net analog extension could negate any real savings gained in utilizing DDS. A network arrangement in the form of Fig. 2.28, on the other hand, could easily achieve the high-performance characteristics inherent in DDS while reducing the overall costs of creating two independent data links.

In this example we have incorporated a split stream unit (SSU) which combines up to four streams (channels) of data into a 9.6-kbps high-speed line for transmission over digital data systems. This device can be viewed as a limited function synchronous multiplexer and plugs directly into the DSU, with operational settings at one-half or one-quarter the specified DDS data rate. The unit provides local loop and remote loop testing of each individual channel and very effectively lifts the four speed restrictions of DDS service.

Fig. 2.27. Analog Extension to DDS

In order to obtain an analog extension to a digital network a device known as a data auxiliary set, which provides an interface between a modem and a service unit, must be installed.

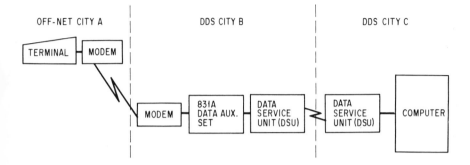

Fig. 2.28. Multiplexing over DDS Utilizing Split-Stream Units

An inexpensive split-stream unit, or limited function synchronous multiplexer, can offer considerable flexibility when interfacing into the DDS network.

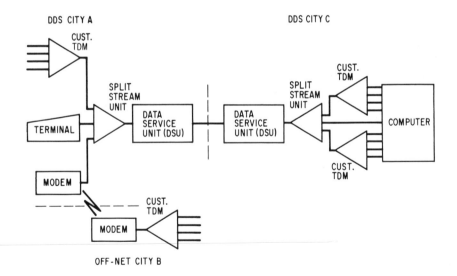

2.8. Parallel Interface Extenders

When an application arises that will require batch processing at a site remotely located from the computer, several approaches can be considered to satisfy this requirement.

A traditional approach is the establishment of a remote batch processing operation. The establishment of this type of operation normally requires the procurement of several communications components in addition to the remote batch terminal. First, a communications controller must be installed and interfaced to the computer if such a device does not already exist at the computational facility. This controller, in conjunction with the computer, performs such tasks as character assembly and disassembly, transmission error checking by generating check characters from the received data blocks, and comparing the check character to the check character generated by the remote batch terminal, as well as performing numerous traffic management functions. Next, a teleprocessing software module will be added and integrated to the computer's operating system to perform and control the transmission discipline. This software may not only be costly but may affect computer performance since it typically requires between 10,000 and 40,000 memory locations, depending upon complexity. Last, a transmission medium and either a high-speed modem or DSU to translate the signals into an acceptable form for transmission must be installed. This traditional remote batch processing operation is illustrated in Fig. 2.29.

Another problem which may arise is the compatibility of the remote batch terminal to the computer system already installed. If the terminal obtained does not support the protocol of the computer's teleprocessing software, an emulator may be required to provide an acceptable transmission link. In any event, transmission from the computer to the terminal will most likely require code conversion, since most terminals cannot accept the computer's native code. Realizing these problems, a device was introduced which permits transmission from selected computers to a variety of computer peripherals without the necessity of the addition of special teleprocessing software or a communications controller. This device is called a parallel interface extender.

Fig. 2.29. Traditional Remote Batch Processing
A large portion of the computer's memory may be reserved for teleprocessing software.

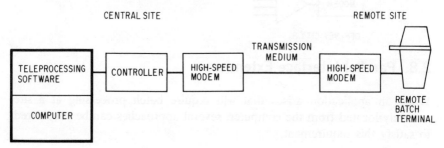

Operation

A parallel interface extender is a device which translates the parallel protocol of an input/output (I/O) channel from such devices as a computer or selected computer peripheral units into a serial protocol which is suitable for transmission over a normal serial communications link. At the other end of the link, another parallel interface extender or similar operating device translates the serial protocol formed by the first parallel interface extender back into the original parallel protocol transmitted by the I/O channel for reception by devices similar to the standard peripherals used for local data processing at a computer center. From a broad viewpoint, a parallel interface extender can be compared as being similar in performance to a multiplexer, combining the data from a number of leads of the parallel I/O channel into a single bit stream for transmission over a serial communications link, as shown in Fig. 2.30.

By permitting a computer to utilize its regular I/O channel when communicating with a remotely located peripheral device, the necessity of obtaining specialized communications software is alleviated, and communications with remote peripheral units can then take place with the same software which is regularly used for communicating with the local peripherals at the computer center. Depending upon the computer configuration in use, a parallel interface extended may reduce operating system software requirements from 10 to 30 percent or more, when compared with communicating to remote devices by using a line controller and the required teleprocessing software modules. Another advantage obtained through the use of parallel interface extenders is the ability to program remote applications in FORTRAN, COBOL, or other higher level languages, as well as in Assembly language, using the READ, WRITE statements of FORTRAN and COBOL or the GET and PUT macros of Assembly language to per-

Fig. 2.30. Parallel Interface Extender Operation

Operates similarly to a multiplexer, combining the data from a number of leads from a computer or peripheral I/O channel into a single bit stream for transmission.

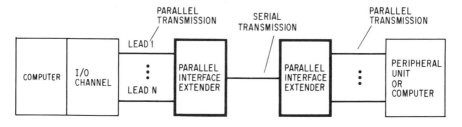

form input and output remote peripheral functions. In addition to the translation of parallel to serial and serial to parallel data, to perform remote peripheral functions the device encodes commands and status information into a serial bit stream at the transmission end of the link while the device at the receiving end of the link performs a decoding function to reconstruct the original commands, status, and data before passing such information to the remote peripheral unit.

Extender Components

A parallel interface extender consists of a control unit and one or more line module groups, as shown in Fig. 2.31. The control unit of the extender connects to the multiplexer channel of a computer and emulates the functions of several peripheral control units, such as card readers, card punches, magnetic tapes, and line printers, thus supporting the computer's standard software, as previously mentioned. Each line module group is connected to the control unit of the extender on one side and provides an interface for the connection of dedicated, switched, or leased lines on the opposite side. The line module contains all necessary line control and error control components, as well as a built-in modem which alleviates the necessity of having special communications software such as IBM's basic telecommunications access method (BTAM) or synchronous data link control (SDLC), a communications controller, line adapter, and a separate modem. For alternate high-speed data transfer in either direction, half-duplex line modules can be used while full-duplex line modules provide data transfer in both directions at the same time. For data transfer over the switched network, half-duplex line modules are normally used while either half-duplex or full-duplex line modules can be used with dedicated or leased 4-wire lines.

Fig. 2.31. Parallel Interface Extender Components
A parallel interface extender consists of a control unit and one or more line module groups. In addition, some manufacturers provide modems built in to the device.

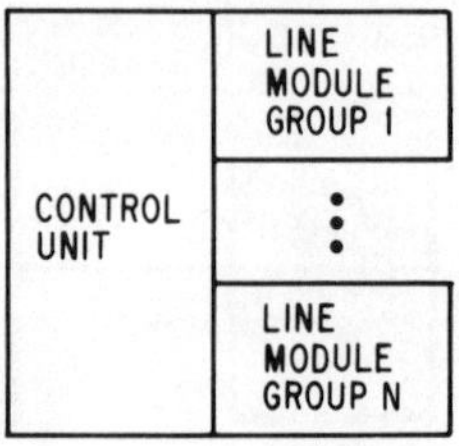

Fig. 2.32. Intercomputer Communications Using a Parallel Interface Extender

Using a parallel interface extender the parallel transmission of the byte multiplexer channel of a computer is converted into a serial data stream for transmission.

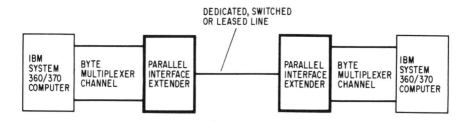

Fig. 2.33. Local and Remote Peripherals as Well as Computers Can Be Serviced

Through the utilization of a parallel interface extender, remote peripherals as well as remote computers are referenced by the central computer as if they were local devices.

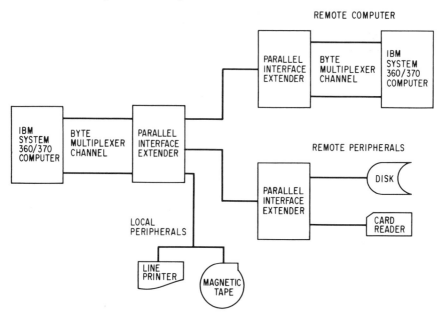

Applications Examples

The parallel interface extender manufactured by Paradyne Corporation can accommodate sixteen half-duplex or eight full-duplex line modules. This unit connects to either an IBM system 360 or IBM system 370 central processing unit via the systems byte multiplexer channel and can be used for such diverse applications as permitting two computers to communicate with each other in their native code (Fig. 2.32) or to connect a computer to a variety of local or remotely located peripheral units, as shown in Fig. 2.33.

With data transmission rates of 4,800, 7,200, 9,600, 19,200, and 56,000 bps, the parallel interface extender permits a level of data transfer that can be matched to the operating speed of most peripheral devices. Since the use of such a device permits what may be unused or limited used peripherals to be transferred to remote locations to be used for other applications than originally acquired, the use of such equipment warrants detailed examination.

chapter 3
data concentration
equipment

Although the nine components included in this chapter perform a variety of functions which govern their utilization for selected application areas, their inclusion here is based upon their common function of concentrating data. In this chapter, the operation and utilization of components designed primarily to accomplish data concentration will be covered. Specific devices to be investigated in this chapter include a variety of multiplexing equipment, concentrators, and front-end processors, as well as components which permit modems, lines, and the ports of computers and other devices to operate on a shared use basis. In addition, a device which splits a data stream into two streams for transmission to take advantage of the difference in the tariff between wideband and voice-band leased lines will also be covered.

3.1. Multiplexers

With the establishment of distributed computing, the cost of providing the required communications facilities became a major focus of concern to users. Numerous network structures were examined to determine the possibilities of using specialized equipment to reduce these costs. For many networks where geographically distributed users accessed a common computational facility, a central location could be found which would serve as a hub to link those users to the computer. Even when terminal traffic was low and the cost of leased lines could not be justified on an individual basis, quite often the cumulative cost of providing communications to a group of users could be reduced if a mechanism was available to enable many terminals to share common communications facilities. This mechanism was provided by the utilization of multiplexers whose primary function is to provide the user with a reduction of communications costs. This device enables one high-speed line to be used to carry the formerly separate transmissions of a group of lower speed lines. The use of multiplexers should be considered when a number of data terminals communicate from within a similar geographical area or when a number of leased lines run in parallel for any distance.

Comparison with Other Devices

In the past, differences between multiplexers and concentrators were pronounced, with multiplexers being prewired, fixed logic devices which produced a composite output transmission by sharing frequency bands (frequency division multiplexing) or time slots (time division multiplexing) on a predetermined basis, with the result that the total transmitted output was equal to the sum of the individual data inputs. Multiplexers were also originally transparent to the communicator, so that data sent from a terminal through a multiplexer to a computer was received in the same format and code by the computer as its original form. In comparison, concentrators were developed from minicomputers by the addition of specialized programming and originally performed numerous tasks that could not be accomplished through the use of a multiplexer. First, the intelligence provided by the software in concentrators permits a dynamic sharing technique to be employed instead of the static sharing technique used in traditional multiplexers. If a terminal connected to a concentrator is not active, then the composite high-speed output of the concentrator will not automatically reserve a space for that terminal as will a traditional multiplexer. This scheme permits a larger number of terminals to share the use of a high-speed line through the use of a concentrator than when such terminals are connected to a multiplexer, since the traditional multiplexer allocates a time slot or frequency band for each terminal, regardless of whether the terminal is active. For this reason, statistics and queuing theory play an important role in the planning and utilization of concentrators. Next, due to the stored program capacity of concentrators, these devices can be programmed to perform a number of additional functions. Such functions as the preprocessing of sign-on information and code conversion can be used to reduce the burden of effort required by the host computer system.

The advent of intelligent multiplexers, which are discussed later in this section, has closed the gap between concentrators and multiplexers. Through the use of built-in microprocessors, intelligent multiplexers can now be programmed to perform numerous functions previously available only through the use of concentrators. The reader should refer to Sec. 3.4, "Concentrators and Front-end Processors," as well as the portion of this section which covers intelligent multiplexers, for additional information on these devices.

Device Support

In general, any device that transmits or receives a serial data stream can be considered a candidate for multiplexing. Data streams produced by the devices listed in Table 3.1 are among those that can be multiplexed. The intermix of devices as well as the number of any one device whose data

**Table 3.1.   Candidates for Data
Stream Multiplexing**

Analog network private line modems
Analog switched network modems
Digital network data service units
Digital network channel service units
Data terminals
Data terminal controllers
Minicomputers
Concentrators
Computer ports
Computer-computer links
Other multiplexers

stream is considered for multiplexing is a function of the multiplexer's capacity and capabilities, the economics of the application, and cost of other devices which could be employed in that role, as well as the types and costs of high-speed lines being considered.

Multiplexing Techniques

Today, two basic techniques are commonly used for multiplexing: frequency division multiplexing (FDM) and time division multiplexing (TDM). Within the time division technique, two versions are available—fixed time slots which are employed by traditional TDM and variable use of time slots which are used by intelligent TDM.

In the FDM technique, the available bandwidth of the line is split into smaller segments called data bands or derived channels. Each data band in turn is separated from another data band by a guard band which is used to prevent signal interference between channels, as shown in Fig. 3.1.

Physically, an FDM contains a channel set for each data channel as well as common logic, as shown in Fig. 3.2. Each channel set contains a transmitter and receiver tuned to a specific frequency, with bits being indicated by the presence or absence of signals at each of the channel's assigned frequencies. In FDM, the width of each frequency band determines

Fig. 3.1. FDM Channel Separations

In frequency division multiplexing the 3-kHz bandwidth of a voice-grade line is split into channels or data bands separated from each other by guard bands.

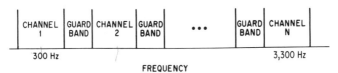

FREQUENCY

Fig. 3.2. Frequency Division Multiplexing

Since the channel sets modulate the line at specified frequencies, no modems are required at remote locations.

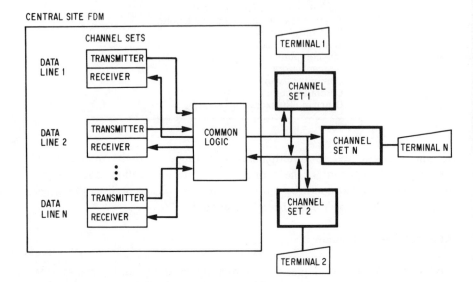

the transmission rate capacity of the channel, and the total bandwidth of the line is a limiting factor in determining the total number or mix of channels that can be serviced. Although a multipoint operation is illustrated in Fig. 3.2, FDM equipment can also be utilized for the multiplexing of data between two locations on a point-to-point circuit. Currently, data rates up to 1,200 bps can be multiplexed by FDM. Typical FDM channel spacings required at different data rates are listed in Table 3.2.

Since the physical bandwidth of the line limits the number of devices which may be multiplexed, FDM is mainly used for multiplexing low-speed asynchronous terminals. An advantage obtained through the use of

Table 3.2.   FDM Channel Spacings

Speed (bps)	Spacing (Hz)
75	120
110	170
150	240
300	480
450	720
600	960
1,200	1,800

such equipment is its code transparency. Once a data band is set, any terminal operating at that speed or less can be used on that channel without concern for the code of the terminal. Thus, a channel set to carry 300-bps transmission could also be used to service an IBM 2741 terminal transmitting at 134.5 bps or a Teletype 110-bps terminal. Another advantage of FDM equipment is that no modems are required since the channel sets modulate the line at specified frequencies, as shown in Fig. 3.2. At the computer site, the FDM multiplexer interfaces the computer ports through channel sets. The common logic acts as a summer connecting the multiplexer channel sets to the leased line. At each remote location, a channel set provides the necessary interface between the terminal at that location and the leased line. When using FDM equipment, individual data channels can be picked up or dropped off at any point on a telephone circuit. This characteristic permits the utilization of multipoint lines and can result in considerable line charge reductions based upon developing a single circuit which can interface multiple terminals. Each remote terminal to be serviced only needs to be connected to an FDM channel set which contains bandpass filters that separate the line signal into the individual frequencies designated for that terminal. Guard bands of unused frequencies are used between each channel frequency to permit the filters a degree of tolerance in separating out the individual signals.

Although FDM normally operates in a full-duplex transmission mode on a 4-wire circuit by having all transmit tones sent on one pair of wires and all receive tones return on a second pair, FDM can also operate in the full-duplex mode on a 2-wire line. This can be accomplished by having the transmitter and receiver of each channel set tuned to different frequencies. For example, with 16 channels available, one channel set could be tuned for channel 1 to transmit and channel 9 to receive while another channel set would be tuned to channel 2 to transmit and channel 10 to receive. With this technique, the number of data channels is halved. However, the cost differential between a 4-wire and a 2-wire circuit may justify its use if one has only a small number of terminals to service.

FDM Utilization

As mentioned previously, one key advantage in utilizing FDM equipment is the ability afforded the user in installing multipoint circuits for use in a communications network. This can minimize line costs since a common line, optimized in routing, can now be used to service multiple terminal locations. An example of FDM equipment used on a multipoint circuit is shown in Fig. 3.3, where a four-channel FDM is used to multiplex traffic from terminals located in four different cities. Although the entire frequency spectrum is transmitted on the circuit, the channel set at each terminal location filters out the preassigned bandwidth for that location, in

Fig. 3.3. Frequency Division Multiplexing Permits Multipoint Circuit Operations

Each terminal on an FDM multipoint circuit is interfaced through the multiplexer to an individual computer port.

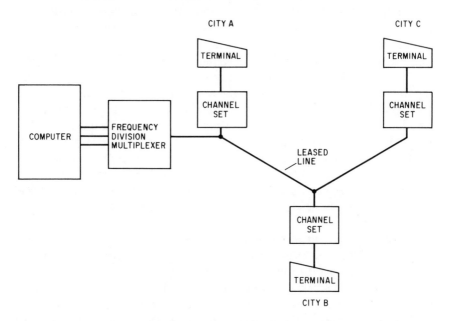

effect producing a unique individual channel that is dedicated for utilization by the terminal at each location. This operation is analogous to a group of radio stations transmitting at different frequencies and setting a radio to one frequency so as always to be able to receive the transmission from a particular station. In contrast to poll and select (time division) multipoint line operations where one computer port is used to transmit and receive data from many buffered terminals connected to a common line, FDM used for multipoint operations as shown requires one computer port for each terminal. However, such terminals do not require a buffer area to recognize their address. When buffered terminals are available, polling by channel can take place, as illustrated in Fig. 3.4. In this example, channels 1 and 2 are each connected to a number of relatively low-traffic terminals which are polled through the multiplexer system. Terminals 3 through 6 are presumed to be higher traffic stations and are thus connected to individual channels of the FDM or to individual channel sets.

Time Division Multiplexing

In the FDM technique, the bandwidth of the communications line serves as the frame of reference. The total bandwidth is divided into smaller bandwidths, each of which is used to form an independent data channel. In the

Fig. 3.4. FDM Can Intermix Polled and Dedicated Terminals in a Network

Of the 6 channels used in this network, channels 1 and 2 service a number of polled terminals, while channels 3 through 6 are dedicated to service individual terminals.

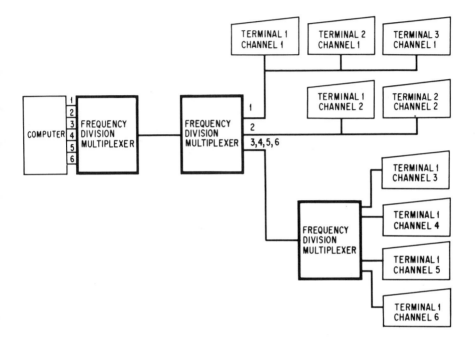

TDM technique, the aggregate capacity of the line is the frame of reference, since the multiplexer provides a method of transmitting data from many terminals over a common circuit by interleaving them in time. The TDM divides the aggregate transmission on the line for use by the slower speed devices connected to the multiplexer. Each device is given a time slot for its exclusive use so that at any one point in time the signal from one terminal is on the line. In the FDM technique, in which each signal occupies a different frequency band, all signals are being transmitted simultaneously.

The fundamental operating characteristics of a TDM are shown in Fig. 3.5. Here, each low- to medium-speed terminal is connected to the multiplexer through an input/output (I/O) channel adapter. The I/O adapter provides the buffering and control functions necessary to interface the transmission and reception of data from the terminals to the multiplexer. Within each adapter, a buffer or memory area exists which is used to compensate for the speed differential between the terminals and the multiplexer's internal operating speed. Data is shifted from the terminal to the I/O adapter at different rates (typically 110 to 7,200 bps), depending upon the speed of the terminal, but when data is shifted from the I/O

Fig. 3.5. Time Division Multiplexing

In time division multiplexing, data is first entered into each channel adapter buffer area at a transfer rate equal to the device the adapter is connected to. Next, data from the various buffers are transferred to the multiplexer's central logic at the higher rate of the device for packing into a message frame for transmission.

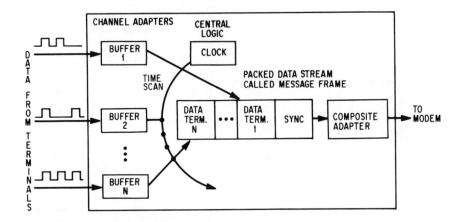

adapter to the central logic of the multiplexer, or from central logic to the composite adapter, it is at the much higher fixed rate of the TDM. On output from the multiplexer to each data terminal, the reverse is true, since data is first transferred at a fixed rate from central logic to each adapter and then from the adapter to the terminal at the data rate acceptable to the terminal. Depending upon the type of TDM system, the buffer area in each adapter will accommodate either bits or characters.

The central logic of the TDM contains controlling, monitoring, and timing circuitry which facilitates the passage of individual terminal data to and from the high-speed transmission medium. The central logic will generate a synchronizing pattern which is used by a scanner circuit to interrogate each of the channel adapter buffer areas in a predetermined sequence, blocking the bits of characters from each buffer into a continuous, synchronous data stream which is then passed to a composite adapter. The composite adapter contains a buffer and functions similar to the I/O channel adapters. However, it now compensates for the difference in speed between the high-speed transmission medium and the internal speed of the multiplexer.

The Multiplexing Interval

When operating, the multiplexer transmits and receives a continuous data stream known as a message train, regardless of the activity of the terminals connected to the device. The message train is formed from a continuous series of message frames which represents the packing of a series of input data streams. Each message frame contains one or more synchronization characters followed by a number of basic multiplexing intervals whose number is dependent upon the model and manufacturer of the device. The basic multiplexing interval can be viewed as the first level of time subdivision which is established by determining the number of equal sections per second required by a particular application. Then, the multiplexing interval is the time duration of one section of the message frame.

For the vast majority of applications, the section rate is established at 30 sections per second, which then produces a basic multiplexing interval of 0.033 s* or 33 ms. Setting the interval to 33 ms makes the multiplexer directly compatible to a 300-baud asynchronous channel which transmits data at up to 30 characters per second (cps). With this interval the multiplexer is also compatible with 150-baud (15-cps) and 110-baud (10-cps) data channels, since the basic multiplexing interval is a multiple of those asynchronous data rates.

TDM Techniques

The two TDM techniques available include bit interleaving and character interleaving. Bit interleaving is generally used in systems which service synchronous terminals, whereas character interleaving is generally used to service asynchronous terminals. When interleaving is accomplished on a bit-by-bit basis, the multiplexer takes 1 bit from each channel adapter and then combines them as a word or frame for transmission. As shown in Fig. 3.6 (top), this technique produces a frame containing one data element from each channel adapter. When interleaving is accomplished on a character-by-character basis, the multiplexer assembles a full character into one frame and then transmits the entire character, as shown in Fig. 3.6 (bottom). Although a frame containing only one character of information is illustrated in Fig. 3.6, to increase transmission efficiency most multiplexers transmit long frames containing a large number of data characters to reduce the synchronization overhead associated with each frame. Thus, while a frame containing one character of information has a synchronization overhead of 50 percent, a frame containing four data characters has its overhead reduced to 20 percent, and a frame containing nine data characters has a synchronization overhead of only 10 percent, assuming constant slot sizes for all characters.

For the character-by-character method, the buffer area required is considerably larger, and although memory costs have declined, TDM character interleaving is still slightly more expensive than TDM bit interleaving systems. Since the character-by-character interleaved method preserves all

---

* s = second

Fig. 3.6. Time Division Interleaving Bit by Bit and Character by Character

When interleaving is accomplished bit by bit (top), the first bit from each channel is packed into a frame for transmission. Bottom: Time division multiplexing character by character. When interleaving is conducted on a character by character basis, one or more complete characters are grouped with a synchronization character into a frame for transmission.

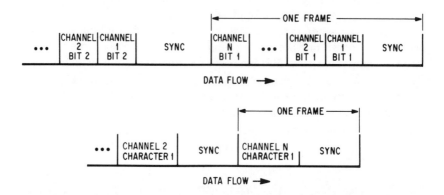

bits of a character in sequence, the TDM equipment can be used to strip the character of any recognition information that may be sent as part of that character. An example of this would be the servicing of a terminal such as a Teletype Model 33, where a transmitted character contains 11 bits which include a start bit, 7 data bits, a parity bit, and 2 stop bits. When the bit-interleaved method is used, all 11 bits would be transmitted to preserve character integrity, whereas in a character-interleaved system, the start and stop bits can be stripped from the character, and only the 7 data bits and the parity bit warrant transmission.

To service terminals with character codes containing different numbers of bits per character, two techniques are commonly employed in character interleaving. In the first technique, the time slot for each character is of constant size, designed to accommodate the maximum bit width or highest level code. Making all slots large enough to carry American Standard Code for Information Interchange (ASCII) characters makes the multiplexer an inefficient carrier of a lower level code such as 5-level Baudot. However, the electronics required in the device and its costs are reduced. The second technique used is to proportion the slot size to the width of each character according to its bit size. This technique maximizes the efficiency of the multiplexer, although the complexity of the logic and the cost of the multiplexer increases. Due to the reduction in the cost of semiconductors over the last several years, most character-interleaved multiplexers currently marketed are designed to operate on the proportional assignment method.

While bit interleaving equipment is less expensive, it is also less efficient when used to service asynchronous terminals. On the positive side, bit-interleaved multiplexers offer the advantage of faster resynchronization and shorter transmission delay, since character-interleaved multiplexers must wait to assemble the bits into characters, whereas a bit-interleaved multiplexer can transmit each bit as soon as it is received from the terminal. Multiplexers which interleave by character use a number of different techniques to build the character, with the techniques varying between manufacturers and by models produced by manufacturers. A commonly utilized technique is the placement of a buffer area for each channel adapter which permits the character to be assembled within the channel adapter and then scanned and packed into a data stream. Another technique which can be used is the placement of a central memory within the multiplexer so that it can be used to assemble characters for all the input channels. The second technique makes a multiplexer resemble a concentrator since the inclusion of central memory permits many additional functions to be performed in addition to the assembly and disassembly of characters. Such multiplexers with central memory are referred to as intelligent multiplexers and are discussed later in this chapter.

TDM Applications

The most commonly used TDM configuration is the point-to-point system, which is shown in Fig. 3.7. This type of system, which is also called a two-point multiplex system, links a mixture of terminals to a centrally located multiplexer. As shown, the terminals can be connected to the multiplexer in a variety of ways. Terminals can be connected by a leased line running from the terminal's location to the multiplexer, by a direct connection if the user's terminal is within the same building as the multiplexer and a cable can be laid to connect the two, or terminals can use the switched network to call the multiplexer over the dial network. For the latter method, since the connection is not permanent, several terminals can share access to one or more multiplexer channels on a contention basis. As shown in Fig. 3.7, the terminals in cities B and C use the dial network to contend for one multiplexer channel which is interfaced to an automatic answer unit on the dial network. Whichever terminal accesses that channel maintains access to it and thus excludes other terminals from access to that particular connection to the system. For a network which contains, as an example, 50 terminals within a geographical area of which only between 10 and 12 are active at any one time, one method to deal with this environment would be through the installation of a 12-number rotary interfaced to a 12-channel multiplexer. If all of the terminals were located within one city, the only telephone charges that the user would incur in addition to those of the leased line between multiplexers would be local call charges each time a terminal user dialed the local multiplexer number.

Fig. 3.7. Time Division Multiplexing Point to Point

A point-to-point or two-point multiplexing system links a variety of data users at one or more remote locations to a central computer facility.

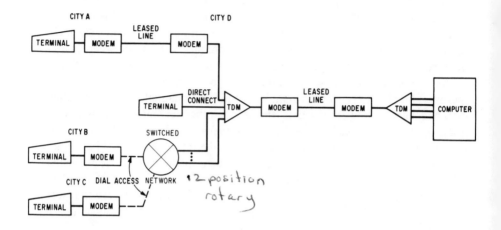

Series Multipoint Multiplexing

A number of multiplexing systems can be developed by linking the output of one multiplexer into a second multiplexer. Commonly called series multipoint multiplexing, this technique is most effective when terminals are distributed at two or more locations and the user desires to alleviate the necessity of obtaining two long distance leased lines from the closer location to the computer. As shown in Fig. 3.8, four low-speed terminals are multiplexed at city A onto one high-speed channel which is transmitted to city B where this line is in turn multiplexed along with the data from a

Fig. 3.8. Series Multipoint Multiplexing

Series multipoint multiplexing is accomplished by connecting the output of one multiplexer as input to a second device.

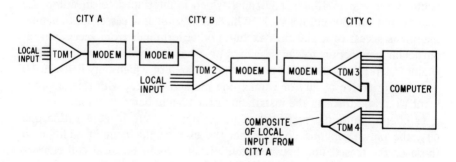

number of other terminals at city B. Although the user requires a leased line between city A and city B, only one line is now required to be installed for the remainder of the distance from city B to the computer at city C. If city A is located 50 miles from city B, and city B is 2,000 miles from city C, 2,000 miles of duplicate leased lines are avoided by using this multiplexing technique.

Although multipoint multiplexing requires an additional pair of channel cards to be installed at multiplexers 2 and 3 as well as higher speed modems interfaced to those multiplexers to handle the higher aggregate throughput when the traffic of multiplexer 1 is routed through multiplexer 2, in most cases the cost savings associated with reducing duplicate leased lines will more than offset the cost of the extra equipment. Since this is a series arrangement, a failure of either TDM2 or TDM3, or a failure of the line between these two multiplexers, will terminate service to all terminals connected to the system.

Hub-bypass Multiplexing

A variation of series multipoint multiplexing is hub-bypass multiplexing. To be effectively used, hub-bypass multiplexing can occur when a number of remote locations have the requirement to transmit to two or more locations. To satisfy this requirement, the remote terminal traffic is multiplexed to a central location which is the hub, and the terminals which must communicate with the second location are strapped into another multiplexer which transmits this traffic, bypassing the hub. Figure 3.9 illustrates one application where hub bypassing might be utilized. In this example, eight terminals at city 3 require a communications link with one of two computers; six terminals always communicate with the computer at city 2, while two terminals use the facilities of the computer at city 1. The data from all eight

Fig. 3.9. Hub-bypass Multiplexing

When a number of terminals have the requirement to communicate with more than one location, hub-bypass multiplexing should be considered.

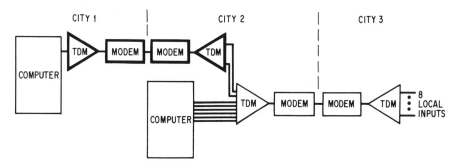

terminals are multiplexed over a common line to city 2 where the two channels that correspond to the terminals which must access the computer at city 1 are strapped to a new multiplexer, which then remultiplexes the data from those terminals to city 1. When many terminal locations have dual location destinations, hub bypassing can become very economical. However, since the data flows in series, an equipment failure will terminate access to one or more computational facilities, depending upon the location of the break in service.

Front-end Substitution

Although not commonly utilized, a TDM may be installed as an inexpensive front end for a computer, as shown in Fig. 3.10. When used as a front end, only one computer port is then required to service the terminals which are connected to the computer through the TDM. The TDM can be connected at the computer center, or it can be located at a remote site and connected over a leased line and a pair of modems. Since demultiplexing is conducted by the computer's software, only one multiplexer is necessary. However, due to the wide variations in multiplexing techniques of each manufacturer, no standard software has been written for demultiplexing, and unless multiple locations can use this technique, the software development costs may exceed the hardware savings associated with this technique. In addition, the software overhead associated with the computer performing the demultiplexing may degrade its performance to an appreciable degree and must be considered.

Inverse Multiplexing

A multiplexing system which is coming into widespread usage is the inverse multiplexing system. As shown in Fig. 3.11, inverse multiplexing permits a high-speed data stream to be split into two slower data streams for transmission over lower cost lines and modems.

Due to the tariff structure associated with wideband facilities, these devices permit a user to transmit data at rates up to 19,200 bps over two voice-grade lines at a fraction of the cost which would be incurred when

Fig. 3.10. TDM System Used as a Front End
When a TDM is used as a front-end processor, the computer must be programmed to perform demultiplexing.

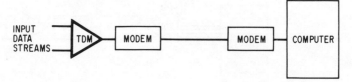

Fig. 3.11. Inverse Multiplexing

An inverse multiplexer splits a serial data stream into two individual data streams for transmission at lower data rates.

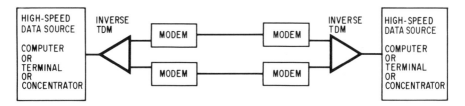

using wideband facilities. The reader should refer to Sec. 3.3 for additional information on these devices.

Multiplexer Economics

The primary motive for the use of multiplexers in a network is to reduce the cost of communications. In analyzing the potential of multiplexers, one should first survey terminal users to determine the projected monthly connect time of each terminal. Then, the most economical method of data transmission from each individual terminal to the computer facility can be computed. To do this, direct dial costs should be compared with the cost of a leased line from each terminal to the computer site. Once the most economical method of transmission for each individual terminal to the computer is determined, this cost should be considered the "cost to reduce." Then telephone mileage costs from each terminal city location to each other terminal city location should be determined in order to compute and compare the cost of utilizing various techniques, such as line dropping and the multiplexing of data by combining several low- to medium-speed terminals' data streams into one high-speed line for transmission to the central site.

In evaluating multiplexing costs, the cost of telephone lines from each terminal location to the "multiplexer center" must be computed and added to the cost of the multiplexer equipment. Then, the cost of the high-speed line from the multiplexer center to the computer site must be added to produce the total multiplexing cost. If this cost exceeds the cumulative most economical method of transmission for individual terminals to the central site, then multiplexing is not cost justified. This process should be reiterated by considering each city as a possible multiplexer center to optimize all possible network configurations. In repeating this process, terminals located in certain cities will not justify any calculations to prove or disprove their economic feasibility as multiplexer centers, due to their isolation from other cities in a network.

An example of the economics involved in multiplexing is illustrated in Fig. 3.12. In this example, the volume of terminal traffic from the de-

Fig. 3.12. Multiplexing Economics

On an individual basis, the cost of five terminals accessing a computer system (top) can be much more expensive than when a time division multiplexer is installed (bottom).

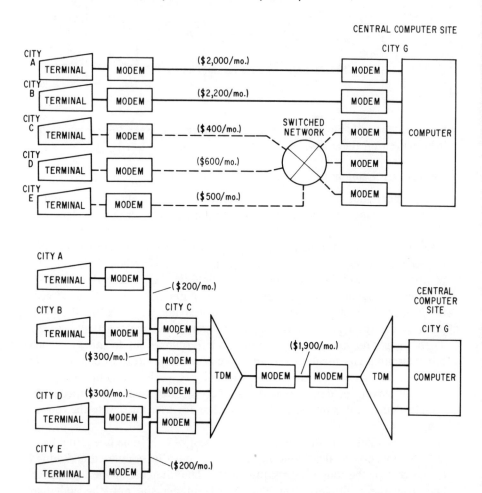

vices located in cities A and B would result in a dial-up charge of $3,000 per month if access to the computer in city G was over the switched network. The installation of leased lines from those cities to the computer at city G would cost $2,000 and $2,200 per month, respectively. Furthermore, let us assume that the terminals at cities C, D, and E only periodically communicate with the computer, and their dial-up costs of $400, $600 and $500 per month, respectively, are much less than the cost of leased lines between those cities and the computer. Then, without multiplexing, the network's most economical communications cost would be:

Location	Cost per month
city A	$2,000
city B	2,200
city C	400
city D	600
city E	500
Total cost	$5,700

Let us further assume that city C is centrally located with respect to the other cities so we could use it as a homing point or multiplexer center. In this manner, a multiplexer could be installed in city C, and the terminal traffic from the other cities could be routed to that city, as shown in the bottom portion of Fig. 3.12. Employing multiplexers would reduce the network communications cost to $2,900 per month which produces a potential savings of $2,800 per month, which should now be reduced by the multiplexer costs to determine net savings. If each multiplexer costs $500 per month, then the network using multiplexers will save the user $1,800 each month.

Exactly how much saving can be realized, if any, through the use of multiplexers, depends not only on the types, quantities, and distributions of terminals to be serviced but also on the leased line tariff structure and the type of multiplexer employed.

Mixing Multiplexers

While FDM equipment is limited by the telephone lines' 3-kHz bandwidth, the main limitation on a TDM system is the transmission capability of the high-speed modem attached to the multiplexer. FDM service is usually limited to sixteen 110-bps or eight 150-bps channels, while TDM systems can service a mixture of low- and high-speed terminals whose composite speed is less than or equal to the attached modem's rated speed. Thus, a single TDM system could service sixty-four 150-bps terminals when interfaced to a 9,600-bps modem, whereas eight 8-channel FDM systems might be necessary to provide equivalent service. Although FDM systems service only low-speed terminals, TDM systems can service a mixture of low- and high-speed lines, providing the user with more flexibility in both network design and terminal selection. As mentioned previously, while TDM systems favor point-to-point applications, FDM systems are well suited for multidrop configurations where a number of widely separated terminals can be serviced most economically over a single multipoint line. Although terminal quantities, locations, and transmission rates will often dictate which type of system to use, often a mixture of systems should be considered to provide an optimum solution to network problems.

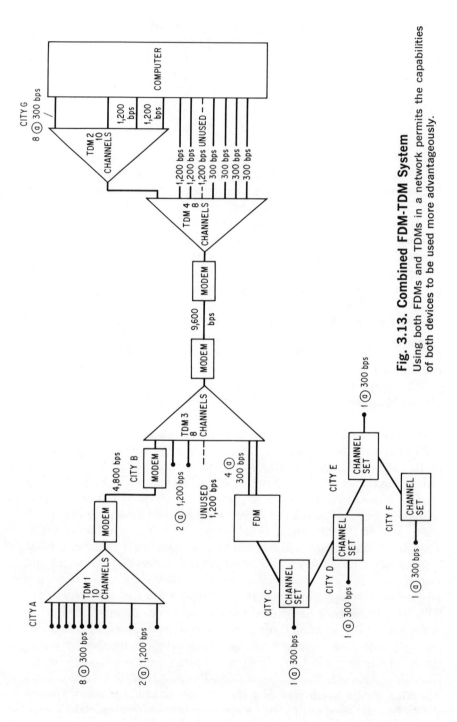

Fig. 3.13. Combined FDM-TDM System

Using both FDMs and TDMs in a network permits the capabilities of both devices to be used more advantageously.

Thus, in many networks, TDM systems will be used for transmission at high data rates between two widely separated locations, while FDM will often be used in the same system to provide multidrop servicing to terminals, which because of transmission rates and locations are best serviced by an FDM system. Such a combined system is shown in Fig. 3.13. In developing this system, the terminal requirements were first examined and denoted as follows:

City	Terminal quantity	Terminal speed	Aggregate terminal speed
A	8	300	2,400
A	2	1,200	2,400
B	2	1,200	2,400
C	1	300	300
D	1	300	300
E	1	300	300
F	1	300	300

In examining the terminal requirements of city A, the total aggregate throughput of the eight 300-bps terminals and the two 1,200-bps terminals becomes 4,800-bps. Since this exceeds the typical capacity of FDM systems, city A becomes a candidate for TDM. Although the two terminals at city B may lie within the upper range of servicing by an FDM system, further examination of the terminals located in cities C, D, E, and F makes them ideal candidates for FDM. If an FDM system is installed to service those cities, based upon geographical distances, we may then desire to install a TDM at city B which we can use to service the two terminals at that city, as well as servicing the output of the TDM in city A and the FDM system. Thus, instead of three long distance leased lines, city B can act as a homing point for all the multiplexers in the system. Since the aggregate throughput of TDM3 will be 8,400 bps, an extra channel card(s), depending upon manufacturer, may be required to make the system run at a standard 9,600-bps data rate. Although this channel will not be utilized by any terminal, the extra 1,200-bps capacity is available for servicing additional terminals at a later date. This extra channel card can be one 1,200-bps card (as shown in Fig. 3.13) or a number of channel cards whose total capacity adds up to 1,200 bps.

At city G only two TDMs are necessary. Since the output of the FDM system is four 300-bps lines which are input to TDM3, TDM4 now demultiplexes this data into four 300-bps channels which are then interfaced to the computer. TDM4, in addition, separates a 4,800-bps channel from the 9,600-bps composite speed, and this channel is further demultiplexed by TDM2 into its original 10 channels which were provided by TDM1. In addition, TDM4 separates the two 1,200-bps channels which were multiplexed by TDM3. Thus, the 10 data channels of TDM1 and the four channels of the FDM system are serviced by the eight-channel TDM3 (which includes one 1,200-bps unused channel for timing). At city G, TDM4 contains 8 channels (again, one 1,200-bps channel is unused and provides timing) of which the 4,800-bps channel is further demultiplexed by the 10-channel TDM2 system. Due to the similarity in channels, TDM4 can be considered the mirror image of TDM3, and TDM2 would be the mirror image of TDM1. With the advent of new families of multiplexers produced by several vendors, only one multiplexer may be required at city G to demultiplex data from all remote sites.

Intelligent Multiplexers

In a traditional TDM, data streams are combined from a number of devices into a single path so that each device has a time slot assigned for its use. While such TDM are inexpensive, reliable, and can be effectively employed to reduce communications costs, they make inefficient use of the high-speed transmission medium. This inefficiency is due to the fact that a time slot is reserved for each connected device, whether or not the device is active. When the device is inactive, the TDM pads the slot with nulls and cannot use the slot for other purposes.

An intelligent multiplexer is in many respects very similar to a concentrator since both devices combine signals from a number of connected devices in such a manner that there is a certain probability that a device will have access to the use of a time slot for transmission. Whereas a concentrator may require user programming and always requires special software in the host computer to demultiplex its high-speed data stream, intelligent multiplexers are built around a microprocessor that is programmed by the vendor, and no host software is required for demultiplexing since another intelligent multiplexer at the computer site performs that function.

By dynamically allocating time slots as required, intelligent multiplexers permit more efficient utilization of the high-speed transmission medium. This permits the multiplexer to service more terminals without an increase in the high-speed link as would a traditional multiplexer. The technique of allocating time slots on a demand basis is known as statistical multiplexing and means that data is transmitted by the multiplexer only from the terminals that are actually active. Another technique used by intelligent multiplexers which permits more efficient use of line capacity is data compression. Here, the different frequencies of different characters are used to reduce the average number of bits per character via the use of codes. Thus, when numerical data is transmitted, the digits might be translated into 4-bit codes instead of the normal 7 or 8 bits required on a traditional TDM. Through the use of statistical multiplexing and data compression, between two and four times as much traffic may be supported over a high-speed line as a traditional multiplexer can support. For most intelligent multiplexers being marketed, asynchronous terminal data traffic can be supported in a 4:1 ratio, commonly referred to as a 4:1 compression ratio. This compression ratio should not be confused with the data compression of transmitted characters, as the ratio also includes the benefits derived from statistical multiplexing in addition to the actual data compression. Thus, with a compression ratio of 4:1, four 1,200-bps terminals connected to a statistical multiplexer would have a composite high-speed output of 1,200 bps. For synchronous terminal data traffic, compression ratios of between 1.5 and 2.0 to one are normally produced by the statistical multiplexer. Prior to the utilization of intelligent multiplexers, the transmission characteristics of the terminals to be supported must be carefully investigated.

Since intelligent multiplexers contain a memory area for the temporary storage of traffic when an excessive number of terminals become active, it is important that the terminals do not approach a steady-state operation condition, or the multiplexers storage area will fill and data can be lost. Some intelligent multiplexers preclude this storage area overfill condition by temporarily inhibiting one or more terminals from transmitting as traffic volumes reach a critical point. For these reasons, terminals used to sample data continuously are normally not connected to intelligent multiplexers.

An example of the effective utilization of intelligent multiplexers can be obtained from a comparison of methods used to link terminals to a computer, as shown in Fig. 3.14. In the top portion of Fig. 3.14, a tradi-

Fig. 3.14. Comparing Multiplexers and Intelligent Multiplexers

The use of intelligent multiplexers permits greater line utilization.

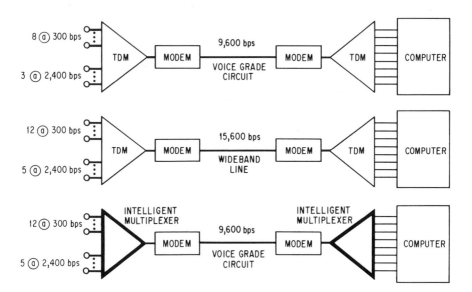

tional TDM multiplexes three 2,400-bps and eight 300-bps terminals from a remote location to a central computer. Suppose an expansion required the addition of two 2,400-bps terminals and four 300-bps terminals. Since the multiplexer uses all available time slots to run the high-speed line at 9,600 bps, even if the multiplexer can accommodate the additional devices a high-speed line and higher speed modems will be required. Since wideband service costs four times or more per mile than leased voice-grade lines, the transmission over any significant distance could result in a considerable expense. As shown in the middle section of Fig. 3.14, a wideband line capable of supporting 15,600-bps transmission would be required to support the new terminals.

While other techniques (see Sec. 3.3) exist to preclude the use of wideband transmission, they inevitably require additional communication devices to be employed on the circuit. The use of an intelligent multiplexer can permit more data to be transferred over an existing link without additional equipment, as shown in the lower portion of Fig. 3.14. Here, the 9,600-bps modems can continue in operation, even though the conventional TDM would require modems capable of transferring data at 15,600 bps. Depending upon the technique employed for data compression and the statistical nature of the activities of the terminals, 7,200-bps modems might also be considered. Although the use of intelligent multiplexers can be considered on a purely economic basis to determine if the increased cost of such devices is offset by the reduction in line and modem costs, the statistics that are computed and made available to the user of such devices should also be considered. Although many times intangible, these statistics may warrant consideration even though an economic benefit may at first be hard to visualize. Some of the statistics normally available on intelligent multiplexers are listed in Table 3.3. Through a careful monitoring of these statistics, network expansion can be preplanned to cause a minimum amount of potential busy conditions to users. In addition, frequent error conditions can be noted prior to user complaints and remedial action taken earlier than normally transpired when conventional devices are used.

TDM Options

Numerous options are available for both traditional and intelligent TDM. A partial list of such options will be found in Table 3.4. Auto speed detect permits the multiplexer to have the capability of automatically adjusting to the speed and character format of asynchronous data. This option lets the multiplexer dynamically configure itself and thus lets a single terminal channel support a variety of asynchronous terminal speeds without an operator manually reconfiguring the multiplexer each time a different terminal desires to use a channel. Autoecho permits a multiplexer to serially echo received data from an asynchronous terminal channel back to the terminal. Its utilization provides a primitive form of error control since

Table 3.3.   Intelligent Multiplexer Statistics

Multiplexer loading: % of time device not idle
Buffer utilization: % of buffer storage in use
Number of frames transmitted
Number of bits of idle code transmitted
Number of negative acknowledgments received

$$\text{Traffic density} = \frac{\text{nonidle bits}}{\text{total bits}}$$

$$\text{Error density} = \frac{\text{NAKs received}}{\text{frames transmitted}}$$

$$\text{Compression efficiency} = \frac{\text{total bits received}}{\text{total bits compressed}}$$

$$\text{Statistical loading} = \frac{\text{number of actual characters received}}{\text{maximum number which could be received}}$$

$$\text{Character error rate} = \frac{\text{characters with bad parity}}{\text{total characters received}}$$

Table 3.4.   Multiplexer Options

Auto speed detection	Multinode operation
Audio alarm	Redundant common logic
Autoecho	Redundant power supply
BYSYNC Terminal support	Synchronous test cards
Asynchronous test cards	Statistical display
Port contention	

the user can see the character transmitted. Binary synchronous (BISYNC) terminal support is an option required on some multiplexers to support terminals that transmit data under that protocol. Port contention is an option that enables a multiplexer to make originating remote terminals contend for one or more of a group of available computer ports. This option makes the multiplexer function as a port selector in addition to its multiplexing role. To support the interconnection of more than one node in a network, the multinode operation option should be considered. A variety of multinode configurations can be established so that the user can have the capability of altering the interconnections of source and destination data flow. The other options listed in Table 3.4 should be self-explanatory, and the user should check vendor literature for specific options available for use on different devices.

3.2. Group-band Multiplexers

A group-band multiplexer is a TDM which has been specifically designed to permit multiple channel usage of group-band (wideband) data circuits. Although the capabilities and capacities of group-band multiplexers vary by manufacturer, basically they provide the user with the ability to intermix different speed-synchronous data streams in order to obtain a composite synchronous data stream that is suitable for transmission over group-band (wideband) facilities. Typical group-band multiplexer servicing speeds can range from 2,400 bps through 56 kbps, with such intermediate speeds as 4,800, 7,200, 9,600, and 19,200 bps being acceptable to most devices. The composite transmission speed developed by the group-band multiplexer for transmission over the wideband facilities can range from 19.2 kbps through 1.544 Mbps, with intermediate data rates of 38.4, 40.8, 50.0, 56.0, 64.0, and 230.4 kbps commonly used.

Operation

Similar in operation to a traditional TDM developed to service synchronous data streams, a group-band multiplexer uses a bit interleaving process to combine two or more channels of synchronous digital data onto a single synchronous wideband facility. Although techniques vary by manufacturer, one or more channels are usually utilized as a synchronization channel within the group-band multiplexer. Due to the utilization of channels for synchronization, a portion of the high-speed data rate in effect becomes reserved for system overhead. While this overhead is not significant when compared to the total data transmission rate of the system, it must be taken into consideration when configurating the channel utilization of a group-band multiplexer. Thus, while a traditional TDM would develop a 9,600-bps output data rate when it multiplexes two 4,800-bps input data streams, a group-band multiplexer used to service thirty-one 2,400-bps data streams would produce a composite speed in excess of 74,200 bps due to the synchronization overhead. This is shown in Fig. 3.15, where a group-band multiplexer is used to combine thirty-one 2,400-bps data streams. In this example, one additional channel is used only for synchronization, which makes the composite speed rise to 76.8 kbps although the usable data transmission capacity of the circuit is 74.2 kbps.

Fig. 3.15. Group-band Multiplexer Overhead
An allowance for one or more synchronization channels must be considered when group-band multiplexers are employed.

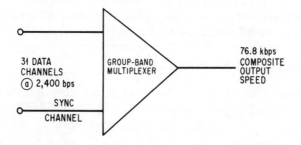

Since synchronization techniques vary, manufacturers' literature should be consulted to determine the number of synchronization channels which must be used at different data rates. In addition, the user should check vendor literature to determine the number and speed of the synchronous data channels that are supported. Some devices have a program pin on each channel module so that the user can select the needed speed as long as it is some multiple of 2,400 bps, up to 19,200 bps. On other devices a change in channel rates may require a return of the equipment to the factory or service by field engineers.

Applications

In addition to providing a link between two computer centers where a requirement may exist for multiple computer-to-computer communications, group-band multiplexers are adaptable for a number of communication network applications. An example of their application would be in a communications network where one or more regional areas are distant from the computer center so that the charges for leased lines connecting individual terminals and multiplexers to the computer center cumulatively exceed the cost of providing wideband service between a central point in that region and the computer center. An example of this type of situation is shown in Fig. 3.16. Here, TDM are installed in cities A and C to multiplex four 2,400-bps synchronous data streams in each city and transmit the multiplexed data over voice-grade lines at 9,600 bps to the group-band multiplexer which is installed in city B. At city B, the group-band multiplexer services eight additional 2,400-bps data streams which originate at that location, in addition to the two 9,600-bps data streams from cities A and C. If the group-band multiplexer being utilized requires one 2,400 bps synchronization channel as shown, although data is transmitted on the wideband facility at 40,800 bps, only 38,400 bps is actually used for data transmission with the difference being allotted to synchronization overheads.

Although not commonly used, group-band multiplexers can be pyramided at one location to make it possible for the user to combine the transmissions from 1,000 or more low-speed terminals for transmission over a Bell System circuit at a speed of 1.536 or 1.544 Mbps. Due to the limited number of organizations which have 1,000 terminals in a regional area, yet alone in a city, a more common pyramiding technique is to use a mixture of TDM and group-band multiplexers to service a few hundred terminals within a regional area as well as providing a computer-to-computer link over the same circuit used to service the terminals. An example of this type of application is shown in Fig. 3.17. In this example, a TDM services eight 1,200-bps terminals in city A and produces a 9,600-bps synchronous data stream which is input to the group-band multiplexer at city D. This group-band multiplexer acts as a pyramid, servicing the

Fig. 3.16. Group-band Multiplexer Servicing Regional Area

The capacity of a group band multiplexer can be utilized by employing the device to serve as a hub or data transmission focal point at regional locations.

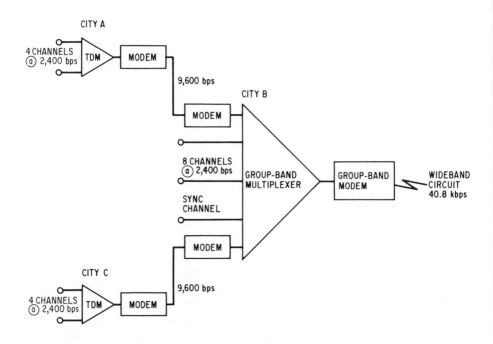

40.8-kbps data stream of the group-band multiplexer in city B and the 76.8-kbps data stream of the group-band multiplexer in city C. At city D, two computers, each transmitting at 19,200 bps as well as twenty-six 2,400-bps terminals are serviced by the group-band multiplexer. With 1 channel used for synchronization, this group-band multiplexer produces a composite output of 230.4 kbps which now contains the traffic of eight 1,200-bps terminals, seventy-three 2,400-bps terminals, two computers at 19.2 kbps, and three synchronization data streams at 2,400 bps. Although it may be hard to visualize, one advantage of pyramiding group-band multiplexers is that monitoring, cabling, and troubleshooting can be simplified through the installation of functionally identical units at cities B, C, and D.

Options

Like most communications equipment, group-band multiplexers can be obtained with either a data terminal equipment (DTE) interface, a data communications equipment (DCE) interface, or a combination of the two interfaces. Thus, if the terminals to be serviced by the group-band multi-

Fig. 3.17. Pyramiding

Group-band multiplexers can simplify monitoring and trouble-shooting by permitting functionally identical units to be installed at many locations.

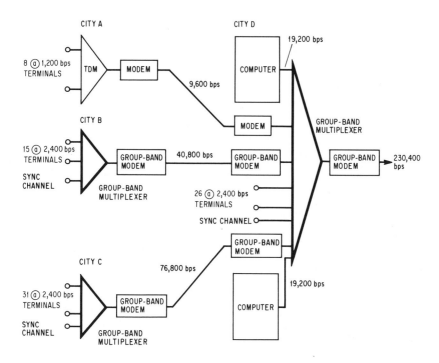

plexer are within the cable length specifications of the RS-232 interface, they can be directly connected to the group-band multiplexer and the user does not have to obtain modems. By using the data communications equipment interface, the group-band multiplexer can service distant data streams via modems, as shown in the previous examples.

Group-band Modems

While group-band multiplexers multiplex data streams for transmission over group-band facilities, group-band modems provide the mechanism for the transmission of that data over the facilities at speeds ranging from 9.6 kbps through 1.544 Mbps. Usually, the group-band multiplexer derives its wideband send and receive clock from the attached modem and by integer division divides the clock into the individual lower data rates. Some manufacturers offer group-band modems which have strap selectable rates, whereas on some group-band modems the data transmission rate is fixed. In selecting a group-band modem the user should investigate what options are available, as well as their cost. Some common options include strap selectable rates as previously mentioned, simultaneous voice channel capability where a plug-in card allows simultaneous usage of the 104- to 108-kHz segment of the available bandwidth for voice communications, Bell System 303 data set interface adapters, as well as buffers which will permit the group-band modem to operate on a digital network.

Similar Functional Devices

Prior to the selection of group-band multiplexers for a particular application, a number of similar functional devices should be checked to determine their applicability and cost of usage.

First, inverse multiplexers present an economic alternative to the use of wideband transmission at speeds up to 19,200 bps. Next, if a large number of asynchronous terminals are to be multiplexed, another potential device that should be considered is an intelligent multiplexer. This device will strip away the start and stop bits associated with asynchronous transmission, perform selected data compression for transmission, and reverse the compression and reinstitute the start and stop bits at the destination. Through these techniques, between four and eight 300-bps terminals can effectively share one time slot that would normally require four to eight such slots on a traditional multiplexer. The reader should refer to Secs. 3.1 and 3.3 for additional information on these devices.

3.3. Inverse Multiplexers

Through the introduction of a new class of data communications equipment, network users can now obtain transmission at wideband rates through the utilization of two voice-grade lines. These devices also provide network configuration flexibility and provide reliable back-up facilities during leased line outage situations. In addition, since wideband transmission is not available at many locations, these devices have the extra advantage of extending wideband service to every location where the more available leased line service can be obtained.

Operation

An inverse multiplexer splits a data stream at the transmitting station, and two substreams travel down different paths to a receiving station. Such a data communications technique has several distinct advantages over single-channel wideband communications lines. Using leased lines increases network routing flexibility and permits the use of the direct distance dialing (DDD) network as a back-up in the event of the failure of one or both leased lines.

Similar in design and operation, devices produced by several manufacturers permit data transmission at speeds up to 19,200 bps by combining the transmission capacity of two voice-grade circuits. Their operation can be viewed as reverse time division multiplexing. Input data streams are split into two paths by the unit's transmitting section. Although this chapter will concentrate in greater detail on the general operation of these devices, two specific units are described in more detail in Figs. 3.18 and 3.19.

The inverse multiplexer produces two serial bit streams by dividing all incoming traffic into two paths. All odd bits are transmitted down one path and all even bits down the other. At the other end, the receiver section continuously and adaptively adjusts for differential delays caused by 2-path transmission and recombines the dual bit streams into one output stream, as illustrated in Fig. 3.20.

Each inverse multiplexer contains a circulating memory that permits an automatic training sequence, triggered by modem equalization, to align the memory to the differential delay between the two channels. This differential delay compensation allows, for example, the establishment of a 19,200-bps circuit consisting of a 9,600-bps satellite link, and a 9,600-bps ground or undersea cable, as shown in Fig. 3.21. In this type of application, the failure of one circuit can be compensated by transmitting the entire data load over the remaining channel at one-half the normal rate.

Typical Applications

As stated previously, one key advantage obtained by using inverse multiplexers is the cost savings associated with two voice-grade lines in place of wideband facilities. Another advantage afforded by these devices gives the user the ability to configure and reconfigure the network based upon the range of distinct speeds available to meet changing requirements. If synchronous 9,600-bps speed-selectable modems are installed with the inverse multiplexers, four possible throughput bit rates can be transmitted, as shown in Table 3.5. For transmission over two voice-grade circuits at

Table 3.5.   Wideband Transmission Combinations Available (bps)

Modem A	Modem B	Transmission speed
9,600	9,600	19,200
9,600	7,200	16,800
7,200	9,600	16,800
9,600	4,800	14,400
4,800	9,600	14,400
7,200	4,800	12,000
4,800	7,200	12,000

Fig. 3.18. Biplexer

The Codex Biplexer provides full-duplex transmission at speeds as high as 19,200 bps (composite) over two type 3002 C2 conditioned voice-grade lines by combining the capacity of two independent channels. These channels may be diversely routed with differential delays of up to 800 ms. The Biplexer contains monitor circuits that detect modem degradations and/or failures so that the Biplexer can always maintain at least one-half the normal data rate. Other data rates per channel are 2,400, 4,800, and 7,200 bps.

Features include automatic compensation for differential transmission paths; adaptation to changing line delays; automatic restoral over the direct distance dialing (DDD) network in the event of dedicated line failure; remote and local loop backs; complete fault isolation; and system-monitoring capabilities.

Interface. For high-speed terminals, four interface configurations are available—Bell 303B, EIA RS-232-C/CCITT V.24, CCITT V.35 for standard European wideband modems, and MIL STD 188 for military specifications.

Physical specifications. Power supply: ac inputs of either 115 or 230 V ± 10 percent; 47–63 Hz, switch-selectable. The internal oscillator provides stability within 1 part in 10^6 per year. The Biplexer unit is 7 in high, 19 in wide, and 21 in deep.

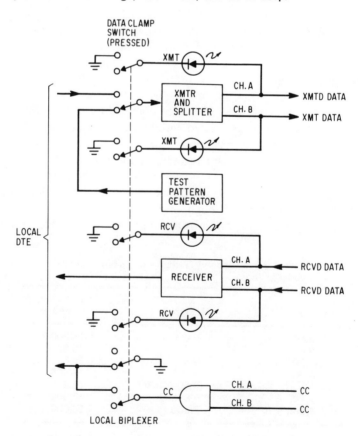

LOCAL BIPLEXER

Fig. 3.19. Lineplexer II

The Rancal–Milgo, Inc. Lineplexer II operates in a full-duplex mode to transmit and receive odd bits down one type 3002 voice-grade channel at speeds up to 9,600 bps while it simultaneously uses a second voice-grade channel to transmit and receive even bits at the same rate. Recombination of "plexed" data results in a composite speed that is double the rate on the individual channels.

The Lineplexer II features a total backup system over the direct distance dialing (DDD) network, reconfiguration for day-night operations that allows system rearrangement of port configuration and operating speed via front-panel switches and displays, unattended operation through a self-monitoring system that causes the associated modem to fall back to a lower speed if the line degrades, automatic alternate-route selection, and diagnostic capabilities.

Specifications. Technical specifications include: data-transfer rate of 19,200 bps on high-speed channels interfacing with RS-232-C, MIL STD 188C, Bell 300 series, CCITT V.24, and CCITT V.35. Voice-band channels at speeds from 4,800 bps to 9,600 bps for composite speeds of 9,600 bps to 19,200 bps over the DDD network are available with interfaces to RS-232-C, MIL STD 188C, and CCITT V.24. Modes of operation include channel A only, channel B only, channel A and B (normal operation), and channel A or B (both channels handle identical data, but only one is used, according to signal quality). Primary power is from an ac input at 105–125 or 210–250 V ac, 47–63 Hz.

Signal restoration. Speed is reduced after receipt of a low signal quality indication from either modem by external command, by using the manual Lineplexer switch, or through the operation of the Lineplexer sync monitor, special circuitry that stops transmission completely until both channels are resynchronized. Reestablishment of the high rate is automatic.

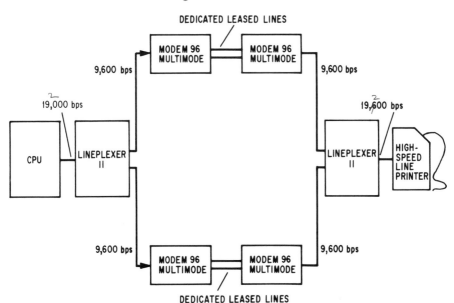

9,600 bps for a composite rate of 19,200 bps, utilization of inverse multiplexers at this speed may be considered to provide a computer-to-computer transmission path. This is illustrated in Fig. 3.22. Another application for such a device could be to connect a high-speed remote batch terminal to a computer at a lower but still wideband transmission rate, as shown in Fig. 3.23.

Another possible use of such devices is to permit time-sharing operations and computer-to-computer or remote batch terminal-to-computer transmissions to occur over common leased lines. This sharing of the transmission medium can be accomplished through the use of multiport modems, as illustrated in Fig. 3.24.

In the example shown in Fig. 3.24, sixteen 300-bps terminals have their data multiplexed by two 8-channel TDM at the remote site. Each TDM produces a 2,400-bps synchronous data stream which is connected to one port on a multiport modem. The remote batch terminal or computer transmits data at 14,400 bps which is split into two 7,200-bps data streams by the inverse multiplexer. Each 7,200- and 2,400-bps data stream is then multiplexed by the multiport modem for transmission at 9,600 bps to the central site. At the central site the process is reversed, with the inverse multiplexer recombining the 7,200-bps output from one port of each modem into a single 14,400-bps data stream that is transferred to the computer. Each 2,400-bps output is demultiplexed by the TDM into eight 300-bps channels and connected to the computer to provide a total of 16 low-speed terminal paths that are transmitted over the same facility as the computer or remote job entry (RJE) data.

Contingency Operations

If the user is faced with the problem of channel degradation, rather than a total outage, an automatic fallback capability allows the pair of channels to be switched to a slower speed until the return of good signal quality permits the resumption of higher speed transmission. Another important

Fig. 3.20. Inverse Multiplexer Operation
An inverse multiplexer splits a transmitted data stream into odd and even bits which are transmitted over two voice-grade circuits and recombined at the distant end.

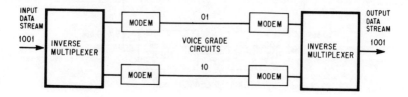

Fig. 3.21. Inverse Multiplexing Using Satellite-terrestrial Circuits

One type of "plexing" configuration could involve the use of a satellite link for one data stream with a ground or undersea cable link for the other.

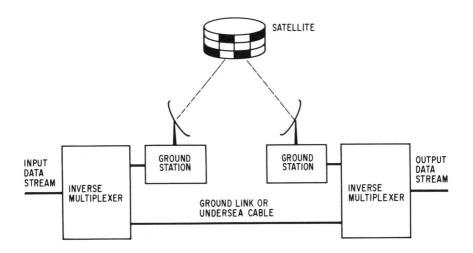

Fig. 3.22. Computer-to-computer Transmission

Inverse multiplexer at remote computer site splits data stream into odd and even bit streams that travel at 9,600 bps over conditioned voice-grade lines and recombine at the CPU located at the central site.

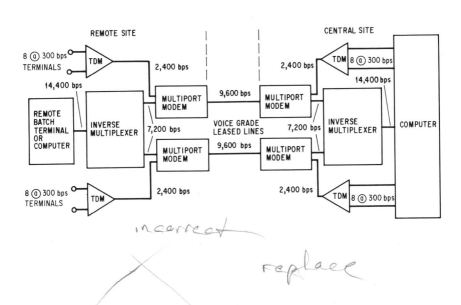

Fig. 3.23. Reduced but Still Wideband Transmission

Lower transmission rates at wideband speeds can be maintained by the use of inverse multiplexers.

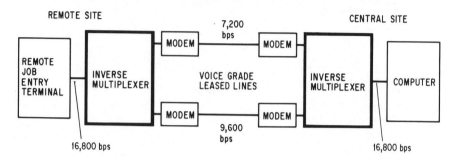

capability not available on wideband facilities is that service can be restored to one or both voice channels by dialing over the voice network during a dedicated line outage. This restoral capability provides for the configuration of the network in such a way as to develop a wide range of contingency plans, in addition to the range of inherent equipment speeds and the combination of line speeds available. If one or both of the leased lines should fail or transmission degrades on a circuit to a point where the continued use of that circuit is unacceptable, circuit compensation can be achieved in a variety of ways. Figure 3.25 details two possible methods of circuit compensation. In the first example, data throughput may be maintained at 19,200 bps by the utilization of the dial-up or switched voice network. If

Fig. 3.24. Shared Use of Wideband Facilities

A number of configurations can be developed by using inverse multiplexers and multiport modems to permit shared use of wideband facilities.

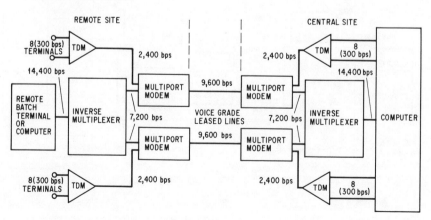

Fig. 3.25. Methods of Circuit Compensation

Top: Dial restore to compensate failure of leased line. Bottom:
Continued operations on one line at a data rate of 9,600 bps or
less. Leased-line failure can be remedied directly over the DDD
network. If this is not possible, transmission can continue at half
speed on the remaining channel.

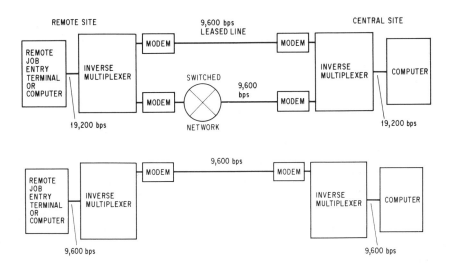

the quality of the dial-up connection is such that 9,600-bps transmission
cannot be maintained, a drop in the transmission to 7,200 bps may become
necessary. Even at this speed, total aggregate throughput will be 16,800
bps. In the second example, it is postulated that, because of high cost, the
DDD network would be unavailable, as would be the case in the failure of
a satellite channel. The remaining circuit permits the maintenance of a data
transmission rate as high as one-half the normal 19,200 bps.

Economics of Use

An advantage in the use of an inverse multiplexer is the cost savings associated with using two voice-grade lines. In 1978, wideband transmission, as
regulated by the Federal Communications Commission (FCC) Tariff 260
for series 8000 channels, was priced at $16.20 per mile for the first 250
miles, $11.40 per mile for the next 250 miles, and $8.15 per mile for
every mile thereafter. Voice-grade interchange channel tariffs are divided
into three rate schedules, with the schedule used determined by transmission from and to rate center categories. Schedule 1 rates apply to a channel
between two category A rate centers, schedule 2 applies to a channel between a category A rate center and a category B rate center, while schedule
3 rates apply to a channel between two category B rate centers. Voice-

Table 3.6.   Voice-Grade Leased Line Cost per Mile

Mileage	Schedule 1	Schedule 2	Schedule 3
1	51.00	52.00	53.00
2–15	1.80	3.30	4.40
16–25	1.50	3.10	3.80
26–40	1.12	2.00	2.80
41–60	1.12	1.35	2.10
61–80	1.12	1.35	1.60
81–100	1.12	1.35	1.35
101–1000	0.66	0.66	0.68
over 1000	0.40	0.40	0.40

grade leased line costs for each schedule are shown in Table 3.6. In addition to line distance charges, modem charges associated with voice-grade channels can be substantially lower than charges for service stations required by wideband facilities. When a two-station charge of $784 is added to the cost of a 100-mile wideband circuit, the cost to the user of such a facility will be $2,404 per month. Using a lease rate of $1,450 for a pair of inverse multiplexers and four 9,600-bps modems, the cost of two schedule 1 100-mile voice-grade circuits, the inverse multiplexers and modems will be $1,700 per month, indicating a breakeven point of less than 100 miles before inverse multiplexing becomes economically feasible. Through the use of Table 3.6 the reader can compute the economic advantage, if any, of using inverse multiplexers for a particular application.

Another advantage of inverse multiplexer utilization is availability of service. Since wideband transmission is generally available only in major cities, two voice-grade circuits transmitting at a composite rate of 19,200 bps, in effect, extend wideband capacity nationwide.

Because of the ease of channel speed selection and line restoral capability, line utilization should be more efficient and back-up capabilities better than those currently available on wideband transmission facilities.

3.4. Concentrators and Front-end Processors

Integral to almost every data communications network are two devices which, although consisting of many similar hardware components, must be recognized and utilized as distinct entities whose performance is designed for particular applications. These devices are communications concentrators and front-end processors. Substantial confusion concerning the utilization of these devices can occur due to the multitude of functions they perform. A front-end processor in effect performs concentration functions by concentrating a number of lines into a few data transfer paths between that processor and a host computer. Likewise, a remote network processor can be viewed as performing the functions of a front-end processor when its high-speed data link is used to transmit data directly into another processor. To alleviate some of the existing confusion about the utilization of these processors, this section will examine the basic components of these devices, the functions they perform, the characteristics that should be investigated for evaluation purposes, and their placement within a data communications network.

Concentrators

As a general statement, a concentrator is a device which concentrates m incoming lines to n outgoing lines, where the number of incoming lines is greater than or equal to the number of outgoing lines. The incoming lines are usually referred to as concentrator-to-terminal links, whereas the outgoing lines are normally called concentrator-to-concentrator or concentrator-to-host links, as illustrated in Fig. 3.26. Although the concentrator-to-host link implies such lines from the concentrator are connected to the host processor, in actuality they can terminate at a front-end processor which is in turn connected to a host processor or main computer. Depending upon the hardware components and operating software one selects, the concentrator can be used to perform a number of functions. These functions can include concentration, pure contention, store and forward concentration, concentration and message switching, and remote network processing.

When functioning as a concentrator, data from a large number of low- and medium-speed lines are combined for retransmission over one or more high-speed lines. The high-speed output can be transmitted directly to a front-end processor or to another concentrator. In a pure contention role, the concentrator serves as a programmed switch and is also referred to as a port selector or contention unit. Through the addition of on-line storage capacity and appropriate software, the concentrator can be con-

Fig. 3.26. Concentrator Links

In a concentration role m incoming lines (concentrator-to-terminal links) are concentrated onto one or more high-speed lines (concentrator-to-host computer system links).

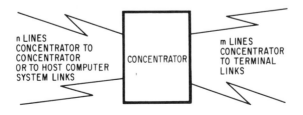

n LINES
CONCENTRATOR TO
CONCENTRATOR
OR TO HOST COMPUTER
SYSTEM LINKS

CONCENTRATOR

m LINES
CONCENTRATOR
TO TERMINAL
LINKS

figured to store and forward messages or to perform message switching alone. Another function rapidly gaining acceptance is that of remote network processing which is a term used to denote concurrent concentration and remote batch processing on one processor.

In a concentration role, concentrators concentrate m low- to medium-speed lines onto one or more high-speed lines, similar to the function performed by a multiplexer. However, concentrators can be programmed to transmit data only from terminals that are active as opposed to a conventional TDM, in which a fixed fraction of the multiplexed channel is reserved for each terminal regardless of whether the terminal is active. By using the memory areas in concentrators for stored programs, changes in terminal speeds, data formats, communications procedures, the number of terminals to be serviced can be accommodated, whereas a traditional multiplexer is primarily an inflexible hardware device configured to accept predetermined data inputs and produce a predetermined data output. Concentrators can also be programmed to make more efficient utilization of the high-speed data link through data compression, making use of the different frequencies of characters to cause a reduction in the average number of bits transmitted per character through the utilization of codes to denote different characters or groups of characters. If the host computer's native code is different from the terminal's code, code conversion can be performed by the concentrator, relieving the host processor of this function. While concentrators provide a significant advantage over the use of traditional multiplexers, users should also explore the capabilities of newer multiplexers, which are referred to as intelligent multiplexers. These devices are built around microprocessors and perform many communications functions previously available only through the use of concentrators. The reader is referred to Sec. 3.1 for additional information on intelligent multiplexers.

Concentrator Components

The typical hardware components included in a concentrator in a concentration role are shown in Fig. 3.27. The single-line controllers provide the necessary control and sensing signals to interface the concentrator to individual data communications circuits. While single-line controllers can be asynchronous or synchronous, the majority are used to transmit synchronous data since each controller is used to provide only one high-speed transmission link from the concentrator to another concentrator or host computer (front-end processor).

Since the support of numerous lines would be expensive and would consume a large amount of physical space if implemented with single-line controllers, most communications support for the concentrator-to-terminal links are implemented through the use of multiline controllers (MLC). These can be categorized by capacity (number of lines and speed of lines

Fig. 3.27. Concentrator Hardware Components

The single and multiline controllers provide the necessary control and sensing signals to interface the concentrator to the communications circuits.

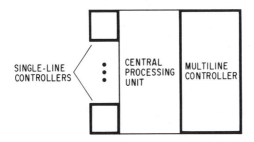

supported) as well as by the type of operation—hardware- or software-controlled and the type of data transfer employed—character at a time or block transfer. Hardware-controlled MLC place no additional burden on the concentrators' central processing unit (CPU), whereas programmed controllers place a large burden on the processor although they have the lowest cost per line by reducing the hardware in the interfaces and the controller to a minimum. For a programmed controller, all sampling control, bit detection, and buffering is performed by the processor with the amount of processing time required by the operational program being the delimiting factor determining the amount of lines that can be connected to the concentrator.

To reduce the complexity of circuits in hardware MLCs as well as to reduce software overhead of programmed controllers, incoming lines must normally be grouped on some controllers. These groupings are by baud rate, code level, and the number of stop bits for asynchronous terminal support. Figure 3.28 illustrates a typical grouping by channel for an MLC that requires a minimum of four groups per class with any mixture of classes until the number of groups multiplied by 4 equals the total number of channels supported by the controller.

Although a complete examination of controllers might warrant the investigation of up to 50 parameters, Table 3.7 denotes the key types of information one should ascertain about the different controllers that may be supported by a concentrator. Another area that can have a major bearing on communications costs is the types of interfaces that the controller supports, as illustrated in Fig. 3.29. If the controller supports directly connected terminals and the concentrator can be located within the vicinity of a number of those terminals, directly connecting those terminals to the concentrator will alleviate the cost of installing line drivers or pairs of modems between the concentrator and each terminal.

Table 3.7.   Controller Selection Factors

Control type: hardware or software
Number of lines supported (MLC only)
Number of lines per group (MLC only)
Number of classes (MLC only)
Maximum throughput (MLC only)
Data codes and speeds supported
   Number of bits per character
   Number of stop bits
   Sync characters support
Number per concentrator
Full-duplex/half-duplex support
Automatic dial/automatic answer support
Modem interface
Line-type serviced
   Leased
   Switched
   Direct connect
Asynchronous/synchronous support
Protocol supported
Parity checking
Expansion capability (MLC only)

Pure Contention Concentrator Applications

In essence, a pure contention concentrator is a programmed switch which is also referred to as a port selector. In performing this function, any of m input lines are connected to any of n output lines as one of the n output lines becomes available. The m input lines are commonly called the line side of the concentrator, whereas the n output lines are referred to as the port side of the concentrator, since a concentrator used for this type of function interfaces the ports of a front-end processor on the output side of the device. The basic hardware components of a contention concentrator is illustrated in Fig. 3.30. Incoming data on each line of the line side of the device is routed through the processor which searches for a nonbusy line on the port side to which the data can be transmitted. Priorities can be programmed so that groups of incoming lines can be made to contend for one or a group of lines on the port side of the device. When all ports are in use, messages can be generated to new terminals attempting to access the system, and through the addition of peripheral devices, jobs can be batched to await the disconnection of a user from the system and then to use the newly available port side line to gain entry to the computational facility. Additional information about port selectors will be found in Sec. 3.7.

Store and Forward Message Concentration

Although some vendors offer a complete concentration package to include controllers and CPU, other vendors permit the customer to select the CPU that is to be used for the concentrator. The evaluation and selection of the

Fig. 3.28. Groupings by Channel

The number of groups and classes permitted by the multiline controller are important constraints that must be determined prior to equipment selection.

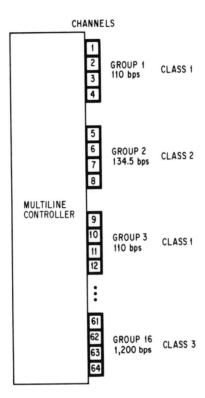

CPU of the concentrator should be accomplished similarly to the evaluation and selection of any standalone computer. Both the hardware and software should be evaluated according to user requirements. Thus, if one has the requirements for a store and forward message concentration system, emphasis should be placed upon peripheral equipment, data transfer rates,

Fig. 3.29. Controller Interfaces

The types of interfaces that the controller supports may have a major bearing on communications costs.

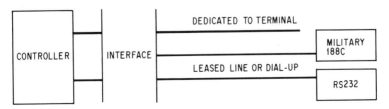

Fig. 3.30. Contention Concentrator Components

A pure contention concentrator functions as a port selector, with *m* input lines contending for access to *n* output lines.

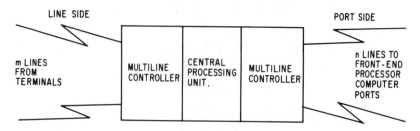

and software appropriate for this particular application. In addition, if the application is critically time dependent, examining hardware reliability may not suffice by itself, and the user will most likely want to consider a redundancy configuration. Figure 3.31 illustrates a redundant store and forward message concentration system, in which both systems are directly connected to each other by an intercomputer communications unit and share access to incoming and outgoing lines and peripherals via electronic switches. During operation, one system is considered the operational processing or master system while the other system is the slave or standby system. Upon a hardware failure or power interruption, the master system signals the slave system to take over processing via the intercomputer communications unit, generates an alarm message, and conducts an orderly shutdown. Since the slave system has been in parallel processing, it resets all switches and becomes the master system, holding the potential of losing data to a minimum. This procedure can usually be completed within 500 ms for processors with a cycle time of 750 ns* or less, since 666 cycles (500 ms/750 ns) or more are then available within that time period to execute the required instructions to transfer control and effect the orderly shutdown. Since instructions normally require two to three processor cycles, this time permits about 220 instructions to be executed to cause the switchover and shutdown.

Message Switching

To effect message switching, incoming data is routed to a central point where messages are concentrated for processing, and based upon some processing criteria, messages are then routed out over one or more lines connected to the system. In a message switching system, all terminals connected to the system can communicate with every other terminal connected to the system once the message has been processed and the destination data is acted upon.

---

* ns = nanosecond

Fig. 3.31. Redundant Store and Forward Message Concentration Hardware

Upon a hardware failure or power interrupt the master system signals the slave system to take over processing via the intercomputer communications unit.

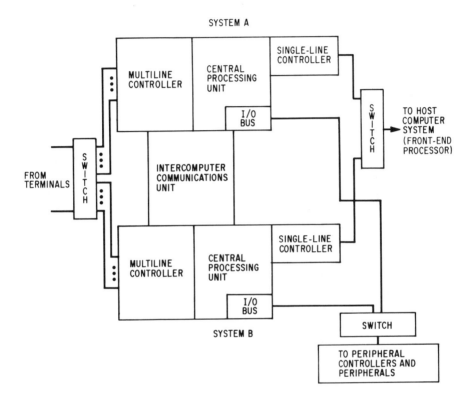

The hardware required for a message switching system is quite similar to that required by a store and forward message concentration system, the primary difference being the application software, the fact that incoming messages are processed and then routed out over one or more of the incoming lines, and that access to peripherals might be accomplished via a data-multiplexed control (DMC) or direct memory access (DMA) option in the concentrator instead of through the use of the lower data transfer rates obtained with the use of the I/O bus. The interface used to transfer data to and from controllers and peripheral devices is normally a function of the required data transfer rate.

The DMC provides peripheral devices with high-speed access to the computer's memory. It is a passive device that responds to the requirements of the devices connected to it. When a particular device has data to input or is ready to accept data, it uses the DMC control lines to request service. The DMC then sends a break request to the CPU, and a DMC cycle is executed when the current instruction is completed. During the DMC cycle the appropriate transfer between the device and the computer's memory occurs with the DMC using the computer's standard I/O bus for data transfer to and from the device. A DMA interface allows data transfers to bypass the I/O bus and thus allows external devices such as line controllers to access memory without program control. All receive characters enter a prescribed table in memory where they are then operated on by the program in the processor. In the DMC and DMA modes, data transfers are effected independent of program control so that other processing may be accomplished during data transfers. A message switching system configured for redundancy of operation is shown in Fig. 3.32. In addition to examining the controller parameters listed in Table 3.7, the line and station characteristics of the message switching system which are a function of both hardware and software should be determined. Table 3.8 lists some of the message switching system characteristics that should be investigated prior to selecting such equipment. The number of stations supported many times is far more important than the number of lines supported, since a number of foreign exchange (FX) lines in diverse cities could each be connected to a channel on the MLC of the message switching system. This

Fig. 3.32. Redundant Message-switching System

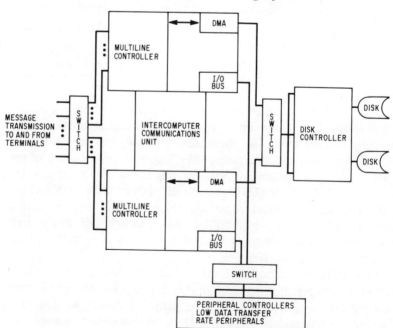

Table 3.8. Message Switching System Characteristics

Number of lines supported
Number of stations supported
Line speeds and codes supported
Station types
Message addressing permitted
Levels of message priority
Message length
Input error checking
Alternate routing
Line and station holds and skips
Journalization capability
Retrieval capability
Intercept and recovery provisions
Alarms and reports

situation would enable a large number of terminals to contend for the FX line in each city, with each terminal having a unique station code. Station type refers to whether full-duplex, half-duplex, or simplex transmission is supported, while message addressing refers to the number of addresses per message as well as the availability of broadcasting a message to a predetermined group of stations or to all stations by using a group addressing scheme. Most message switching software permits message priority of several levels. An example of priorities would be *expedite, normal,* and *deferred,* where a *deferred* priority message is transmitted to its destination after normal working hours, whereas a message of *expedite* priority would terminate any message being transmitted to the addressee of the expedite message until the expedite message transmission is completed. Depending upon vendors, some software packages permit any station to assign any message a priority while other systems can lock out terminal stations from assigning one or more priorities to a message. Normally, the maximum length of any message is a function of disk space and system throughput, but for all practical purposes, users can transmit messages without worrying about their length.

Software for a good message switching system will preprocess the message header as it is entered and inform the user of invalid station codes, invalid group addresses, garbled transmission for both header and text, and other errors prior to routing the message. On some systems, a message denoting these errors will also be routed to the message switching systems' operator's console so that person will be able to ascertain user problems as they occur and furnish assistance, if required. Alternate routing permits supervisory personnel to route all traffic destined to one or a group of stations to some other station. This capability is important if for some reason a communications component or terminal becomes inoperative and there is a station nearby that can handle messages destined for the inoperative terminal. Line and station holds and skips supplement alternate routing as they permit polling to any line to be skipped and permit traffic to any station or line to be held from delivery.

Journalization permits every message transmitted from the system to be recorded on journal storage. This permits message retrieval from the journal. However, the type of retrieval permitted varies from system to system. Some systems permit any station to retrieve messages delivered to itself, while other systems permit any station to retrieve any message by sequence number. On some systems, only the operator can access the journal by either station number, sequence number, or time of day. Intercept permits the operator to have traffic that is routed to specific lines or stations rerouted to intercept storage and to be delivered to the addressed destinations by using a recovery function. These characteristics are especially important if a large number of lines become inoperative at one time and messages cannot be alternate routed to other nearby terminals. Since line drops are of critical importance to a message switching system, events of this type can normally be expected to cause an alarm message being generated to an operator console so he or she can take appropriate action.

Remote Network Processing

A remote network processor (RNP) is in effect a concentrator. However, it also performs the additional function of remote batch processing, thus providing two distinct functions in one package. RNPs vary in capabilities, ranging from basic, single-job stream remote batch processing plus remote message concentration to multiple job stream remote batch processing combined with remote message concentration. Due to the addition of remote batch processing to the concentration function, line utilization to the host computer is extremely high since the RNP may be servicing a variety of devices to include card readers, magnetic tape units, and line printers, in addition to concentrating the data from remote terminals for transmission to the host computer. A typical RNP configuration is illustrated in Fig. 3.33.

As shown in Fig. 3.33, several concurrent remote and local batch processing jobs can be accomplished in addition to the standard concentration function. Remote batch jobs can be entered for transmission to the host computer while completed jobs are printed on the line printer and other jobs are being punched out on the card punch.

Some RNPs have a segment of read only memory which permits down-line loading of operational software from the host computer to the RNP. This is a valuable feature since it permits programming changes for new batch and remote terminal equipment to be performed at the central site and alleviates the necessity of employing programmers at every RNP installation to effect equipment configuration changes.

Fig. 3.33. Remote Network Processor

Both remote batch processing and the concentration of terminal data for transmission are performed concurrently by a remote network processor.

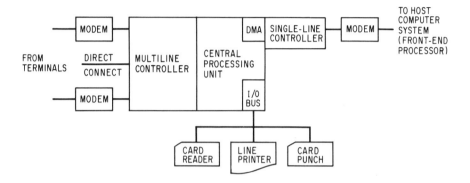

By offloading work from the host computer by blocking the characters transmitted from each terminal into messages, the RNP permits users to better load balance their computational equipment, and in many instances this can alleviate a costly host processor upgrade or the threat of encountering degraded service.

Down-line Loading

Most concentrators being marketed today can be obtained with a READ ONLY MEMORY. This feature can be used to permit dynamic concentrator reconfiguration of the types of terminals serviced or to change processing functions by down-line loading of the concentrator. An example of this is shown in Fig. 3.34.

Although the multiline programmed controller is interfaced to 22 lines, for daytime operations it only services sixteen 300-bps time-sharing terminal lines and four 1,200-bps cathode ray tube (CRT) lines. The data from the lines serviced are transmitted at 9,600 bps to the central computer facility. For nighttime operations, eight of the time-sharing lines and two of the CRT lines are removed from service in order to permit two 2,400-bps printers to be connected via the concentrator to the central computer. This dynamic reconfiguration can be controlled by the central computer by having the central computer down-line load the concentrator. During the down-line loading procedure, instructions are sent to the concentrator which activates the concentrators READ ONLY MEMORY. The READ ONLY MEMORY is a fixed program which then takes the incoming data from the central computer, stores it in a predetermined location as a new program, and then initiates the program into operation. The incoming data can be

Fig. 3.34. Dynamic Reconfiguration by Down-line Loading

Dynamic reconfiguration of terminals serviced by a concentrator can be controlled by the host computer system through the process of down-line loading the concentrator.

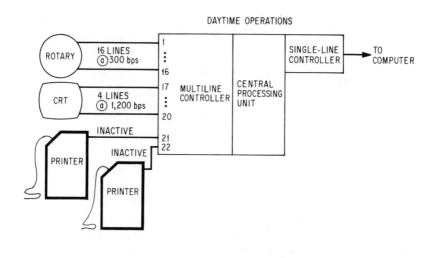

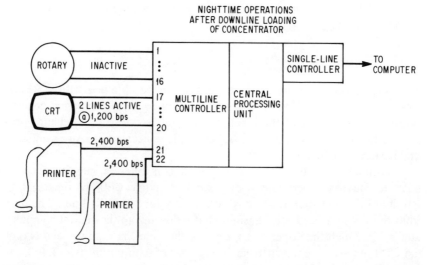

an entirely new program or new tables and commands which alter the previous software configuration and in effect can become a new or revised program. This new program then determines which lines and what types of terminals will now be serviced by the concentrator. The key advantage of this type of operation is that no operator intervention is necessary and the concentrator can also be down-line loaded in the morning to resume daytime requirements before anyone reports to work.

Fig. 3.35. Alternate Link Routing Using Concentrators

One concentrator can be used, to provide an alternate routing capability by permitting the sharing of its primary link to the host computer system.

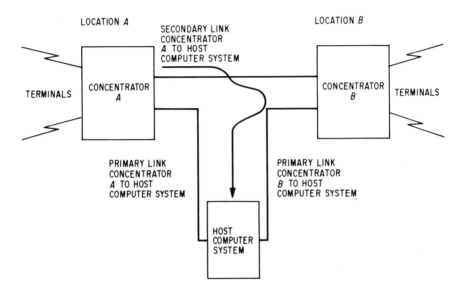

Alternate Routings

Since a concentrator can have several high-speed output lines (single-line controllers), it is possible to configure a network so that one concentrator can be utilized to provide an alternate link routing capability to a second concentrator, as shown in Fig. 3.35. In this example, the remote terminals which are serviced by the concentrator at location A are linked to the computer center on the primary remote concentrator A to computer center line. If this primary link should become inoperative, the central computer can communicate with the remote terminals attached to concentrator A through the secondary link which consists of a high-speed line from concentrator A to concentrator B and the sharing of concentrator B's primary link from concentrator B to the computer center.

Satisfying Average Data Transfer Requirements

Since a concentrator can be used to store input data from the terminals it is connected to until memory is full or by transferring the information to secondary storage such as a disk or tape unit, the high-speed lines from the concentrator to another concentrator or to the computer center only need the capacity to handle the average data rate of the terminals. This permits the condition to occur where the concentrator service's terminal input exceeds the maximum line transmission rate from the concentrator to the computer center. Thus, information is stored in memory or on secondary storage until such time as the concentrator can retrieve the information and transmit it to its destination. For a traditional multiplexer, the absence of terminal activity still requires the multiplexer to take up signal space on the high-speed line, although the activity slot for that terminal is padded with nulls. Since numerous terminal applications have data transmission conducted in burst mode with the terminal activity reduced to a minimum between each burst, a portion of the high-speed line is usually idle for a majority of the time, with the multiplexer transmitting mostly nulls and thus wasting a large portion of the line's capacity. This type of situation can be alleviated to a large degree when concentrators are used. As shown in Fig. 3.36, sixteen 1,200-bps terminals with an average data rate of 500 bps can be serviced by a single concentrator, and depending upon the line overhead (protocol) and buffering techniques employed, transmission from the concentrator to the computer center can occur over one 9,600-bps line. In reality, due to buffering and protocol overhead, only 70 to 90 percent of the high-speed link capacity is normally available for data transfer, reducing the effective data transfer on a 9,600-bps line to between 6,700 and 8,600 bps. Through the addition of a disk, traffic peaks and valleys can be smoothed out, since the disk can be used to provide intermediate storage for the condition where seven or more terminals become active at the peak data rate of 1,200 bps and thus exceed the 9,600-bps transmission capacity of the line from the concentrator to the central computer. To service the same number of terminals with a multiplexer would require the installation of two such devices at the remote location as well as two demultiplexers at the central computer site, with each multiplexer transmitting over a 9,600-bps line. Since multiplexers must be configured to service a terminal's peak data rate, the two multiplexers require double the line capacity which the concentrator needs in transmitting to the central computer. In addition, since a concentrator can be programmed to communicate directly with a high-speed channel of the central computer, no additional hardware may be necessary at the central site, whereas two multiplexers may be necessary to split the high-speed multiplexer traffic back into its original form so that the computer can talk to the remote terminals. This requirement for demultiplexers is due to the fact that multiplexer protocols are unique and computers cannot communicate with the high-speed multiplexer traffic without extensive software modifications.

In determining which type of device to use, the savings in line charges and modem costs achieved by the concentrator's capability must be balanced by the higher cost of the concentrator and its disk subsystem as well as the queuing delay when the average data rate exceeds the transmission line capacity.

Fig. 3.36. Using Concentrators to Satisfy Average Data Rates

Sixteen 1,200-bps terminals with 600-bps average data rate. In addition to servicing more terminals than time division multiplexers, concentrators only require one computer port which may substantially reduce hardware costs at the central computer site.

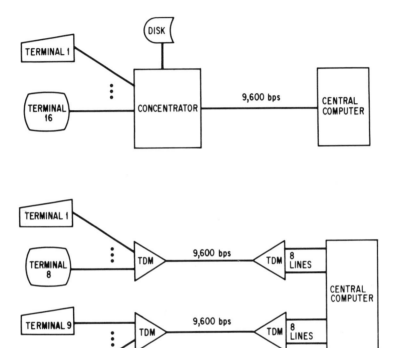

Front-end Processors

A front-end processor provides a large volume of network communications power in support of a particular computer system. Although they are similar in design and have components in common with concentrators, normally they have larger word sizes, faster cycle time, and larger memory, and permit the interfacing of more communications devices to the processor. In addition, front-end processors are usually more "closely coupled" to a particular host computer and may be specifically programmed to operate with that computer and its operating system. A typical front-end processor configuration is illustrated in Fig. 3.37.

Fig. 3.37. Front-end Processors

A front-end processor can be considered the heart of a computer network, relieving the host-computer system of many software burdens, performing such functions as code conversion, character blocking, and character deblocking.

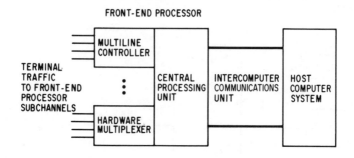

FRONT-END PROCESSOR

Not only are more MLCs available for connection to a front-end processor than for a concentrator, the MLCs are close to being universal in their ability to service a mixture of synchronous and asynchronous data at speeds ranging from 50 to 50,000 bps. Another device encountered on some front-end processors but normally not used on concentrators is a local communications multiplexer which provides for time division multiplexing by character, to and from the front-end processor, for a variety of low-speed terminals at transmission rates up to 300 bps. These local multiplexers can handle terminals with differing communications speeds and code settings, with the character demultiplexing performed by software in the front-end processor. In addition to performing network and communications processing activities that one normally associates with front-end processors, owing to the larger memory and word size, quite often they can be used to perform message switching functions by the addition of modular software.

The operating system which supervises the overall control and operation of all system functions is the key element of a front-end processor. Although numerous software elements must be evaluated, major consideration should be given to determining supported line protocols as well as supported processor communications. In the first area, most vendors divide their supported line protocols into several categories or classes of support. Normally, category 1 refers to vendor-developed and tested software to support certain line protocols. Category 2 usually refers to vendor-developed but nonqualified tested software, while category 3 refers to customer-developed interfaces designed to support certain terminal line protocols. While the features of front-end processors are similar to concentrators, the reliability and redundancy as well as diagnostics should be more extensive since the front-end processor is the heart of a communications network. Figure 3.38 illustrates a typical data communications network consisting of several different types of concentrators and a front-end processor.

At location 1, a standard concentrator is used to concentrate the traffic from 32 terminals onto a high-speed line for transmission to the front-end processor. Since location 2 has a requirement for remote batch processing as well as connecting 12 terminals to the host computer, a remote network processor has been installed to perform these two functions. Since location 3 has a significant number of terminals doing an important application, a redundant store and forward message concentrator was installed at that location. The remainder of the terminals in the network totals 128. However, it was felt that at most only 56 would ever become

Fig. 3.38. Integrating Concentrators and Front-end Processors into a Network

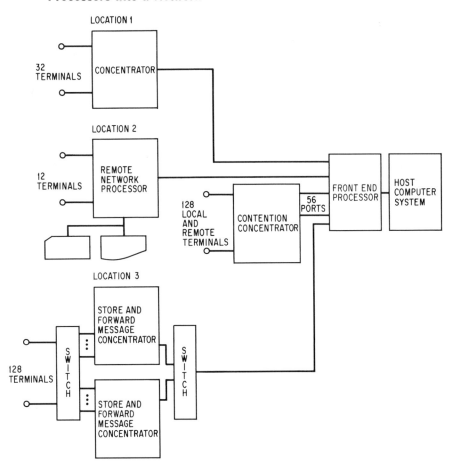

active at any given time. Therefore, to economize on front-end processor ports, a contention concentrator was "front ended" to the front end processor, making 128 lines connected to 128 terminals contend for the use of 56 front-end processor ports.

3.5. Modem- and Line-sharing Units

Cost-conscious company executives are always happy to hear of ways to save money on the job. One of the things a data communications manager can best do to make his or her presence felt is to produce a realistic plan for reducing expenses. It may be evident that a single communication link is less costly than two or more. What is sometimes less obvious is the most economical and effective way to make use of even a single link.

Multiplexing is usually the first technique that comes to mind. But there are many situations where far less expensive, albeit somewhat slower, equipment is quite adequate. Here, terminals are polled one by one through a "sharing device" that acts under the instructions of the host computer. Typically, the applications where this method would be most useful and practical would be those where messages are short and where most traffic between host computer and terminal moves in one direction during any one period of time. The technique, which can be called "line sharing" (as distinct from multiplexing) may work in some interactive situations, but only if the overall response time can be kept within tolerable limits. The technique is not as a rule useful for remote batching or RJE, unless messages can be carefully scheduled so as not to get in each other's way because of the long run time for any one job. Although line sharing is inexpensive, it has some limits to its usefulness, particularly in situations where a multiplexer, most likely a TDM, can be used to produce additional economic leverage.

Operation

A TDM operates continuously to sample in turn each channel feeding it, either bit by bit or character by character, and produces an aggregate transmission at a speed equal to the sum of the speeds of all its terminals.

A conventional TDM operation is illustrated in Fig. 3.39A (top). A multiplexer operating character by character assembles its first frame by taking (for example) the letter A from the first terminal, the letter E from the second, and the letter I from the third terminal. During the next cycle, the multiplexer takes the second character of each message (B, F, and J, respectively) to make up its second frame. And the sampling continues in this way until traffic on the line is reversed to allow transmission from the computer to the terminals. The demultiplexing side of the TDM (operating on the receiving side of the network) assembles incoming messages and distributes them to their proper terminals or computer ports.

Fig. 3.39. Multiplexing Versus Line Sharing

A. Time division multiplex network. B. Modem-sharing network.
Multiplexer needs. A time or frequency division multiplex system
(A) requires one computer port for each terminal and a
multiplexer at each end. A sharing system (B) needs only one
computer port. Because it requires terminals to be polled, a
sharing system can be cost-effective for interactive operation, but
may not be so for long messages such as are likely to move in
remote job entry or remote batch types of applications.

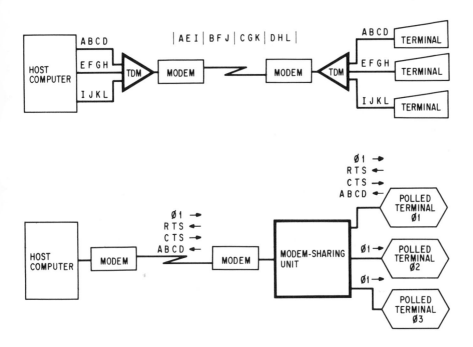

An FDM divides up the transmission link's total bandwidth into a
number of distinct strips, each of which is able to carry a low-speed channel. The FDM accepts and moves transmissions from all of its terminals
and ports simultaneously and continuously.

A line-sharing network is connected to the host computer by a local
link, through which the host polls the terminals one by one. The central
site transmits the address of the terminal to be polled throughout the network by way of the sharing unit. This is illustrated in Fig. 3.39B (bottom).
The terminal assigned this address (01 in the diagram) responds by transmitting a request to send (RTS) signal to the computer, which returns a
clear to send (CTS), to prompt the terminal to begin transmitting its
message (ABCD in diagram). When the message is completed, the terminal
drops its RTS signal, and the computer polls the next terminal.

Throughout this sequence, the sharing device continuously routes the
signals to and from the polled terminal and handles supporting tasks, such

as making sure the carrying signal is on the line when the terminal is polled and inhibiting transmission from all terminals not connected to the computer.

Device Differences

There are two subspecies of device used in this technique: modem-sharing units and line-sharing units. They function in much the same way to perform much the same task—the only significant difference being that the line-sharing unit has an internal timing source, while a modem-sharing unit gets its timing signals from the modem it is servicing.

A line-sharing unit is mainly used at the central site to connect a cluster of terminals to a single computer port, as shown in Fig. 3.40. It does, however, play a part in remote operation, when a data stream from a remote terminal cluster forms one of the inputs to a line-sharing unit at the central site, to make it possible to run with a cheaper single-port computer.

In a modem-sharing unit, one set of inputs is connected to multiple terminals or processors, as shown in Fig. 3.40. These lines are routed through the modem-sharing unit to a single modem. Besides needing only one remote modem, a modem-sharing network needs only a single 2-wire (for half-duplex) or 4-wire (for full-duplex) communications link. A single link between terminals and host computer allows all of them to connect with a single port on the host, a situation that results in still greater savings.

Fig. 3.40. Line-sharing and Modem-sharing Use Compared
Line-sharing units tie central site terminals to the computer, but modem-sharing units handle all the remote terminals. A line-sharing unit requires internal timing, whereas a modem-sharing unit gets its timing from the modem to which it is connected. In either case, access to the host is made through a single communications link—either 2-wire or 4-wire—and a single port at the central site computer.

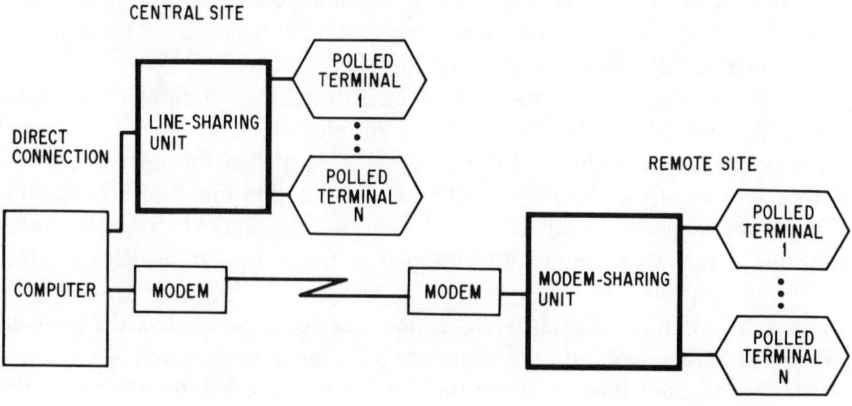

If multiplexing were used in this type of application, the outlay would likely be greater, because of the cost of the hardware and the need for a dedicated host computer port for each remote device. A single modem-sharing unit, at the remote site, is all that is needed for a sharing system, but multiplexers come in pairs, one for each end of the link.

The polling process makes sharing units less efficient than multiplexers. Throughput is cut back because of the time needed to poll each terminal and the line turnaround time on half-duplex links. Another problem is that terminals must wait their turn. If one terminal sends a long message others may have to wait an excessive amount of time, which may tie up operators if unbuffered terminals are used, although terminals with buffers to hold messages waiting for transmission will ease this situation.

Sharing Unit Constraints

Sharing units are generally transparent within a communications network. There are, however, four factors that should be taken into account when making use of these devices: the distance separating the data terminals and the sharing unit (generally set at no more than 50 ft under RS-232-C interface specifications); the number of terminals that can be connected to the unit; the various types of modem with which the unit can be interfaced; and whether the terminals can accept external timing from a modem through a sharing unit. Then, too, the normal constraints of the polling process, such as delays arising from line turnaround and response and the size of the transmitted blocks must be considered in designing the network.

The 50-ft limit on the distance between terminal and sharing unit (RS-232 standard) can cause problems if terminals cannot be clustered closely. A way to avoid this constraint is to obtain a sharing unit with a DCE option. This option permits a remote terminal to be connected to the sharing unit through a pair of modems, as illustrated in Fig. 3.41. This in turn allows the users the economic advantage of a through connection out to the farthest point. Since the advantage of modem-sharing units over a multipoint line is the reduction in the total number of modems when terminals are clustered, only one or at most a few DCE options should be used with a modem-sharing unit, as it could defeat the economics of clustering the terminals to utilize a common modem.

It is advisable to check carefully into what types of modem can be supported by modem-sharing units, since some modems permit a great deal more flexibility of network design than others. For instance, if the sharing unit can work with a multiport modem, the extra modem ports can service remote batch terminals or dedicated terminals that frequently handle long messages. An example of this flexibility of design is shown in Fig. 3.42. Some terminals that cannot accept external timing can be fitted with special circuitry through which the timing originates at the terminal itself, instead of at the modem.

Fig. 3.41. Extending the Connection

Line- or modem-sharing units form a single link between host computer and terminals. This system contains a modem-sharing unit with inputs from the terminals at its own site as well as from remote terminals. A line-sharing unit at the central site can handle either remote site devices or local devices more than 50 ft away from the host computer, which is the maximum cable length advisable under RS-232-C standards.

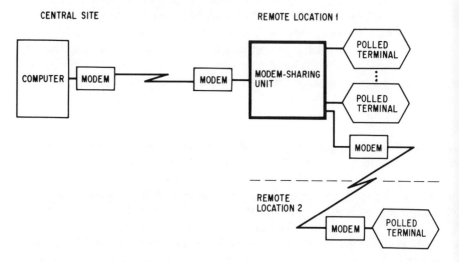

Economics of Utilization

The prices of sharing units range from $500 to $3,000, depending mainly on the number of terminals that can be connected through the unit. At present this number varies, the most versatile units being able to handle up to 32 terminals.

As shown in Table 3.9 (p. 148), a typical multiplexing system containing a line leased at $1,000 a month and designed to service four 1,200 bps terminals (Part A of the table) might cost the user $2,160 a month; a system with a modem-sharing unit designed to service four polled 4,800 bps terminals (Part B of the table) would cost $1,900 a month, or 12 percent less. Because the leased line contributes the largest part of the system's cost, the percentage saved with a less expensive line can be even greater. For instance (Part C of the table), a line leased for $500 a month would increase the overall saving to 16 percent.

Other Sharing Devices

Sections 3.6 and 3.7 cover sharing devices. Section 3.6 explores the use of port-sharing units, which are used in polled networks for the programmed selection of the computer port. Section 3.7 discusses port selection (or port

Fig. 3.42. Multiple Applications Can Share the Line

Through the use of a modem-sharing unit with a data
communications equipment interface, a terminal distant from the
cluster (location 2) can share the same line segment (computer
to location 1) that is used to transmit data to those terminals at
location 1. With a second application that requires a remote batch
terminal at location 1, additional line economies can be derived
by installing multiport modems so both the polled terminals and
the RBT can continue to share the use of one leased line from the
computer to location 1.

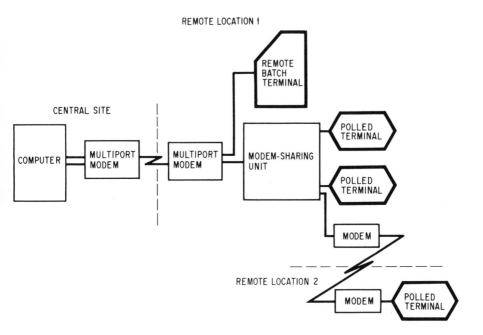

contention) units, where the unit provides random access to the computer
ports under its control. The most significant differences in the different
types of sharing units lies in their placement and function and in the
options available to them. Unlike line-, modem-, and port-sharing units,
the port selection devices operate by time sharing or contention. Access to
any one port is provided on a first-come, first-served basis whenever a port
is available. With port selection, therefore, a large number of lines contend
for a small number of ports. Users let go of a port by signing off in a way
similar to that found in time-sharing and RJE applications. The reader
should refer to these sections for additional information.

3.6. Port-sharing Units

An alternative to the utilization of modem- and line-sharing units in a
communications network can be obtained through the employment of de-

Table 3.9. Comparison of Monthly Rental Costs

A. Multiplexing

		Monthly cost
Two TDM at $90 each		$ 180
Two 4,800-bps modems at $120 each		240
Four computer ports at $35 each		140
Leased line		1,000
Four terminals at $150 each		600
	Total monthly cost	$2,160

B. Using a modem-sharing unit

		Monthly cost
Two 4,800-bps modems at $120 each		240
Computer port		35
Modem-sharing unit		25
Leased line		1,000
Four terminals at $150 each		600
	Total monthly cost	$1,900

C. How percentage savings increase as
   leased line cost decreases

	$1,000 a month leased line	$500 a month leased line
Multiplexing	$2,160	$1,660
Modem-sharing unit	1,900	1,400
Percentage saving	12%	16%

vices known as port-sharing units. In addition, the proper employment of such devices can be used to complement or supplement modem- and line-sharing units and in certain situations may result in large economies being realized.

When to Consider Their Use

Port-sharing units are devices that are installed between a host computer and modem and that control access to and from the host for up to six terminals with the number of terminals currently limited by the capabilities of current hardware. In this way, port-sharing units are able to cut down on the number of computer ports needed for these terminals. The port-sharing unit is versatile, inexpensive (about $500), and available from many modem and terminal manufacturers. Its utilization can save the cost of a relatively expensive computer multiplexer channel that does essentially the same job but may have more capabilities than are needed. Port-sharing units can be used to service both local and remote terminals and so expand the job that can be done by a single port of the host computer.

To put the concept of port sharing into perspective, the user should be aware of related devices designed to cut networking costs. Modem-sharing units and line-sharing units are available to minimize modem and line costs at remote locations, but they do not deal with the problem of overloading the host computer's ports. Modem- and line-sharing units are partial solutions to the high cost of data communications networking, but they are limited to the types of problems they can handle, and they can, by themselves, complicate the life of the network designer.

A problem that surfaces when either modem- or line-sharing units are used by themselves is the distribution of polled terminals within the network. For either kind of sharing unit to be effective, the terminals should be placed so that several are grouped close together. A typical modem-sharing unit employed to connect a number of terminals at a remote location for access to one computer port via a single pair of modems is illustrated in Fig. 3.43. Some modem-sharing units can be obtained with a DCE interface option which is an RS-232-C interface by which remote terminals at two or more locations can be connected to the modem-sharing unit through the installation of a pair of modems between the terminal and the modem-sharing unit. Such a configuration is shown in Fig. 3.44. Although the use of the interface shown in Fig. 3.44 permits the network to have a more flexible configuration, with a number of terminals remote from the sharing unit, the number of such terminals that can be served by any one unit is usually limited to one or two.

Another disadvantage of this arrangement is that it is rather like putting all the eggs in one basket. If either modem on the high-speed link between the computer and the modem-sharing unit should fail, or if the circuit itself goes down, all the remote terminals become inoperative. Multiplexed terminals can use the dial-up network to restore data communications if the dedicated line fails. Polled terminals, however, do not have this advantage, since the host computer software is set up to seek and recognize the addresses of specific terminals in a certain order on the line. Thus, polled terminals must stay in their respective places, relative to each other, along the communications route. Any change in route necessitates changes in hardware at the terminals as well as software at the host computer.

Fig. 3.43. Modem-sharing Unit Usage

A modem-sharing unit permits a number of polled terminals to share the usage of a single line, one pair of modems, and a single computer port.

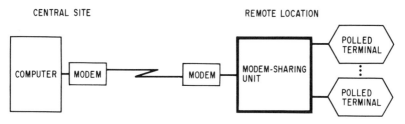

Fig. 3.44. Network Expansion Using Modem-sharing Units with Data Communications Equipment (DCE) Interface

Remote terminals at two or more locations can share a common polled circuit when a DCE interface is present on the modem-sharing unit.

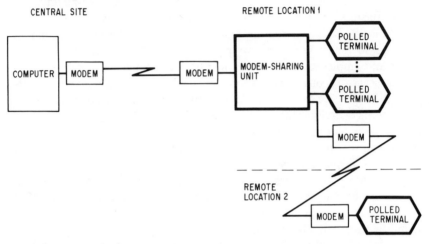

As new applications develop and the number of remote terminals connected to the host computer increases, a situation can arise where the network designer runs out of ports to service the network. If no additional ports are available a costly computer upgrade or the installation of a second computer system would represent a major economic burden. A method to alleviate or postpone these types of equipment upgrades is through the utilization of port-sharing units.

Operation and Usage

Port sharing, then, is presented either as an alternative or as a supplement to modem and line sharing, in networks without multiplexers. A port-sharing unit is connected to a computer port and can transmit and receive data to and from two to six either synchronous or asynchronous modems, as shown in Fig. 3.45.

Data from the computer port is broadcast by the port-sharing unit, which passes the broadcast data from the port to the first modem that raises a receiver-carrier detect (RCD) signal. Data for any other destination will be blocked by the unit until the first modem stops receiving. The port-sharing unit thus provides transmission by broadcast and reception by contention for the port connected to it. Like a modem-sharing unit, a port-sharing unit is transparent with respect to data transmission. Data rates are limited only by the capabilities of the terminal, modem, and computer port.

But, to gain the same results without a port-sharing unit would require a multidrop configuration. Both the port-sharing unit and a multidrop net-

Fig. 3.45. Using a Port-sharing Unit

The port-sharing unit lies between the host computer and the modems at the central site. One advantage is that if a failure occurs on the communications line or at the modem, only the terminal on that particular line goes down. On a polled, multidrop line, a line failure renders all terminals beyond it inaccessible.

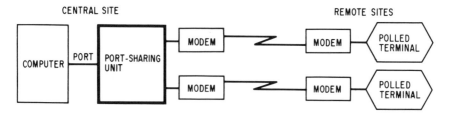

work allow a large number of terminals to be served by one computer port, but in a multidrop network the failure of any part of the circuit will put all terminals beyond the failure out of action. In the configuration in Fig. 3.45, however, failure of modem or outage on the line will only cut out a terminal on that segment. Failure of a computer port or of the port-sharing unit would of course bring down the entire network, but these devices are stable and such failures are fairly unusual.

Port Sharing as a Supplement

Port-sharing units may also be used alongside modem-sharing units. If modem-sharing units alone are used, a situation can arise where there are not enough ports to serve the network, as in Fig. 3.46A. If each modem-sharing unit serves its full complement of terminals, and all the computer ports are in use, expansion of the network, even by just one port, may require a second mainframe computer.

This problem can also be dealt with by the use of a port-sharing unit at the central site which, by cutting down the number of ports currently needed, allows a network to expand without additional computer ports. Figure 3.46B shows how one port-sharing unit with a two-modem interface can free a computer port from the configuration shown in Fig. 3.46A.

One versatile feature of port-sharing units is an option that allows the unit to accept a local interface instead of the normal RS-232-C interface, so that up to two local terminals may be operated without modems at the central site, as shown in Fig. 3.47.

While both modem-sharing units and port-sharing units are similar in the way they are used, there is an important difference in the normal placing of their interfaces. In Table 3.10, a comparison of the characteristics of a port-sharing unit with those of modem- and line-sharing units will be found. For additional information on the latter two devices the reader is referred to Sec. 3.5.

Fig. 3.46. Two Sharing Techniques Combined

When only modem-sharing units are used (A) a time may come when every port is in use and no further expansion on the network is possible. Rather than buy another host computer to serve a single new terminal, the user may prefer to invest in a port-sharing unit (B) that will solve the problem for about $500.

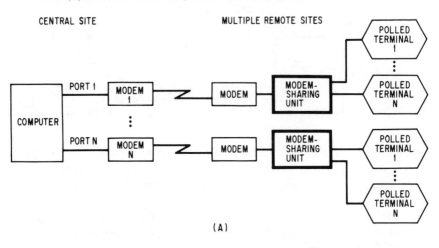

(A)

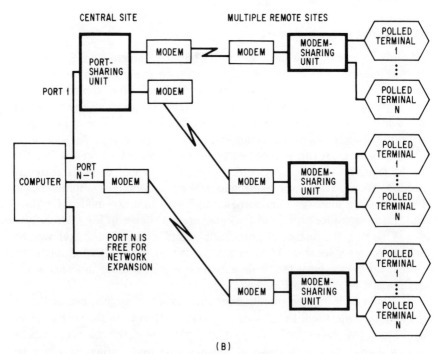

(B)

Fig. 3.47. Connecting Local Peripherals

A local interface option to port-sharing units lets local and remote sites be served by the same port. Peripherals are polled as if they were at remote sites.

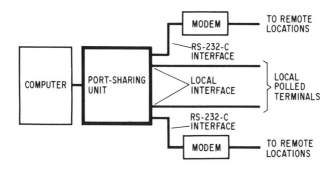

Table 3.10. Features of Sharing Units

Feature	Modem-sharing line-sharing unit	Port-sharing unit
Transmit mode	Broadcast	Broadcast
Receive mode	Contention	Contention
Number of modems interfaced	2–32	2–6
Terminals supported	Polled	Polled
Options	RS-232-C Interface (MSU to modem)	Local interface (PSU to terminal)
Normal interface placement	Between modem and terminal	Between computer port and modem

Comparing Cost with Alternate Components

In Fig. 3.48, the reader is presented with two alternate means of connecting four 2,400-bps remotely located terminals to a central computer facility. In the top portion of that illustration, a port-sharing unit and four individual lines and four pairs of modems are installed to enable the terminals to communicate on a poll and select basis with the computer. For this configuration the failure of any modem or line will only render the terminal connected to the failing modem or line inoperative. In the lower portion of that illustration (Fig. 3.48B), a pair of four-channel synchronous multiplexers has been installed to service the four terminals which are now restricted to being colocated unless other equipment is installed in addition to the devices shown in that illustration. Table 3.11 compares the monthly cost of a four-terminal network in multiplexed and port-sharing configurations. The break-even point comes when the cost of each leased line (x) reaches $103 a month. This figure can be arrived at by taking the

Fig. 3.48. Comparing Port-sharing Units with Multiplexers

A. Port-sharing unit servicing four polled terminals. B. Using multiplexers to service the terminals. When a leased line is equidistant from all terminals to the computer, a cost comparison becomes simple as listed in Table 3.11.

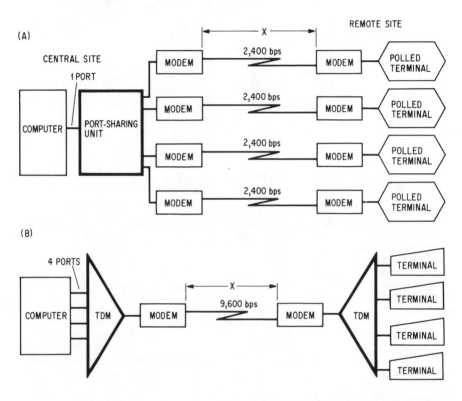

total known costs (for multiplexers, computer ports, modems, and four terminals, at an average of $150 a month apiece), and adding an unknown cost—for the leased line—which remains constant whether the user employs port-sharing units or chooses a multiplexed network configuration. Balanced against this is the somewhat smaller total rental amount for a single port-sharing unit, one computer port, four lower speed modems, and four terminals, all at the same rate of $150 a month.

More Leased Lines

The lower part of the table, however, shows an increase in the number of leased lines from one to four. The upper part of the table, therefore, gives a fixed cost of $1,420 with a variable amount on a one-time basis for a

Table 3.11.   Comparison of Monthly Costs

Multiplexed configuration costs	
Two 4-channel TDM @ $120	$ 240
Four computer ports @ $35	140
Two 9,600-bps modems @ $220	440
Four terminals @ $150	600
One leased line	_x_
	$1,420 + _x_
Port-sharing unit configuration costs	
One port-sharing unit @ $25	$ 25
One computer port @ $35	35
Eight 2,400-bps modems @ $55	440
Four terminals @ $150	600
Four leased lines	4_x_
	$1,110 + 4_x_

Where x = monthly cost of a leased line

single leased line, while the lower part shows a significantly lower equipment cost but gives a variable cost for leased lines four times that for a single-line multiplexed configuration.

In this example, $1,420 less $1,110 equals $310, or $3x$ (with x still representing the variable cost of the leased line). Dividing $310 by 3 gives a break-even point of $103. Thus, until monthly leased line charges total $103 for each line, the use of a port-sharing unit is more economical. Although the preceding cost comparison assumed that the cost of the terminals used on the port-sharing and multiplexer networks illustrated in Fig. 3.48 were equivalent, this may not necessarily be true. Since terminals used on a port-sharing network generally require a buffer area, these terminals may be more expensive than nonbuffered ones that could be used on the multiplexer network. If due to the application requirement buffered terminals become necessary, then the terminal cost can be eliminated from consideration since they would be necessary regardless of the network employed.

In addition, users can (without increasing network costs) add up to two more local or remotely located terminals to a configuration based on a port-sharing unit, since the table is based on the costs related to four terminals, and the average port-sharing unit can support up to six. The only additional cost would be for the rental of the terminal units; none would be incurred for additional modems or leased lines when local terminals are connected.

In order to carry two additional terminals in a multiplexed configuration, however, the user would have to pay substantially more. Not only is an additional $35 per computer port required, but since the multiplexer is operating at the transmission limit of a leased voice-grade circuit, sub-stantially more expensive wideband facilities would have to be installed to service the upgraded multiplexers. In addition, as explained earlier, the cost of adding two computer ports can be further aggravated if all ports are already in use on the host computer, so that any extra load requires another entire processing unit.

The port-sharing unit, therefore, is most evidently a cost-saving tool when the user is already straining the CPU to its limits. While saving money is a full-time preoccupation for all cost-conscious data communica-tions managers, and port sharing should be considered in any polled-terminal situation where instantaneous response is not the most important network condition, there are times, such as when the CPU runs out of capacity, that the cost of any further network expansion takes a leap from a few hundred dollars to perhaps tens of thousands for another CPU.

A Similar Device

Another device which has a function similar to port-sharing units, although its operation and usage differ, is a port selector (or port contention) unit. This unit provides access to a computer port on a first-come, first-served basis. Instead of up to six lines contending for a port, a larger number of lines can reach the same port when it opens up. The availability of a port occurs when a current user of the port disconnects from the system. For additional information the reader is referred to Sec. 3.7.

3.7. Port Selectors

A traditional method used to provide service to new terminals as they are added to a network is through the expansion of the number of front-end processor ports. A variety of approaches can be used to accommodate such terminals. The number of dial-in lines at the computer center can be ex-panded, or additional dedicated or direct connect lines can be installed to service terminals added at the computer facility. For remote locations, the addition or upgrading of multiplexers and the installation of additional leased lines may be required to provide new channels to enable the new terminals to connect and transmit to the computer. Even when such a network expansion is completed, it is unlikely that all ports will be busy at the same time. Thus, while extra lines and additional communications components may be required to provide additional transmission paths to the computer, some front-end processor ports may be operating only a fraction of the day. Port selectors, through their ability to cross-connect incoming transmissions to available ports, permit more efficient front-end processor utilization.

Types of Devices

Many equipment manufacturers sell port selection devices. Most of these products are standalone devices, built to function as an interface between computer ports and lines which may emanate from multiplexers, direct dial lines, or dial-up lines. One manufacturer, however, does offer a port selection option as part of a large multiplexer.

Some port selectors are designed only to contend asynchronous, teletype terminal traffic, while other devices can contend both asynchronous and synchronous traffic within the same unit, with each type of traffic being contended to one or more computer ports servicing that mode of transmission.

Operation

The utilization of port selectors permits terminals to be added to a network with a corresponding increase in the number of computer ports. In addition, the utilization of this device may permit a system contraction whereby a number of computer ports becomes unnecessary and can be returned to the manufacturer.

The basic function performed by a port selector can be viewed as a dynamic data switch similar to telephone rotaries (stepping switches that sequentially search for available outgoing lines), except that the selector provides appropriate interfaces between computers and terminals to route a large calling terminal population to a lesser number of called computer ports. Some selectors have additional features specifically applicable to data networks. Although users tend to confuse port selectors with port-sharing units, their applications are for specific line environments that result from the utilization of different types of terminals for specific applications. Port-sharing units are used in polled networks where the computer controls the traffic flow, and terminals must have a buffer area to recognize polls to their address. Port selection units are used in contention networks, in which terminals transmit to the host on a random basis, and the access to any port is on a first-come, first-served basis.

Computer Site Operations

From a network viewpoint, a port selector is similar to a black box with N line side input connections and n port side output connections, with $N \geq n,$ as shown in Fig. 3.49. The port selector continuously scans all line side connections for incoming data from terminals connected to that side. At the same time, the selector maintains a status check of available ports so that when a terminal becomes operational and requests access, the selector connects the terminal to an available port. Some port selectors can

Fig. 3.49. Port Selector at Computer Site

At line side, port selectors can interface a variety of channels—from multiplexers, dial-in lines, leased lines and direct connect lines. As terminal traffic becomes active, the port selector attaches the circuit to a predefined or randomly selected computer port for the duration of the transmission.

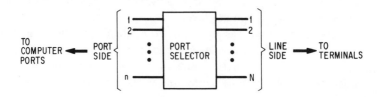

be arranged to form subgroups of contending terminals and ports, so that certain terminals can only be connected to one or more of an assigned group of ports. This capability is discussed more fully under "Selector Features" at the end of this section. If all of the designated ports are taken, the selector will continue to scan until a port becomes available, or until the request for access ceases. Another option is a "busy out" feature whereby the port selector signals new callers that all available ports are in use.

Remote Operations

Port selectors can be used at remote locations to make input terminals contend for a lesser number of communications lines or multiplexer ports. Consider a remote location with 32 terminals, each communicating with the central computer at 300 bps, as illustrated in Fig. 3.50. If all terminals at the remote location can be directly connected to the multiplexer to avoid telephone line and modem charges, one economical method to move the data is to multiplex the transmission from the 32 terminals over a single leased line, at an aggregate transmission speed of 9,600 bps. This system

Fig. 3.50. Traditional Multiplexer Utilization

When multiplexers are used for data concentration, one computer port is required for each multiplexer channel.

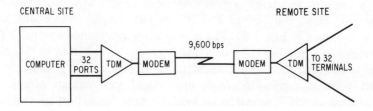

Fig. 3.51. Servicing 48 Terminals Using a Remotely Located Port Selector

Port selector can be used to perform a remote concentration function by providing a 48 to 32 contention rate from the 48 terminals connected to the line side of the device to the 32 ports which are connected to the input side of the multiplexer.

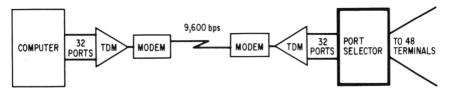

requires two 32-port multiplexers and 32 computer ports. Assume that 16 additional 300-bps terminals must be added to the remote site after the system is installed. Since the leased line is already operating at its 9,600-bps limit, one alternative is to upgrade the multiplexers by adding 16 ports to each and to replace the modems and voice-grade communications link with wideband facilities. This method requires 16 additional computer ports to service the additional terminal traffic. But, the added line capacity would be very expensive, because wideband facilities are far more costly than voice-grade lines.

Another option would be to install a pair of 16-port multiplexers, one additional leased line between them, and two 4,800-bps modems to transmit on the new line. But 16 additional computer ports would still be required to service the additional terminals. Increasing the number of terminals that can be handled by the central site by means of a port selection arrangement may indeed be less expensive than doing it by expanding the capacity of the multiplexing equipment. To find out if port selection is the practical answer to a particular situation, the user should first assess the demands the present terminals are making on the network, then estimate the additional demands that will arise because of the proposed new terminals.

Let us assume a study was conducted and it was determined that although 48 terminals are necessary at the remote site, due to time-dependent applications and terminal use habits (coffee breaks, different department shift schedules, etc.), a reasonable expectation is that with the exception of 2 h* per week, no more than 32 terminals will simultaneously use the computer. For the 2-h high utilization period per week, the study concluded that at most 35 terminals will access the system. If we are willing to sacrifice three terminals from accessing the computer 2 h per week, then a port selector can be installed to service 48 lines and bring those lines to 32 ports on a contention basis, as illustrated in Fig. 3.51.

---

* h = hours

Fig. 3.52. Using Telco Rotaries for the Expansion

Although the installation of a telephone company rotary and lines will permit an infinite number of terminals equipped with modems to contend for the 32 multiplexer channels, the cost of such equipment may not prove to be the most economical method to employ.

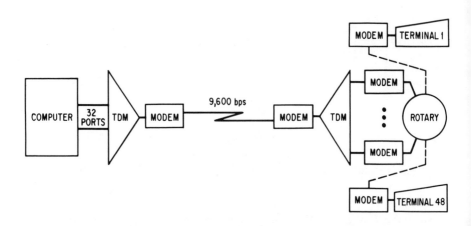

The port selector then offers a contention ratio of 48:32, or 3:2 (48 terminals connected to the line side of the selector and 32 outputs to the multiplexer ports). It eliminates the need to add 16 computer ports, to upgrade or add multiplexers, or to upgrade or add communications links. Although a telephone company rotary could be used for the port selection process, as shown in Fig. 3.52, 80 modems would then be needed (48 for the terminals and 32 for the business lines connected to the multiplexer). A port selector can thus cut back on the number of modems needed for port selection by rotaries, as well as the expense of 48 communications links. By directly connecting the terminals to the line side of the port selector it becomes possible to do away with the low-speed modems. A port selector that can make 48 lines contend for 32 ports might cost about $15,000. But the rotary system cost of $1,359 per month for the components enumerated in Table 3.12 would equal the cost of a port selector in a little less than 1 year.

Another device which should be considered for this type of terminal expansion is an intelligent multiplexer. This type of multiplexer strips the start and stop bits of each asynchronous transmission and through code conversion permits the transmission of several terminals to occur on what would be one reserved time slot for an individual terminal when data is multiplexed on a traditional TDM. The use of this device could alleviate the necessity of installing additional line facilities. However, when terminals are directly connected to the multiplexer at the remote site, a corresponding number of computer ports will still be required at the computer site, unless

Table 3.12. Monthly Rotary Equipment Charges

80	Modems @ 12.50	$1,000
32	1FB Business lines @ 10.00	320
2	Data cabinets @ 4.50	9
1	804T Autoanswer device @ 30.00	30
	Monthly cost	$1,359

the composite high-speed data link was demultiplexed by specialized software in the front-end processor, in which case only one port would be required. Due to the cost associated with developing specialized software, as well as the memory requirements for the program, this technique is not normally employed unless the economics of scale can justify the effort and cost involved. The reader is referred to Sec. 3.1 of this book for additional information on the use and applications of intelligent multiplexers.

Usage Decisions

A typical computer network, as in Fig. 3.53, indicates what must be taken into account in coming to a decision about port selectors. In this example, 48 computer ports handle messages from two multiplexers and a local

Fig. 3.53. Traditional Computer Network

In a typical computer network a 48-port front-end processor would permit the 32 remote terminal and 16 local terminals to reach the computer simultaneously. This configuration insures that no terminal user ever meets a busy signal—but it is expensive.

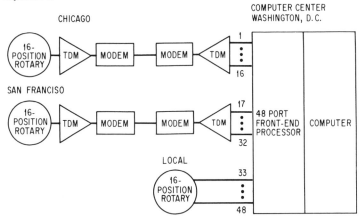

rotary. Each multiplexer provides 16 terminal-to-computer connections, as well as 16 dial-in ports at the computer site. If the network is distributed over several time zones, peaks in utilization of the terminals will occur at different times in different places.

Fig. 3.54. Utilization Profiles

Users of a nationwide network are not likely all to be in their offices or doing the same amount of work at the same time. This situation works in favor of a port selection configuration; it will readily be seen that peak usage rarely coincides in the different, widely separated centers served by a large communications network.

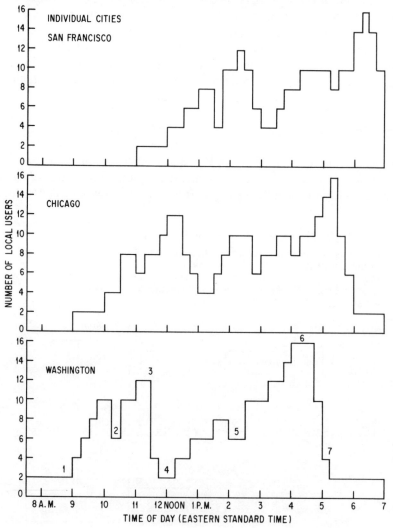

A typical profile of the number of users logged onto the network from each geographical area can be computed with statistical software packages provided by computer manufacturers. Profiles of the system's utilization are shown in Fig. 3.54. While other networks may not reveal exactly the same patterns, they may be similar, because normal working habits are a significant factor in the fluctuations of network utilization.

At the start of working hours (Fig. 3.54, point 1 on the third profile), use gradually builds as people arrive at the office and settle down to work. During the morning coffee break period (point 2), the number of users decreases temporarily, with the length of time and the degree of the dropoff varying from place to place. Morning peak use (point 3), is followed by a drop in activity during the lunch period (point 4). Use then builds up until the afternoon break (point 5) and peaks again as people rush to complete the day's work (point 6). As the close of business approaches (point 7), activity tapers off until only a few terminals remain on-line.

By combining the three local profiles, an overall network profile can be developed (Fig. 3.55) which presents the number of terminals on-line as the day moves forward (Eastern Standard Time). The smooth curves above this profile plot activity in the 95th and 99th percentiles, and indicate

Fig. 3.55. The Total Network Profile

The curves represent the 95th and 99th percentiles of use for the entire network. They show that at peak periods only 37 or 40 terminals, respectively, will be either on-line or seeking access. The curves also show that during these same periods of peak use a substantial number of the remote terminals will inevitably be idle.

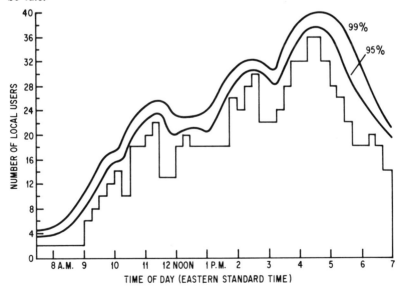

the maximum number of terminals that can be expected to be on-line for 95 and 99 out of every 100 observations. Put another way, 95 percent of the time there will be up to 37 terminals on-line or seeking access between 4:15 P.M. and 4:45 P.M., and 99 percent of the time there will be as many as 40 users (between 4 P.M. and 5:30 P.M.).

Returning to the network in Fig. 3.53, it is now apparent that 99 percent of the time, eight or more of the 48 computer ports are not in use, and that 95 percent of the time, 11 or more ports will be idle. Thus, the use of a port selector becomes a question of economics against inconvenience. Is the cost of a number of mostly idle computer ports worth the seldom used advantage of being able to connect all terminals, simultaneously and without delay? A related question that the network designer must answer is whether the computer can process all messages rapidly enough when all terminals are on-line.

Let us assume that instead of installing the equipment illustrated in Fig. 3.53, a port utilization study was conducted and that the 90th percentile of port usage was decided on. This would mean that a 48-line by 32-port port selector would be required. After calculating the cost savings possible with such a port selector we can determine if the sacrifice of 16 continuously available ports is justifiable. Assuming such justification, the revised network which incorporates a port selector is illustrated in Fig. 3.56. Other port selector configurations could result from an investigation into the savings possible with a 48-line by 37-port selector (95th percentile, Fig. 3.55) or a 48-line by 40-port selector (99th percentile).

Fig. 3.56. Network Revision to Incorporate a Port Selector

This network provides almost the same performance as the network shown in Fig. 3.53. However, through the use of the port selector, only 32 computer ports are required. Because of the different time zones, it is unlikely that a remote terminal will get a busy signal.

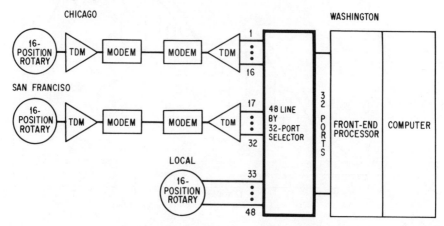

Port Costs

Besides a savings in the circuit boards that make up the ports themselves, other computer costs are reduced because of the fewer ports. Let us assume that the user has a Honeywell Series 60 computer and a Honeywell DATA-NET 6000 front-end network processor (FNP) which provides the network communications power for the Honeywell Series 60 computer system. The basic configuration of the DATANET 6000 FNP is shown in Fig. 3.57. Each FNP can contain up to two general purpose communications bases (GPCB), each of which can accommodate up to 16 communication dual channel boards (up to 32 concurrently operating ports) at speeds of 50 to 50,000 bps and up to six asynchronous communications bases (ACB), each of which can service up to 17 ports at 30 characters per second through the installation of nine communication dual channel boards. Thus, the 32 ports from the port selector can be interfaced to one GPCB containing 16 communication channel boards or two ACB containing eight communication channel boards apiece. Without a port selector to accommodate all 48 ports, an additional ACB or GPCB and eight communication channel boards would be required. The additional cost associated with servicing a 48-port configuration by using either type of communications base is shown in Table 3.13.

Since a 48-line by 32-port port selector costs approximately $15,000, the installation of such a device should save between $35,000 and $40,000 when compared to installing an additional ACB or GPCB and their associated ports. The user must decide whether this saving outweighs the value of the extra ports. If the network serves an in-house computer system, productivity lost when terminals are denied access to the computer must be considered. If the network is used by outside customers, a possible loss of revenue should also be taken into account.

Although a saving of $35,000 or $40,000 is considerable for a single computer installation, additional saving is possible for installations that have redundant computers, because every excess computer port that can be

Fig. 3.57. DATANET 6000 FNP Basic Configuration

The Honeywell 6000 front-end network processor contains one or more communications bases with each base containing one or more communication boards.

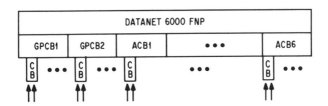

Table 3.13.   Incremental Costs on FNP Going from 32 to 48 Ports

For General Purpose Communications Base (GPCB)
8 DCF 6010 Channel interfaces (2 ports each) @ 3120 — $24,960
1 GPCB — 30,000

Total — $54,960

For Asynchronous Communications Base (ACB)
8 DCF 6010 Channel interfaces (2 ports each) @ 3120 — 24,960
1 ACB — 24,800

Total — $49,760

eliminated on one front-end processor can also be eliminated on the other. In addition, reductions may also be possible in the capital outlay for devices that switch between central processing units. One such redundant processor configuration is shown in Fig. 3.58.

The installation of a port selector to front end the line transfer device is shown in Fig. 3.59. Note that not only are the number of front-end processor ports reduced by 32 (16 per processor) but also that the size of the line transfer device can be reduced, since a 32 by 64 switch is now needed instead of a 48 by 96 switch (Fig. 3.58) if a selector was not used.

Load Balancing

A key advantage obtained from the utilization of port selectors is the ability to balance the communications load when an installation has two or more front-end processors. This load balancing can be accomplished

Fig. 3.58. Redundant Processor Configuration
Savings in excess of twice the savings of a single processor may be obtained since a portion of the switching arrangement may be removed.

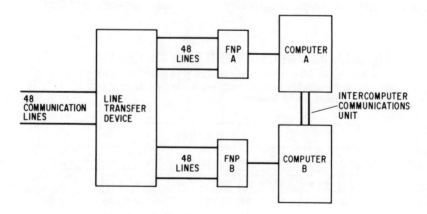

Fig. 3.59. Port Selector Increases Savings for Redundant Configurations

Using a port selector to front-end the line transfer device of a dual processor not only doubles the number of ports that can be eliminated but also reduces the size of the switch required.

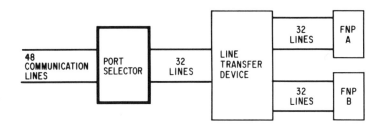

simply by wiring the cables from the port side of the selector in an alternate manner to each front-end processor. Thus, an installation with dual front-end processors would cable the leads from ports 1, 3, 5, 7, 9, . . . , $N - 1$ from the port selector to the first front-end processor and the leads from ports 2, 4, 6, 8, . . . , N to the second front-end processor.

Selector Features

A wide range of standard and optional selector features should be considered. First, the basic size or capacity of the port selector and its expansion capability, if any, should be determined. Selectors are offered as a base unit, with a predetermined number of calling channels and called ports available for interface. By the addition of line and port nests and adapters the capacity of the selector can be increased.

Another feature to consider is the ability to partition the selector for interface to fixed speed front-end or multiplexer channels. This feature is illustrated in Fig. 3.60, where port contention is accomplished within each of three speed/code groupings for transmission to a lesser number of fixed speed front-end processor ports.

Even when using a speed-transparent selector where all incoming traffic transmits at the same rate, one may wish to consider assigning priorities for access to the computer by grouping certain incoming lines so that they contend for a different number of ports, thereby providing a higher access probability for certain users of the system. This is shown in Fig. 3.61. Instead of being preconfigured to seek available ports within a predetermined group or groups of ports, automatic group selection is an option which permits the selector to determine which of the port groups a given user requires based upon the transmission of a control character from the user's terminal.

Fig. 3.60. Speed-partitioned Port Selector

The 48 incoming lines are contended in groups of 16 for 24 ports of which each group can contend for eight predefined speeds.

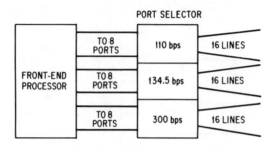

Additional features available on selectors include diagnostic modules, busy-out switches, and automatic computer select. Selector diagnostic modules are used to determine which line is connected to which port and to display key diagnostic information for that particular cross-connect. Busy-out switches permit user flexibility in changing existing contention ratios, and the automatic computer select features permit incoming traffic to be contended and routed to two different processors based upon the interpretation of a special character transmitted from the user's terminal.

Fig. 3.61. Grouping Selector Contention

Users from New York City always require immediate access so no contention is performed. Although 32 local terminals are connected to the selector, management has decided that at most 24 will be active at one time and has directed a 4:3 contention ratio be established for this group, and a 3:2 ratio for the terminals from Washington, D.C.

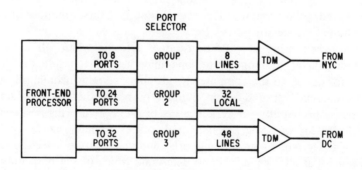

chapter 4
redundancy and
reliability aids

Although a variety of network configurations can be designed to attain specific levels of redundancy and reliability, basic to such designs will be two communications components—switches and line restoral units. Initially developed as devices to assist technical control center personnel in a wide range of operational tasks, data communications switches were recognized as an economical and simplistic series of devices that could be used to reconfigure network components and replace failing devices with alternate components simply by the turn of a switch. As networks became more complex and more emphasis was placed on the duration of component outages, a series of automatic and semiautomatic switches were developed to provide network users with a lower failed component replacement time. At the same time that component failures were addressed, manufacturers recognized the desirability of providing devices which could detect leased line failures and automatically provide an alternate communications path over the switched network until the leased line outage was alleviated. This category of equipment is commonly referred to as line restoral units and can be used to provide an automatic alternate communications path for a variety of components normally connected to a central·computer via the installation of a leased line.

4.1. Data Communications Switches

Communications switches are bringing a new freedom and economy to network design and operations. Until recently, they were found mainly in technical control rooms, where they help in on-line monitoring, fault diagnosis, and digital and analog testing. But now they are also being used to reroute data quickly and efficiently and to replace several dedicated backup units with just one, enabling a single terminal to act as standby for several on-line terminals.

The kinds of switches available, and how they may be combined or chained to fulfill different functions, are described in the first portion of this section. The second portion of this section will concentrate on applications, in particular on the use of switches to assure network uptime without a heavy investment in redundant equipment.

The four basic categories of switches are fallback, bypass, cross-over, and matrix. Of these, two or more from the same or different categories may be chained to serve still other data communications requirements. Furthermore, within each category there are two types of switches: the so-called telco switches, which transfer 4-wire leased or 2-wire dial-up telephone lines, and the Electronics Industry Association (EIA) switches, which transfer all 24 leads of an EIA RS-232 interface.

Fallback Switches

The fallback switch is a rapid and reliable means of switching other network components from on-line to standby equipment. The EIA version selects either a pair of 24-pin-connected components, which, as shown in Fig. 4.1, may be terminals, modems, or channels on a front-end processor.

In the first example, two terminals share a single modem. This configuration might be required, for example, when terminals have the same transmission speed but use different protocols, so that each communicates with a different group of remote terminals or computers.

In the second example, one terminal is provided with access to two modems, one of which is redundant but needed for uptime reliability. Alternatively, the first modem might enable the terminals to transmit to another terminal at 2,000 bps during one portion of the day, while the second lets it talk to a central computer at 9,600 bps during other periods of the day. Then, depending on operational requirements, one terminal

Fig. 4.1. Fallback Switches

Top: EIA (24-pin) fallback switch. Bottom: Telco fallback switch. The EIA fallback switch transfers 24 leads at a time, while the telco switch transfers the two or four leads associated with telephone lines.

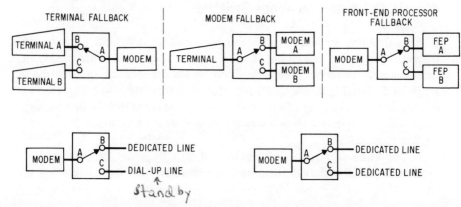

with a fallback switch for modem selection could be more practical than installing two terminals.

In a third application, an EIA fallback switch (Fig. 4.1, top right) permits a modem to be transferred between front-end processors. Although called a line-transfer device by some manufacturers, in effect what one obtains is a device that selects which front-end processor will service the modem.

A telco fallback switch similarly allows the user to select one of two sets of telephone lines. As shown in Fig. 4.1 (bottom), it can select one line from among various combinations of dedicated and dial-up lines that may have been installed to fit the needs of a particular application. Thus, for a large data transfer application which is of a critical nature, the telco fallback switch could be connected to a pair of leased lines, one of which is used as an alternative circuit in the event of an outage on the primary circuit.

Bypass Switches

The EIA bypass switch connects several EIA interfaces of one type (say, modems) to the same number plus a spare of another EIA interface type (say, terminals) and can switch any member of the first group to the spare member of the second group. One application for bypass switches is at a computer installation (Fig. 4.2, top left). Here, one front-end channel is reserved as a spare in case any of the existing channels, which normally service predetermined modems, should need to be connected quickly to a spare channel.

In another application (Fig. 4.2, top right), the EIA bypass switch can substitute a standby spare terminal for a failed on-line terminal and do away with the need for a spare modem. Although seldom used for multiple terminal access, a bypass switch can also enable many terminals to share a single modem and line.

A telco bypass switch transfers any one of a group of 2-wire or 4-wire telco lines to a spare communications component. For example, as shown in Fig. 4.2 (bottom left), if modem 1 should fail, line 1 can be switched to the spare modem. Conversely, a telco switch may transfer a spare line to an operational communications component like a modem (Fig. 4.2, bottom right). Telco bypass switches can be used to switch leased or dial-up lines to modems, automatic dialers, or acoustic couplers.

Cross-over and Matrix Switches

Cross-over switches provide the user with an easy method of inter-changing the data flow between two pairs of communication components. Four connectors are associated with each switching module, one for each of the two pairs of communication components connected to that module.

Fig. 4.2. Bypass Switches

Top: EIA bypass switch. Bottom: Telco bypass switch. Bypass switches transfer either EIA or telco interfaces to spare components with a similar interface on the other side of the switch.

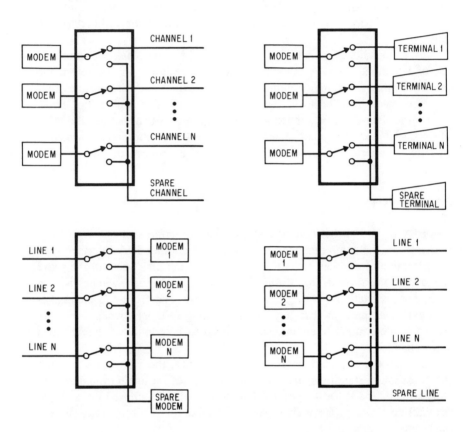

As shown in Fig. 4.3 (top), an EIA cross-over switch permits the data flow to be reversed between two pairs of EIA interfaced components. In the example shown in Fig. 4.3 (top), modem A, which is normally connected to the front-end processor channel A, and modem B, which is connected to front-end processor channel B, are reversed when the switch is moved from the normal to the cross-over mode of operation. Thus, modem A then becomes connected to channel B and modem B is connected to channel A upon cross-over.

Similarly, a telco cross-over switch permits the user to interchange the data flow between two telco lines and two modems. Although two dedicated lines are shown connected to the cross-over switch in Fig. 4.3 (bottom), one can also connect one dedicated line and one dial-up line,

Fig. 4.3. Cross-over Switches

Top: EIA cross-over switch. Bottom: Telco cross-over switch.
Cross-over switches, either EIA or telco, make it easy for the
operator to reroute the flow of information between pairs of
identical components.

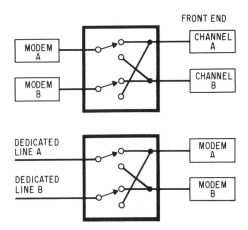

or two dial-up lines to the switch. Here, upon cross-over, line A, which is
normally connected to modem A, becomes connected to modem B, and
vice versa.

With a matrix switch the user can interconnect any combination of a
group of incoming interfaces to any combination of a group of outgoing
interfaces. Matrix switches are manufactured as a n-by-n matrix, with
4-by-4, 8-by-8, and 16-by-16 combinations typically available. The user of
a manual matrix switch makes an interconnection by depressing two push
buttons on the switch simultaneously, one representing the incoming interface and the other representing the outgoing interface.

As shown in Fig. 4.4. (top), an EIA 4-by-4 matrix switch is a quick
and efficient way of connecting any combination of four modems to any
combination of four front-end processor channels. The circles represent
the depressed switch combinations, so that, in this case, modem 1 serves
front-end processor channel 1, modem 2 serves front-end processor channel
3, modem 3 serves front-end processor channel 2, and modem 4 serves
front-end processor channel 4. Further, with this configuration the user is
free to designate one or more modem or front-end processor channels as
spares or a combination of modems and channels as spares.

The telco 4-by-4 matrix shown in Fig. 4.4 (bottom) similarly permits
the transfer of any combination of four incoming lines to any combination
of four outgoing lines.

A type of application warranting investigation of telco matrix
switches arises when remote terminals require access to two or more

Fig. 4.4. Matrix Switches

Top: 4-by-4 EIA matrix switch. Bottom: 4-by-4 telco matrix switch. Matrix switches make fast work of connecting any combination of a group of incoming interfaces to any combination of outgoing interfaces.

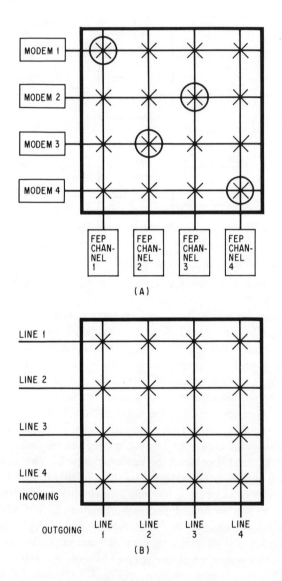

adjacent computeis. If the terminals are used heavily enough to justify installing leased lines from the remote sites to the central computers, the telco matrix switch enables the user to switch the incoming leased lines to outgoing cables which, via modems, are connected to different computers.

Additional Derivations

From the four categories of switches previously discussed, a number of additional switching functions have been developed. For instance, a spare component backup switch is basically a pair of fallback switches contained in one housing. As shown in Fig. 4.5 (top left), this switch permits a normal and a backup mode of operation. The normal mode permits data to be transferred through the primary component, whereas the backup mode switches the data flow through the spare components.

In another configuration (Fig. 4.5, top right) a pair of modems are the primary and spare components connected to one terminal, and the switch selects the modem to be used in transferring data between the terminal and the telco line. Because three EIA interfaces are involved, this configuration is called a 3-of-4 EIA interface bypass switch. In a 4-of-4 EIA interface (Fig. 4.5, bottom), four interface devices are connected to the switch. In this configuration the switch selects one of two encoders to encode terminal data for transmission through an attached modem.

A second common switch derivation is a multiple fallback switch

Fig. 4.5. Backup Switch Variations

Top: Backup switch. Center: Backup switch, 3-of-4 EIA interface. Bottom: Backup switch, 4-of-4 EIA interface. Paired EIA and telco fallback switches, which often come in one package, provide both a backup and a normal mode of operation.

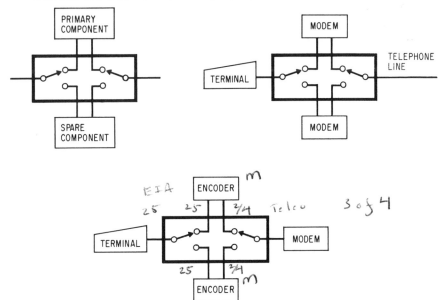

(Fig. 4.6). Besides the EIA and telco versions, this switch is manufactured in a 1-of *n* version, with *n* being the number of possible selections. Figure 4.6 (top) shows two possible configurations for a 1-of-4 EIA fallback switch. At the left, the switch allows the terminal to be connected to any one of four modems, while at the right, any one of four terminals may be connected to a single modem. Similarly, Fig. 4.6 (bottom) shows how the 1-of-4 telco fallback switch allows either four modems to share a single line or four lines to share a single modem.

Chaining Switches

No manufacturer produces a complete line of ready-made switches, but it is often more convenient to deal with and install switches from a single maker. The user can do so by developing the switching functions required

Fig. 4.6. Multiple Fallback Switches

Multiple fallback switches, either EIA or telco, allow many terminals to share one modem or many modems to share one telephone line.

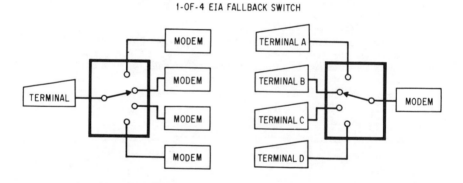

1-OF-4 EIA FALLBACK SWITCH

1-OF-4 TELCO FALLBACK SWITCH

from combinations of one vendor's switches. In Fig. 4.7 (left), for instance, four fallback switches are chained together to perform the function of a bypass switch. A single backup terminal can be used to replace any one of four primary terminals. In Fig. 4.7 (right), four fallback switches are chained so that a single backup modem may be used by any terminal if its primary modem fails.

Other switches can be similarly chained to develop additional switching functions or to increase the capacity of existing network devices. Even more usefully, different categories of switches and different types of switches within the same category can be chained. Figure 4.8 shows a 4-by-4 telco matrix switch chained to a 4-by-4 EIA matrix switch so that the user may interconnect any combination of lines, modems, and front-end processor channels to arrange the information path desired. For this example, the number of possible configurations is increased to n^3 from the normal n^2 combinations available with a single n-by-n matrix switch.

Fig. 4.7. Chaining Fallback Switches

Chaining of simple switches yields a variety of functions, for instance, permitting any of several terminal locations to select a single spare modem.

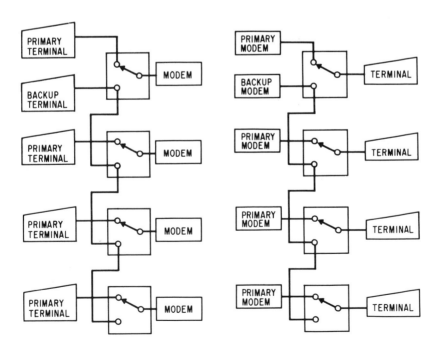

Fig. 4.8. Chaining Telco and EIA Matrix Switches

Here, an EIA matrix switch and a telco matrix switch are chained so the user may interconnect any combination of lines, modems, and front-end processor channels.

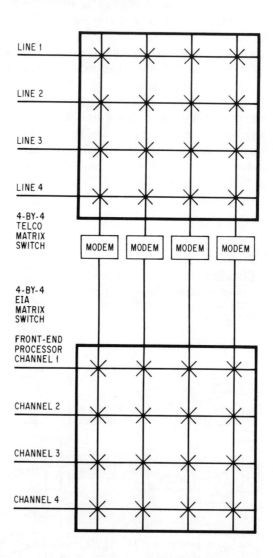

Switch Control

The four most common methods of transferring a switch are local and remote manual, American Standard Code for Information Interchange (ASCII) unattended remote, and via a business machine or central host computer. A local manual switch usually has a toggle or toggles, but a few are now manufactured with pushbuttons and corresponding indicator lights. For a remote manual switch one manufacturer produces a remote control panel equipped with a pushbutton and a cable connecting it to the remote switch. This setup also has the advantage that shorter cable lengths can be run from communications components to the switch. Although toggle-operated units can be rack mounted, they are normally available only in single-channel modules. Remote-control units, on the other hand, are normally manufactured in 4-, 8-, or 16-unit configurations, and all units are master switched from the remote control simultaneously, rather than one at a time.

The ASCII unattended remote control permits a switch to be controlled or monitored at any remote site at which a telephone line can be installed. An adapter interfaces the switch (or switches) to the telephone line and turns it on or off upon receiving a coded message consisting of the switch number and the state to which to transfer. The adapter then reports back the switch's new status. Also available is a query mode which allows the operator to check out a remote switch's position.

When a business machine (computer) is involved, switching is controlled directly by the machine, normally through a 5-V transistor-transistor logic (TTL) logic circuit. Let us now examine how such switches can be a cheaper alternative to obtaining overall network availability than is the installation of typical redundant equipment. Furthermore, the cost of switches themselves can be kept low if the application allows a reasonable time interval for an operator to perform manual switching compared with the higher cost of master-controlled remotely operated switches.

Switching Applications

When network equipment fails, a variety of communications switches can get the network back into operation, fast. They quickly bring redundant equipment into place to meet established requirements for overall network availability. The cost of providing the switches can range from less than a few hundred dollars to well over $50,000. What makes the price vary so much rests on the answers to such questions as:

> Which devices are most likely to fail?
> What tangible and intangible effects will a failed network device, such as a concentrator, have on the organization's operation?
> Would the operational loss be so great that it warrants the cost of including backup equipment and transmission lines?
> When a network component goes down, how much downtime, if any, is allowable to activate backup devices and get the network back into full-scale operation?

To obtain speedy network recovery, what are the best types of switches for the application, and where should they be placed in the network?

The significance of these and similar questions, and their answers, will become apparent during the discussions of typical redundancy/switching configurations that follow.

The four basic types of communications switches—fallback, bypass, cross-over, and matrix—come in two versions: EIA for switching digital signals and telco for switching 2-wire and 4-wire telephone lines. Chaining these switches provides a variety of extended switching functions. Furthermore, the switches can be activated or controlled in local or remote manual modes, in an unattended remote mode in which the switch is actuated by a specified ASCII-character code, and in a computer-controlled remote mode. Switches become more expensive in going from local manual mode up to computer-controlled mode. But changing a network from primary to backup mode manually may take 10 or 15 min, while a computer-controlled switch can actuate all switch connections essentially instantaneously and automatically from a remote location.

In the first portion of this section, the use of switches to substitute spares for such devices as modems and terminals was discussed. In the second part, the discussion will center around the ramifications of switching between dual-colocated concentrators. Here, one concentrator may be assigned completely to back up the other unit, or each concentrator may be servicing its own terminals during normal operation. In either case, on failure of one concentrator, the other takes over all duties if it has enough capacity to do so. In the latter case, if the reserve capacity is not available, then a secondary job, such as driving a line printer, may be suspended as long as concentrator downtime continues.

In the basic setup of the 10 following applications, each concentrator location services a number of relatively local low- and medium-speed terminals, so that each has a number of terminal-to-concentrator links. Each concentrator merges all traffic from its terminals and sends it on a high-speed line to a remote host computer.

As will be seen, the applications tend to become more complex and more expensive. The actual choice depends to some extent on network application and to some extent on the severity of the consequences of a device failure.

Hot-start Configuration

The two main methods of integrating colocated concentrators to service remote terminals are commonly called "hot-start" and "cold-start." The hot-start approach, Fig. 4.9, means that a backup computer is energized,

Fig. 4.9. Hot-start Configuration

In this hot-start configuration, when the primary concentrator fails, a computer-controlled switch puts the backup concentrator in control.

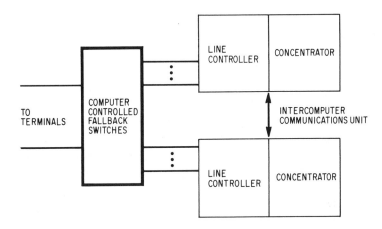

fully programmed with a duplicate of the software in the primary concentrator, and may be continuously tracking the traffic in and out of the primary concentrator. When the primary computer fails, a computer-controlled switch can put the backup concentrator in control substantially instantaneously.

Full effectiveness of such a hot-start arrangement requires the installation of an intercomputer (that is, interconcentrator) communications unit. When a failure such as memory–parity errors or power loss occurs, the concentrator experiencing difficulty sends appropriate software commands through the communications unit. Additionally, an automatic command to a bank of computer-controlled telco fallback switches provides instantaneous transfer of the line from each terminal to the line controller of the operating concentrator.

The near-instantaneous switching and the minimization of the loss of data are the important advantages of the hot-start configuration. However, there are significant hardware costs associated with the computer-controlled switches and the intercomputer communications unit. In addition, the necessary software modifications to permit the desired switching are complex, involving experienced personnel, much patience, and large amounts of machine time for testing the developed software. Overall, the cost for a hot-start configuration may well reach over $100,000, not counting the cost of the concentrator itself. But it may be well worth the money to assure that the network remains continuously operational and available.

The remainder of this section will focus on variations of the cold-start redundancy configuration, with different methods of switchover available from manual (local toggles) and remote-control (pushbutton) switches into a communications network. However, computer-controlled switches can be used in any of these configurations with a consequent increase in complexity and cost combined with a salutary improvement in network uptime.

Cold-start Configuration

Telco fallback switches represent one method of providing an alternate path between the remote terminals and the two concentrators (Fig. 4.10). Here, the occurrence of a concentrator failure or a concentrator-to-host link failure will require manual intervention. When one or both failures occur, it becomes necessary to switch the telco units to insure that the remote terminals are connected to the operating concentrator. Furthermore, the standby concentrator must have its programs bootstrapped from a high-speed storage unit such as a disk. Thus, if the concentrators are initially sharing the terminal workload, the failure of one concentrator may require the other concentrator's software to be reconfigured to service the entire workload. This configuration can be completed in a few minutes by manually throwing the switches and reading the backup programs from the disk into the operational concentrator's memory.

Some data being transmitted through the concentrator may be lost during the reconfiguration time. But the low cost of the cold-start configuration may justify the extra time associated with satisfying retransmission requests for lost messages.

Fig. 4.10. Cold-start Configuration
In the cold-start configuration, failure of a concentrator or a concentrator-to-host link requires manual intervention by the operator.

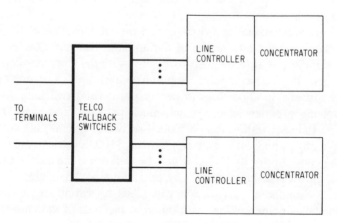

Sharing a Backup Concentrator

The availability requirements of the network may be such that neither operating concentrator has the reserve to serve as backup for the other. But it may be possible to service both devices with a single backup concentrator, as shown in Fig. 4.11. Here, telco fallback switches allow the terminals in building 1 or building 3 to be connected to the backup concentrator in building 2. The number of modems interfaced to the telco switching units in building 2 only need equal the maximum of the number of such devices in either building 1 or building 3. Thus, if the possibility of two concentrators failing at the same time is disregarded, the cost of the fallback switches is more than offset by the savings due to the lesser number of modems necessary at the backup concentrator.

Fig. 4.11. Sharing a Backup Concentrator
Here, both primary concentrators, neither of which can completely take over for the other, is serviced by a third backup concentrator.

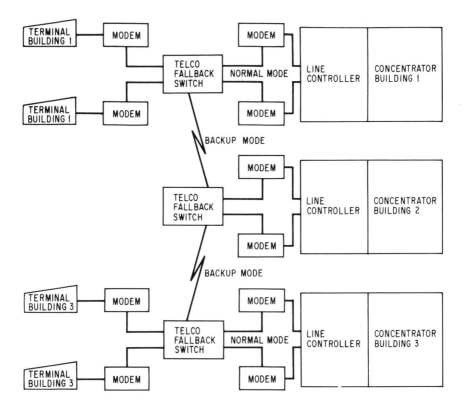

Backup with EIA Switches

An alternative approach to servicing the terminals in buildings 1 and 3 by the backup concentrator in building 2 can be obtained through the use of EIA fallback switches (Fig. 4.12). Instead of installation between the modems as with the telco switches in the preceding application, the EIA switches are between the modem and the line controller of the concentrator. Depending on the distance between either primary concentrator and the backup concentrator, line drivers or modems become necessary to permit an undistorted output signal to reach the backup concentrator. Assuming

Fig. 4.12. Backup with EIA Switches
Another way to back up a failed concentrator is by using EIA fallback switches between the modem and the line controller of the concentrator.

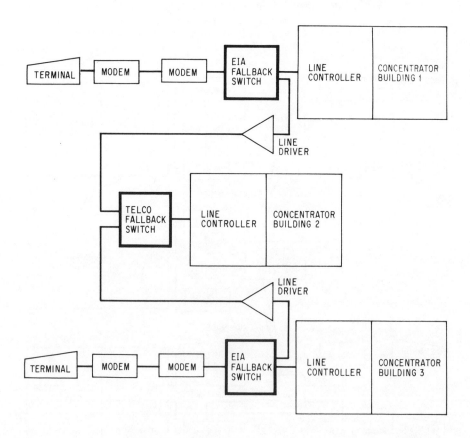

relatively short distances that permit the use of lower cost line drivers, rather than modems, a telco fallback switch will suffice in building 2 for each pair of terminal-to-concentrator links in the other buildings.

In the normal mode of operation, the terminals in building 1 or 3 communicate with their respective concentrator via a pair of modems and an EIA fallback switch. Should either concentrator fail, the operator must position the fallback switch into its backup mode and position the telco switch in building 2. Doing this provides a new set of circuits from the affected terminals to the concentrator in building 2.

This and the previous application have a concentrator added to the basic configurations of two such devices. In either case, the user may set up a network of three primary concentrators that share the backup duties. As well as connecting terminals directly to the concentrator in building 2, the user would have to install EIA or telco fallback switches to transfer the new data paths to either of the other two concentrators when backup service is needed.

Concentrator to Central Computer

If data transfer from each concentrator to the central computer is via a few high-speed lines, EIA fallback switches permit the transfer of modems and lines between the concentrators. In Fig. 4.13, two switches permit each concentrator to communicate over its own dedicated link to the central

Fig. 4.13. Concentrator-to-computer Backup

Two EIA fallback switches permit each concentrator to communicate over its own dedicated link going to the central
computer complex in the primary mode of operation. When a
fallback switch is activated, the concentrator can be connected to
the other concentrator's modem and line.

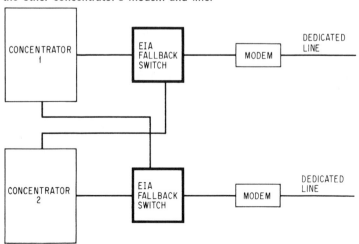

computer complex. This type of configuration compensates for a concentrator failure by permitting the remaining concentrator to communicate with the host computer over its line and the line of the other device. However, the failure of either one of the dedicated lines or of a modem would require selection of one of the concentrators to use the remaining data communications link.

Adding a Third EIA Fallback Switch

If the user wants to overcome the shortcomings of the preceding configuration, the inclusion of a third EIA fallback switch and another modem interfaced to the dual-concentrator configuration can either prevent or minimize the failure of a modem or of a dedicated line as shown in Fig. 4.14.

In the normal mode of operation, each concentrator communicates with the central computer via its own dedicated line. If a modem or dedicated line should fail, the proper positioning of two of the switches allows the concentrator to communicate with the central computer via the middle modem over an alternative path, either a dial-up network or another dedicated line. A disadvantage of this configuration is that each concentrator has access to only one line at a time, unlike the configuration in the previous application.

Adding More Switchable Lines

Access to more than one dedicated line at a time may be obtained by adding lines for each concentrator and reconfiguring the EIA fallback switches, as shown in Fig. 4.15. If one concentrator should fail, the other can com-

Fig. 4.14. Adding a Third EIA Fallback Switch
A third EIA fallback switch and another modem interfaced to the dual concentrators can prevent or minimize modem or line failure effects.

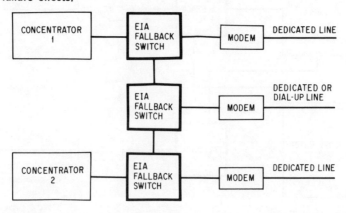

Fig. 4.15. Adding More Switchable Lines

If one concentrator should fail, the other concentrator can communicate over both dedicated lines and still have access to the backup line.

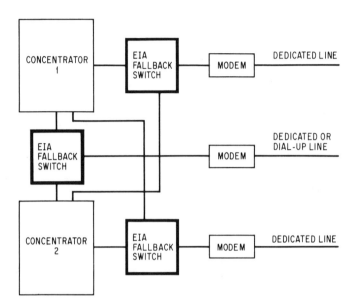

municate over both dedicated lines, and it still has access to the backup line. In this manner, throughput degradation should be minimized.

Chaining Adds Options

Chaining two EIA fallback switches results in another way of providing an alternative central computer link for a dual-concentrator installation (Fig. 4.16). Only one channel is required for each concentrator. In normal operation, each switch interfaced to each concentrator channel remains in the primary modem position. If the dedicated line or the primary modem of either concentrator should fail, the associated switch is positioned so that a path is provided to the backup modem. As in the other application, this backup modem can use a dial-up network or a dedicated line to communicate with the central computer.

This configuration requires only one concentrator channel to provide a link in the event of modem or dedicated-line failure. However, should a concentrator fail, the other one is not provided with access to the failing device's line. Thus, if terminals from the failing concentrator are switched to the operational concentrator, the operational link to the computer may

Fig. 4.16. Chaining Adds Options

Chaining two EIA fallback switches is another way of providing an alternative central computer link for a dual-concentrator installation.

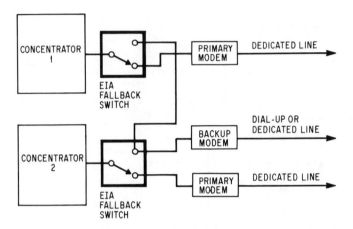

not be sufficient to satisfy the increased terminal traffic. Redundancy for this link through the use of EIA fallback switches can become rather complicated when more than a few lines require multiple access.

Access to Other Lines

Use of one or more EIA matrix switches, as shown in Fig. 4.17, can alleviate switching complexity as well as provide each concentrator access to the other dedicated line. For example, with a single 4-by-4 switch, each concentrator can have easy access to the spare modem and to any modem and line connected to the other concentrator. Although only one spare modem is shown here, a second modem and its associated line facilities could be added, since the output side of the 4-by-4 switch can interface one additional device.

As shown by the circles, concentrator 1 normally transmits data through modem 2 to the central computer, and concentrator 2 via modem 1. Either concentrator can be connected to the spare modem and associated line, should its primary modem or line fail. If a concentrator fails, the other one can be connected to the failing device's primary modem and line, thus insuring the continuation of full throughput to the central computer. If each concentrator communicates with the central computer through more than one link, the use of an 8-by-8 or a 16-by-16 switch, or the chaining of more than one matrix switch, should be explored.

Fig. 4.17. Access to Other Lines

One or more EIA matrix switches can alleviate switching complexity as well as provide each concentrator access to the other dedicated line.

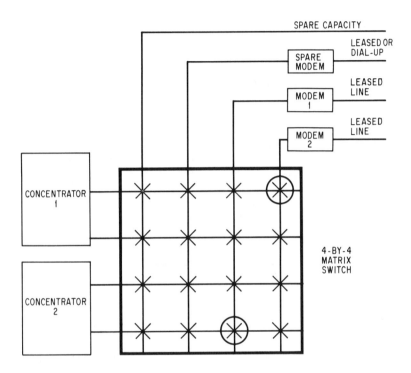

Integrating Switches into Both Links

Although the number of concentrators and of communications lines from each concentrator to the host computer depends upon such factors as the number of terminals serviced by each concentrator in both primary and backup modes of operation, terminal traffic patterns, and line protocol overhead, the configuration in Fig. 4.18 represents one possible way of integrating switches into both the terminal-to-concentrator and the concentrator-to-host computer links. It provides an alternate path for both links when dual concentrators are within about 50 ft of each other.

Here, it is assumed that the remote terminals are in two buildings. However, because the distances between each terminal and the concentrators preclude direct attachment or the use of line drivers, modems are necessary. An equipment study established each terminal's need for access to a second concentrator in order to maintain the desired level of backup. At the same time, to maintain throughput at the full transmission speed after the failure of one concentrator, it was found necessary to have the

Fig. 4.18. Integrating Switches into Both Links

Integrating switches into both the terminal-to-concentrator and concentrator-to-host links provides an alternate path for both links,

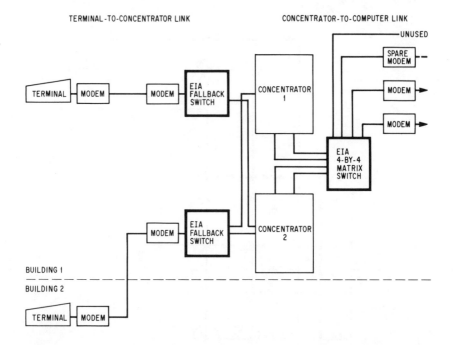

capability to switch the links of the failing device to the other one. Furthermore, should any modem or line of the concentrator link to the computer become inoperative, an easy switch to a spare modem communicating with the host computer via the dial-up network was desirable.

If the equipment study shows that each concentrator requires one channel for communicating with the host computer, then two channels become necessary on each device in order for each to use the other's link as well as its own at the same time. Thus, as shown here, the failure of concentrator 1 can be compensated for by positioning the EIA fallback switches on the terminal-to-concentrator link so that the terminals in building 1 connect to the second concentrator. In addition, each concentrator link to the computer is connected via a 4-by-4 EIA matrix switch to the other concentrator. The same procedure applies to the failure of the second concentrator.

Should a modem or line from either concentrator link to the computer become inoperative, the 4-by-4 matrix switch permits an easy reconfiguration to the spare modem and the dial-up network.

The procedures discussed here apply to a network with any number of terminal and host links. From the preceding examples, the utilization of switches provides the system designer with a low-cost option when designing a teleprocessing network that requires a level of redundancy which can range from a single redundant component requirement through multilayers of redundancy.

4.2. Line Restoral Units

A recurring problem facing network designers is the method to employ in providing backup facilities when transmission is over a leased line. Consider a typical time-sharing network where numerous remote locations are linked to a central computer facility by multiplexers which combine the low-speed transmission of numerous terminals for retransmission over leased lines.

If a leased line outage occurs during normal working hours, several possibilities exist for reestablishing communications. If a number of dial-in lines are available at the computer center, remote users could use the switched network to continue. However, long distance telephone charges may become prohibitive. Even if we disregard telephone charges, the number of dial-in lines may not be sufficient to provide service to a group of remote users whose primary communications path has failed. If a technique is available to reestablish the high-speed link, the time from when the outage is reported until someone physically effects a transfer to an alternate communications path for the multiplexed data can frustrate the remote users to the point where they may consider the use of another computer facility. For other types of applications, such as a remote minicomputer monitoring telemetry signals and transmitting those signals to a distant computer, the loss of a leased line could result in the loss of data. Although switches can be used to provide backup for many applications, as discussed in Sec. 4.1, several problems are encountered if they are used for the applications previously discussed.

First, manually operated switches would result in the loss of a period of transmission time which is proportional to the time the line failure occurs until someone effects the switchover. Even if two leased lines are installed for critical applications, the switchover to the second line may not have the desired effect if they are similarly routed by the telephone company. Thus, a main cable failure or a fire such as the one at the American Telephone and Telegraph (AT&T) building in New York City could render both lines inoperative. One method to alleviate the problems associated with leased line outages is through the installation of line restoral units.

Operation

A line restoral unit is a device which monitors the signal strength on a leased line. If the signal strength should drop below a set level, the unit will automatically initiate a call over the switched network and route data via this new transmission path until the signal level and jitter on the leased line return to normal. Several modes of operation can be considered by line restoral unit users. Instead of internal control, where the device initiates switchover, the transfer to the switched network can occur under company control with the restoral unit then serving as an automatic dialer. If the leased line is a 4-wire circuit used for full-duplex transmission, the restoral unit can be configured to initiate two calls over the switched (2-wire circuit) network to reestablish a 4-wire connection. At the disant end a similar unit connects to the dialed calls, as shown in Fig. 4.19.

Prior to the initiation of transmission to the dialed path, the restoral unit will sample transmission quality and continue redialing over the switched network until a good link is established. Once a good connection is established the modems are switched from the failed to the newly dialed connection. In addition, restoral units continuously monitor pilot tones put on the nonoperating leased line, checking for phase jitter and signal strength until the line recovers. As soon as the leased line is restored to normal operations, the backup connections are either automatically or manually terminated and transmission can proceed once again over the leased line. An audio alarm is built into these units to notify personnel in the vicinity that a switchover is occurring. In addition, delay circuits are built into these units to prevent constant switching between the switched network and the leased line. A strap option is available on some units which prevents the automatic return of transmission to the leased line. This option is most useful when one wants to delay the system from returning transmission to the leased line until that line has been fully diagnosed and repaired by the telephone company.

Fig. 4.19. Line Restoral Unit Operation

To reestablish communications when a 4-wire leased line fails, two calls are placed over the switched (2-wire) network.

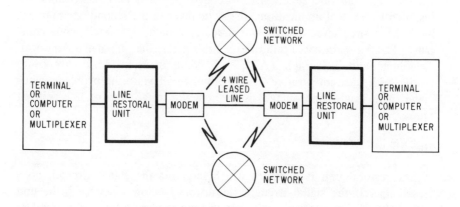

When placed into a network, one unit acts as a master while the second unit is strapped to operate as a slave. Although both master and slave units monitor the leased line, only the master unit can initiate the dial-up procedure. When the master unit senses a degradation in its received signal it initiates the dial-up procedure. At the other end, if the slave unit finds a degradation of its received data it will stop its transmission of carrier to the master, which will then serve as a signal for the master unit to start the dial-up procedure.

Problems of Utilization

Although the integration of restoral units into a network can alleviate a large percentage of leased line backup problems, for certain network configurations new problems can arise through the use of this equipment. A common problem associated with restoral units occurs when the transmission rate used over the leased line is greater than the transmission rate that

Fig. 4.20. Alternate Communications Problems

If the switched network cannot accommodate 9,600-bps transmission, the dial-backup may not be effective.

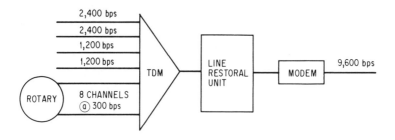

Fig. 4.21. Automatic Dial-backup and Speed Fallback

To accomplish automatic dial-backup and a reduction in the modem's transmitting speed, a number of multiplexer channels must be "busied" out.

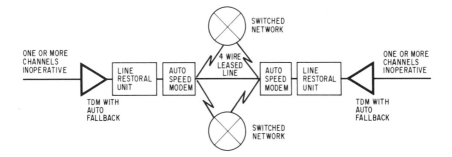

can be established over the switched network. For the remote site shown in Fig. 4.20, the 9,600-bps composite speed developed by the multiplexer can represent a problem if the restoral unit cannot reestablish communications on the switched network at that speed.

If 9,600-bps transmission cannot be established on the switched network, even restoral units that have the capability to switch speed-selectable modems to a lower data rate may prove ineffective. This is because most multiplexers require the physical strap out of one or more channels at both locations to produce a lower composite speed. Some new multiplexers have been designed with these problems taken into account and can be integrated with restoral units to permit both dial backup and automatic transmission rate fallback in the event transmission cannot proceed at the rate previously used on the leased line. To effect the speed fallback, a predetermined number of channels are automatically "busied out," as shown in Fig. 4.21.

chapter 5
automatic assistance devices

To reduce the necessity of operator intervention two automatic assistance devices have been developed: automatic answering units and automatic calling units. In addition to reducing the requirement for operator intervention, these devices permit network components to operate at a high level of utilization since such devices can be used to effect data transmission after normal office hours when all employees have left but when communications rates are reduced.

Automatic answering units are normally integrated into modems which are interfaced to a computer. The answering unit detects the incoming telephone ring and automatically provides a connection to the calling party so that data transmission between a remote terminal's user and the computer can proceed without the intervention of the computer operator or other members of the computer room staff. Conversely, automatic calling units permit a business machine or computer to automatically dial the telephone number of other computers or business machines. Both the telephone numbers and time of call can be programmed in the computer, as well as such additional data as the number and sequence of redials if one or more busy numbers are encountered.

Automatic answering units are normally used in modems at computer time-sharing installations where a large calling population calls a number of computer dial-in lines on a random basis. Automatic calling units are usually employed for applications where it is desired to have equipment at a central location poll a number of remote locations during certain times of the day, but where the cost of installing leased lines is uneconomical since the transmission from each remote site is of short duration.

5.1. Automatic Answering Units

Although some manufacturers produce automatic answering units on a card, such devices are known as an original equipment manufactured (OEM) component which will be integrated into another device at a later

Fig. 5.1. Automatic Answer Modem Employment

Modems equipped with automatic answering units enable remote terminals to communicate with time-sharing computers using the telephone dial-up network without requiring operator intervention at the computer site.

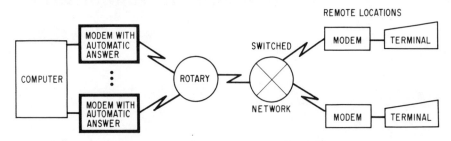

date. When integrated into a modem, the automatic answering unit provides automatic answer capability for the modem. The use of modems equipped with an automatic answering unit permits data transmission to occur between remote terminals and a computer or another terminal interfaced to an automatic answering modem without operator intervention at the called end of the link. A typical employment of automatic answer modems is illustrated in Fig. 5.1.

Operation

When integrated into a modem, the automatic answering unit will place the modem in the answer mode upon the receipt of a ring indicator signal. Depending upon the device selected, the absence of an incoming carrier signal or its delay for a predetermined amount of time after the ring indicator signal is received can be used to disconnect the calling party. After the call is answered and data transmission is in effect, the automatic answering unit will send a disconnect immediately in response to a data terminal ready signal going off or when the incoming carrier signal is lost for greater than a predetermined amount of time, if the disconnect options on the device are strapped for those events. Some of the typical options which are strap selectable for automatic answering units are listed in Table 5.1.

Alleviating Problems

To prevent a tie-up of expensive computer facilities through the use of computer ports and lines due to such problems as wrong number calls, failure of the distant party to disconnect from a time-sharing system, or line failures, a number of techniques can be employed. The timer abort option permits the device to disconnect if a carrier signal is not received

Table 5.1.   Automatic Answering Unit Options

ANSWER MODE INDICATOR
   Ring indicator OFF: ring indicator circuit follows ringing only
   Ring indicator ON: ring indicator circuit follows ringing and remains on
   for the duration of the incoming call
TIME ABORT
   YES: automatic answering unit disconnects if incoming carrier is not
   received within a predetermined time after call is answered
   NO: automatic answering unit does not disconnect with absence of incom-
   ing carrier
LOSS OF CARRIER DISCONNECT
   YES: Automatic answering unit disconnects when incoming carrier is lost
   for longer than a predetermined amount of time
   NO: automatic answering unit does not disconnect on carrier loss
DISCONNECT IMMEDIATELY
   YES: automatic answering unit disconnects immediately in response to
   data terminal ready OFF
   NO: automatic answering unit transmits a spacing signal prior to discon-
   necting in response to data terminal ready OFF

within a predetermined amount of time after the call is answered. This option can be effectively employed to resolve the situation where the modem answers a wrong number call. While the devices can be interfaced to a computer so that they will disconnect on command when the computer receives a special terminal signal, such as a sign-off command from the terminal user, quite often such users forget to do so and merely lift their telephone handset out of the acoustic coupler when they complete their terminal session. The loss of carrier disconnect option is valuable for this situation, since the answering unit disconnects when the incoming carrier is lost for a period longer than a predetermined amount of time.

5.2. Automatic Calling Units

In trying to obtain a telecommunications link between a computer or business machine and another computer or business machine, the establishment of the link can be made manually or automatically, as shown in Fig. 5.2. To initiate automatic calling, the business machine or computer directs a connected device known as an automatic calling unit to initiate and execute the call.

Although originally offered only by telephone companies, the growth of data communications has led a number of independent firms to offer equivalent-type devices, which in some cases exceed the capabilities offered by telephone company equipment. In addition, devices produced by independent firms can be purchased, whereas telephone company equipment is only available on a monthly lease basis.

The basic function of an automatic calling unit is to perform electronically for a business machine, such as a computer, what a human

Fig. 5.2. Call Origination

Call origination can occur normally by having an operator dial a switched network number, or it can be performed automatically through the use of an automatic calling unit.

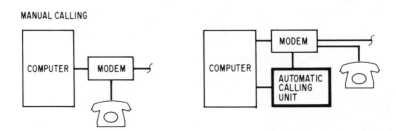

operator does by hand when he or she places a telephone call. In examining the functions performed by an automatic calling unit (ACU), these functions are electronically equivalent to operator functions when making a call, including lifting the telephone headset (referred to as going off-hook), waiting for the correct dial tone or tones, dialing each digit of the telephone number desired in its proper sequence, waiting while the phone rings until the dialed number answers, hanging up and possibly redialing at a later date if the number is busy or if the call is not answered after a reasonable length of time, and hanging up the headset at the end of the completed call. When properly configured into a data communications network, automatic calling units dramatically increase line utilization while correspondingly reducing communications charges.

Types of Calling Units

There are two basic types of calling units which correspond to the type of dialing unit the equipment is connected to. The dc dial pulse type of calling unit is commonly referred to as a Data Auxiliary Set 801A Automatic Calling Unit by the telephone company and permits dialing through rotary dialing connections. The second type of calling unit, the Data Auxiliary Set 801C Automatic Calling Unit, permits calls to be made over a Touch-Tone® telephone in about one-tenth of the time required when using the older rotary dial. For those sections of the country where Touch-Tone® dialing is available, the use of an 801C-type calling unit can shorten the required dialing time by about 10 s per call in comparison to using a 801A-type of calling unit. Calling units manufactured by independent firms are commonly referred to as 801A or 801C replacement devices, with the general designation of an 801 device used to designate some type of automatic calling unit.

Utilization of Calling Units

The most common utilization of automatic calling units is in a distributed network, where one or more computers are used to poll many remote terminals on a periodic basis, as shown in Fig. 5.3.

One of the many users of the configuration shown in Fig. 5.3 is the insurance industry. Most major insurance firms have offices scattered throughout the country. To assist their policy illustration effort, a number of firms have their sales personnel fill out a policy illustration worksheet that specifies the type of policy under consideration, the amount of coverage desired, the name, age, address, sex, and occupation of the potential insuree, as well as insurance options, such as waiver of premium, that may be desired. This information is then entered by a secretary or by the sales personnel into a terminal's storage device, such as a cassette, at the insurance office.

In the evening, when the office has probably closed for business and also when telephone rates are lower, a computer which may be located at the firm's headquarters or a regional office polls the terminals located in the remote offices via the switched (dial-up) telephone network. If the office where the terminal is located did not have any transaction that day, the data terminal at that location is set so it will not respond to the computer's call, and therefore no toll charge is incurred. For those terminals which have been set to respond to the computer's call, the automatic answering device attached to the remote terminal accepts the call, and the data that has been stored on the terminal's storage device is now transmitted to the computer. This process is repeated until all of the preselected terminals have been called. Later in the night, after the data from the terminals have been processed and the policy illustrations prepared in machine form, the

Fig. 5.3. Polling of Remote Terminals

Calling units can be effectively employed to poll remote terminals at predetermined times to reduce communication toll charges. If the calling unit is not certified, a data access arrangement which serves as a protective device between the customer equipment and the telephone company line may be required.

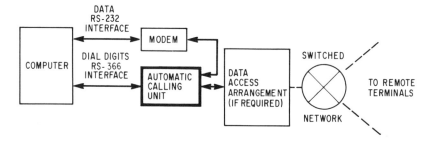

results are returned to the requesting terminals, again by calls originating from the central or regional computer site and occurring over the switched telephone network. The returned data can either be stored on the terminal's storage device for later printout or printed on-line by the terminal's printer as transmission occurs. In either event, the sales personnel entering the office the next morning should find policy illustrations ready to deliver to clients. Since these calls are made without human intervention and at a time when telephone company charges are normally at a minimum, the monthly cost of the automatic calling unit is usually recovered during its first few days of operation during the month.

Depending upon the locations of the remote terminals, the duration of each call, the average number of terminals called each night, and the existing telephone rates for calls over the switched network, either ordinary dialing over the switched network or outward wide area telephone service (WATS) lines may be used. Ordinary dialing over the switched network is most practical when the terminals to be called are geographically dispersed and the connect time required to accept data from each terminal and return the processed information at a later time is of a relatively short duration. For those applications where the connect time is long, WATS lines can be used to keep toll charges down, with a WATS line giving the user a block of hours per month of telephone usage to a specific geographical area at a fixed monthly cost. WATS line areas can be selected from several bands, with one band covering the entire United States with the exception of the state the user is located in, while another band might consist of access to several adjacent states.

Interfacing Automatic Calling Units

Two types of interfaces can be utilized by a system which employs an automatic calling unit. As shown in Fig. 5.3, the more common RS-232 interface is used to connect the automatic calling unit to its associated data set and the data set to the business machine or computer. While some independently manufactured calling units can also be interfaced to the computer according to the RS-232 standard, telephone company provided calling units are interfaced to the computer according to the RS-366 standard which is used to define the interface between a business machine and an automatic calling unit. Within the RS-366 interface standard, five interface classes of automatic calling equipment have been defined, as shown in Table 5.2.

Although five classes of automatic equipment have been defined according to the RS-366 standard, basically the variations can be broken down into versions of type I or type II. Type I defines an automatic calling unit in which the numbers to be dialed are stored internally (stored number dialer), while type II defines one in which the numbers to be dialed are

Table 5.2. Classes of RS-366 Standard Automatic Calling Equipment Interfaces

Class	Data terminal equipment (business machine, computer)	Data communications equipment (automatic calling unit)
Type I	Call request	ACU stores single or multiple telephone numbers which are automatically dialed in sequence; modem separate
Type II	Select numbers stored in ACU by single-digit control	ACU stores single or multiple telephone numbers, however number to be called selected by the data terminal equipment; modem separate
Type III	Number to be dialed stored in the data terminal equipment and passed one at a time to the ACU	ACU receives number from the data terminal equipment a digit at a time via a parallel binary-coded decimal (BCD) interface; modem separate
Type IV	Call request or select numbers stored in the ACU by single-digit control	Combination ACU with built-in modem in one unit; stored number dialer can be type I or type II operation
Type V	Multiline automatic calling unit	Undefined at present time

stored in the memory of the associated business machine or computer. Thus, types III and IV can be considered variations of the first two types.

Interface Lead Description

The interface leads required between an 801 ACU-type device and a business machine according to RS-366 are shown in Fig. 5.4. Here, 13 of the 25 available interface connections are used. Of the thirteen interface leads, six are operated by the computer to signal the automatic calling unit. These leads include CALL REQUEST, four digit leads, and the DIGIT PRESENT lead.

Signals on the CALL REQUEST lead are generated by the business machine to request the calling unit to originate a call. The presence of an ON condition on this lead indicates a request to originate a call, while the OFF condition is used to indicate that the business machine has completed its use of the automatic calling equipment. During the call origination period, this lead must be maintained in the ON condition in order to hold the communication channel "off-hook." This lead is turned OFF between calls or call attempts and should not be turned ON unless the DATA LINE OCCUPIED lead is in the OFF condition.

By presenting parallel binary signals on the four digit leads, the business machine presents to the calling unit a four bit binary representa-

Fig. 5.4. RS-366 Interface Leads

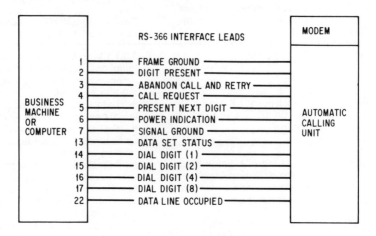

tion of the digit to be dialed. The information presented on these four leads may either be transmitted as the called number or used locally as a control signal, as shown in Table 5.3. As indicated in this table, to request the calling unit to dial a common number such as WE61212, the signals presented by the business machine on the four parallel leads to the ACU would be as shown in Table 5.4.

Signals on the DIGIT PRESENT lead are generated by the business machine to indicate that the calling unit may now read the code combinations presented on the four digit leads. The presence of an ON condition indicates that the business machine has set the states of the digit leads for the next digit. When the calling unit signals the business machine that it is

Table 5.3.   Digit Lead Coding

Digit value	NB8 2^3	NB6 2^2	NB4 2^1	NB2 2^0
0	0	0	0	0
1	0	0	0	1
2	0	0	1	0
3	0	0	1	1
4	0	1	0	0
5	0	1	0	1
6	0	1	1	0
7	0	1	1	1
8	1	0	0	0
9	1	0	0	1
End of number (EON)	1	1	0	0

Table 5.4. Dialing WE61212

Digit	NB8	NB4	NB2	NB1
9	1	0	0	1
3	0	0	1	1
6	0	1	1	0
1	0	0	0	1
2	0	0	1	0
1	0	0	0	1
2	0	0	1	0

ready to accept the next digit by turning ON the PRESENT NEXT DIGIT (PND) lead, the business machine must turn ON, DIGIT PRESENT and keep it in the ON condition until PND goes OFF. Then DIGIT PRESENT must be turned OFF and held in that state until PND comes ON again. When DIGIT PRESENT is ON, the states of the four digit leads are held constant and are changed during the DIGIT PRESENT transitions.

Of the thirteen interface connections which are used, five are operated by the calling unit to signal the associated business machine. As mentioned previously, the PND lead is used by the calling unit to control the presentation of digits on the four digit leads. During dialing, the ON condition indicates that the calling unit is ready to accept the next digit, which will be transmitted by the business machine on leads digit 8, digit 4, digit 2, and digit 1. By placing the PND signal lead in the OFF condition, the calling unit informs the business machine that it must turn OFF the DIGIT PRESENT lead and set the states of the digit leads for the presentation of the next digit. PND cannot revert back to the ON condition as long as the DIGIT PRESENT signal is ON, however it will come ON and remain in the ON condition after the business machine turns DIGIT PRESENT OFF following presentation of the last code combination on the digit leads. If the call is placed by the calling unit, throughout the data transmission interval PND will be in the ON condition. If the call is placed manually or if the business machine is receiving an incoming call, PND will be placed in the OFF condition.

To indicate that power is available within the calling unit, signals are generated on the POWER INDICATION lead by the calling unit. The presence of an ON condition indicates that power is available in the calling unit, while the OFF condition on this signal lead indicates that the calling unit is inoperative because of loss of power.

The DATA LINE OCCUPIED lead is used by the calling unit to indicate the status of the desired communications channel. The presence of an ON condition indicates that the communications channel is in use, while the OFF condition indicates that the business machine may originate a call provided that the POWER INDICATION lead is in the ON condition.

Signals on the DATA SET STATUS lead are generated by the calling unit to indicate the status of the local data communications equipment (i.e., attached data set). The presence of an ON condition indicates that the telephone line is connected to the data set to be used for data communications and that the data set is in the data mode.

The ABANDON CALL AND RETRY signal lead is used to indicate to the business machine that a preset time has elapsed since the last change of state of PND. The timer starts whenever CALL REQUEST is turned ON. The time-out interval on telephone company calling units can be set by a screwdriver operated switch for a period of 7, 10, 15, 25, or 40 s, with a period of 25 to 40 s commonly used to allow sufficient time for the call to go to completion. Any time the business machine, the calling unit, or the telephone network takes more time than the preset timing interval is set to, from the last PND OFF, the ABANDON CALL AND RETRY lead is turned to the ON state. The ON state is a suggestion to the associated business machine to abandon the call and try again at a later time if the connection has not yet been completed. The response to the ON condition of the ABANDON CALL AND RETRY lead is left to the business machine, which can either act upon receipt of the signal or ignore it.

In addition to the previously mentioned signal leads, SIGNAL GROUND and FRAME GROUND leads are part of the 13-lead group utilized in the RS-366 standard. The SIGNAL GROUND provides a common ground reference for the interface circuits and is connected to the frame of the calling unit, while the FRAME GROUND lead provides an electronic bond between the frames of the calling unit and the business machine.

Although telephone company supplied calling units are only interfaced to business machines using the RS-366 interface standard, some independently manufactured calling units permit either RS-232 or RS-366 interfacing. Using a single RS-232 asynchronous data port as shown in Fig. 5.5, data is transmitted serially from the business machine to the calling unit. Using this type of interface, in addition to common ground leads, nine other leads of the 25-pin connector are utilized.

Fig. 5.5. Serial Data Port RS-232 Interface

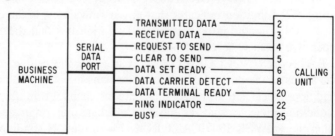

When dial digit data is transmitted via a serial data port, any four of the first six bits after the start bit can be used to define the dial digit, with the remaining bits being ignored by the calling unit. The four bit positions selected must be coded in the same manner as that shown in Table 5.3. An example of an American Standard Code for Information Interchange (ASCII) character for dialing a seven is shown below, where S is START BIT and R is RESET BIT.

$$S \quad 1 \quad 1 \quad 1 \quad 0 \quad 0 \quad 0 \quad 0 \quad R \quad R$$

RS-232 Calling Unit Operation

If the interface is according to the RS-232 standard, the business machine turns the DATA TERMINAL READY (DTR) lead in the ON condition to initiate a call. The calling unit in response goes "OFF-HOOK" and sets a dial tone timer for a few seconds to insure that the dial tone is present before proceeding with dialing. Next, the calling unit turns the CLEAR-TO-SEND (CTS) lead to the ON condition to inform the business machine of a request by the calling unit for a serial dial digit.

Upon receipt of the CTS request from the calling unit, the business machine transfers a serial character to the calling unit via the TRANSMIT DATA lead. The calling unit stores the serial dial digit and turns the CTS lead to the OFF condition after the full character has been received. After receiving the full character, the calling unit outputs dial pulses or tones, times out for a second or for a predetermined number of dial tones if so programmed, and then turns on the CTS lead to request the next dial digit. This process is repeated for all the digits of the number to be dialed.

Depending upon the manufacturer of the calling unit, the transfer of a serial end of number character to the calling unit or the nontransfer of this character for a preset time interval of from 1 to 10 s will perform the end of the number function.

If the ABANDON CALL AND RETRY timer expires before the answer tone or carrier is detected, the calling unit turns OFF the DATA SET READY (DSR) lead to signal the business machine to abandon the call. To abandon or conclude a call, the business machine turns OFF the DTR lead, and the calling unit then turns ON the DSR lead and resets to await the next CALL REQUEST from the business machine.

Calling Unit Operation RS-366 Interface

The business machine originates a call by turning the CALL REQUEST lead in the ON condition. In response to this signal, the calling unit goes OFF-HOOK and "holds" the telephone line in much the same manner as a telephone which is in use. Since the telephone line is now in use, the calling unit turns the DATA LINE OCCUPIED lead in the ON condition. If the DATA LINE OCCUPIED lead was on prior to when the CALL REQUEST was transmitted, the calling unit will not respond since the line would already be in use. Next, the calling unit generates a PND signal which is used to tell the business machine that the calling unit is ready to receive the first digit to be dialed.

Upon detection of the PND condition, the business machine transmits the first digit to be dialed to the calling unit via the four digit leads. When the digit leads have been set, the business machine then places the DIGIT PRESENT lead in the ON condition which tells the calling unit to dial the first digit. After the first digit has been dialed, the calling unit places the PND lead in the OFF condition. This process is repeated until all of the digits have been dialed, after which, either of two actions can occur.

If the calling unit receives a binary 12 (end of number) digit to signify that the preceding digit was the last digit to be dialed, the calling unit will give the telephone line back to the data set and signal the data set to enter the data mode, thus making it ready to send or receive data. If instead of transmitting a binary 12, the business machine fails to output another digit when requested, the calling unit will time out and assume that the last digit has been dialed.

Although the preceding example is rather straightforward, numerous variations in the calling unit's method of operation can occur depending upon the calling unit's selected options as well as the manufacturer of the device. As shown previously, some calling units interface not only with business machines that output dial digit information in parallel according to the RS-366 standard, but also with devices that output the more common RS-232 control signals and asynchronous start-stop data.

Data sets that can be called by the calling unit are not necessarily the same as those data sets which can be connected to a calling unit. One example of this is a network where a calling unit is used to call remote terminals where each terminal is connected to a Bell System 113B (answer only) modem. Here, the data set associated with the calling unit could be a 113A (transmit only) data set but obviously would not be another 113B type modem. Thus, manufacturer's specifications concerning both data sets that can be called as well as data sets that can be connected to the calling unit should be carefully checked. While data sets provided by the telephone company are separate devices, some nontelephone company calling units may be ordered with built-in data sets, making possible savings in space, cabling, and power. However, when using nontelephone company data sets over the switched network, a data access arrangement may be required to serve as a protective device between the modem and the switched network if the modem is not registered. The reader is referred to Chapter 6, Sec. 6.3 for additional information about this device.

Additional Calling Unit Applications

As previously mentioned, the most common type of calling unit application is for the polling of remote terminals, as shown in Fig. 5.3. For this type of application, the business machine conducts automatic polling of remote terminals by utilizing the switched telephone network. This switched network utilization can consist of the ordinary direct distance dialing network or it can be through one or more WATS lines which provide access to the switched telephone network, with the selection based upon such economic factors as the location of the polled terminals, the time the polling occurs, and the duration of each call.

For the situation where only a few cities have to be called but each city contains numerous terminals, an automatic calling unit which can be interfaced to a business machine according to RS-232 standards and thus be remotely located from the business machine should be considered. When equipment is used in this manner, long distance dialing over a leased or foreign exchange line to a remotely located calling unit can be accomplished as shown in Fig. 5.6. The configuration shown in Fig. 5.6 may permit long distance dialing to be made more economical than when using WATS lines or the switched network through direct distance dialing when a large number of terminals to be polled are concentrated in only a few cities and the polling time required for each terminal is of relatively long duration. When compared with ordinary long distance dialing, this configuration would also eliminate the possibility of long distance trunk busy conditions, since

Fig. 5.6. Using Leased Lines to Connect Remotely Located Calling Units

When a large number of terminals to be polled are located in only a few distant cities, it may be more economical to place calling units in each city and connect them to the computer by installing leased lines between the computer and each calling unit.

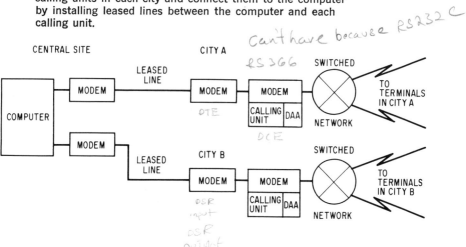

private leased lines are now used to connect the business machine to each remotely located calling unit.

If the number of terminals located within a city or geographical area has a total transmission time that exceeds the computer time available for remote polling due to transmission speed limitations when one calling unit is used, multiple calling units can be used, as shown in Fig. 5.7. If instead of two calling units, several additional units are required, the leased line charges for the configuration shown in Fig. 5.7 could become prohibitive, or result in unnecessary telephone line charges which can be reduced through the utilization of multiplexers. The configuration shown in Fig. 5.7 should also be compared to the cost of both multiple leased line charges as well as multiple WATS line charges. When many channels of low-speed data are to be transmitted to a few cities or geographical areas, this arrangement should be more economical than using multiple WATS lines or multiple leased lines. However, the failure of the leased line between multiplexers would terminate a portion of all remote polling activity and should be taken into consideration by users whose requirements include a method of backup servicing of terminals.

Fig. 5.7. Multiple Long Distance Dialing Using Multiplexers

Multiple remotely located calling units may have their transmissions multiplexed to reduce communications costs.

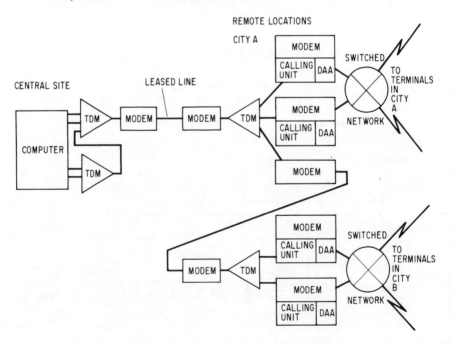

For situations where the duration of each call will be appreciably longer than the time necessary to dial and establish the call, it may be feasible to utilize a single calling unit to dial on several lines. This multiple calling with a single calling unit can be effected through the installation of a device referred to as a calling line selector, and it can be used to switch a single calling unit to a number of lines, with the call being switched to any free line by the calling line selector, as shown in Fig. 5.8.

As shown in the figure, the calling line selector can be effectively used when the terminals to be polled are located within the same city as the business machine or where a number of foreign exchange lines are used to give the business machine located in one city local telephone access to terminals located in different telephone exchange areas. When the calling line selector is used, the business machine may be programmed to select the next line to be dialed by transmitting a parallel 4-bit digit ahead of the first dial digit, or the calling line selector will automatically go to the next free line in sequence if the business machine selection mode is not used. In addition to selecting the next line to be dialed, the calling line selector provides for the automatic answering of incoming calls.

Fig. 5.8. Multiple Calling Using Calling Line Selector and a Single Calling Unit

One calling unit can establish a number of concurrent calls through the use of a calling line selector.

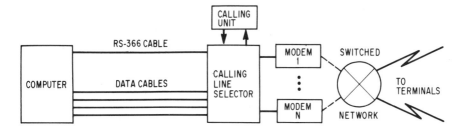

chapter 6
specialized devices

The components explored in this section can be used in a variety of situations. To provide a level of protection to transmitted data, security devices can be installed to encode such data in order to reduce the possibility of the transmission being intercepted and understood by an unauthorized person.

Both speed and code converters and voice adapters can be employed to reduce communications costs. Speed and code converters may permit data communications users both to standardize transmission speeds and reduce the number of lines required for the transmission of data from remote terminals to a central computer. Voice adapters permit a line used for data communications to be alternating or simultaneously used for voice communications, permitting voice contact between remote terminal operators and computer center personnel over common communication facilities.

Although much controversy and many court rulings do provide a colorful history to data access arrangements, basically, such devices can be viewed as a protective component to shield the switched telephone network from the possibility of malfunctioning customer-provided equipment when such equipment has not been registered for usage by the Federal Communications Commission (FCC) or a state regulatory commission.

6.1. Security Devices

As networks expand and proliferate, more and more people have access to them, and the harder it becomes to guard against unauthorized access to the network and entry into data files on computers which normally may be restricted to only a few users. A door that is locked and patrolled is, of course, some measure of security against sabotage or theft, but it offers little protection against the wily, white-collar evil doer for whom entry is no serious problem. Hence, in the absence of adequate operational controls, someone using a time-sharing system may be billed for someone else's transactions, or, more seriously, a company transmitting confidential bid information could have its message intercepted and read by a competitor.

To reduce the possibilities of these events occurring, a number of devices have been introduced by several manufacturers to encrypt both data files and transmitted data. Prior to discussing how these devices operate and where they can be employed, a review of sign-on and data base security features will be undertaken to provide the reader with an insight to the problems associated with unauthorized access as well as some of the methods that can reduce the probability of such access with computer software.

Password Shortcomings

The most frequently employed method of preventing unauthorized access to networks and data bases, that of identification codes, has a number of shortcomings. The code can be glimpsed over a person's shoulder, found on a discarded printout in a trash basket, or on the ribbon of a printer terminal. A remedy, then, is to use characters that are nonprintable. (The term "character" in this context refers to any distinct electrical signal initiated at a terminal and does not necessarily imply a visible figure in the usual sense of the word.) This is the so-called password approach. It is a precaution that is gaining increasing attention among data communications users, and it is also fairly simple, being essentially an extension of the use of terminal identification numbers.

Whether printed or nonprinted, however, careful consideration is required in putting together the elements of an adequate access control system. These include immunity to access by repeated random tries and the ability of the network to report repeated attempts at access.

Practically any element in a network can be the target of unauthorized access, but the most likely point of entry is a remote terminal because it is out of sight of the central office. The sign-on procedure, involving a code that must be keyed in to the terminal to gain clearance, is the standard method of assuring access. Figure 6.1A depicts the normal response of a computer to a sign-on request. If an illegal sign-on is attempted, the response might be as shown in Figure 6.1B.

For example, in a time-sharing system, the procedure starts with the user establishing the telephone connection and identifying the type of terminal (code and transmission speed), usually by sending a carriage return. Typically, after getting a go-ahead from the computer, the user then transmits his or her own personal identification number. If the number is invalid, as might happen if a wrong key is struck accidentally, the user receives a message, such as "illegal sign-on." The computer then allows

Fig. 6.1. Identification Messages

The format of the message requesting the user's identification and password (underlined) is similar to that shown in diagram **A**. Notification that the maximum number of retries has been exceeded is shown in part B. Operator intervention may follow.

```
PLEASE SIGN-ON
?ID U_C U_C U_C V_C V_C V_C V_C
GENERAL TIME SHARING COMPANY
ON AT DATE, TIME
              (A)
```

```
PLEASE SIGN-ON
ID 127 ABCD
ILLEGAL SIGN-ON THRESHOLD EXCEEDED
CONTACT OPERATOR
OFF AT XX/YY
              (B)
```

the user a fixed amount of time, usually several seconds, to send another sign-on. If the time is up or the user exceeds a certain number of allowable retries, the computer automatically disconnects. In this case the user must redial and try again.

This procedure is susceptible to sophisticated attack, however, unless additionally protected, but more on that later. A flow chart outlining a typical sign-on procedure in a time-sharing system is shown in Fig. 6.2.

Legal, but Unprintable

A password approach incorporated into the sign-on procedure following the identification number has the obvious advantage of being less liable to illicit discovery. There are limitations, however. The most obvious limit is the number of characters on the terminal keyboard. For instance, the most common terminal, the Teletype Corporation Model 33-ASR, limits the user to a subset of the American Standard Code for Information Interchange (ASCII). And not all control characters on a keyboard can be used in the password. Some systems reserve certain characters for terminal function control, system control, and communications control. Examples are a carriage return to indicate the end of a line and a backspace to cause deletion of the last character entered. Other characters may turn a paper tape reader on or off. A list of frequently unavailable nonprintable characters is given on Table 6.1. For some terminals there may be a few characters left. In such a case, a long password is needed to provide enough combinations.

Fig. 6.2. Sign-on Procedure

Typical in sign-on procedures for time-sharing systems, the response to a user attempting to gain access is a request for identification and password.

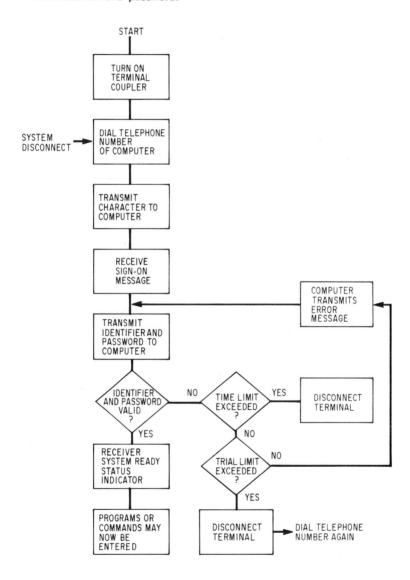

Since the list is extensive, it can easily be seen that not many characters in an average system may really be available for a password. Experience has shown, however, that a three- to six-character password is the optimum length to provide enough characters in most systems to take care of the job. The optimum length, incidentally, is taken to mean one

Table 6.1.   Frequently Unavailable Characters

Character meaning	Possible reserved usage
Break	System interrupt
End of transmission	Communications
Bell	Terminal
Line feed	Terminal
Form feed	Terminal
Carriage return	Terminal, system
X-On	Terminal
Tape	Terminal
Cancel	System or communications
Space (field separation)	System
Delete line	System
Delete character	System
Rub-out	System or communications

that does not defy an average user's ability to remember the password, and one that does not add substantially to computer overhead in the processing of it.

It may appear at first that the number of combinations possible in a password of a given length would simply be C^i, where C is the size of the available character repertoire and i the number of character positions to be filled. Actually, additional combinations are possible by using fewer than the maximum number of positions that one has decided upon. This is accomplished by typing a carriage return immediately following the shortened password to indicate that it is terminated.

Consider, for example, a three-position password in which each position can take either of two nonprintable characters, which are designated A and B in Fig. 6.3. By using all three positions there are eight possible

Fig. 6.3. Code Combinations

By permitting the password to be smaller than the maximum number of chosen positions, extra combinations are possible. A and B denote nonprintable characters, making up to 14 combinations.

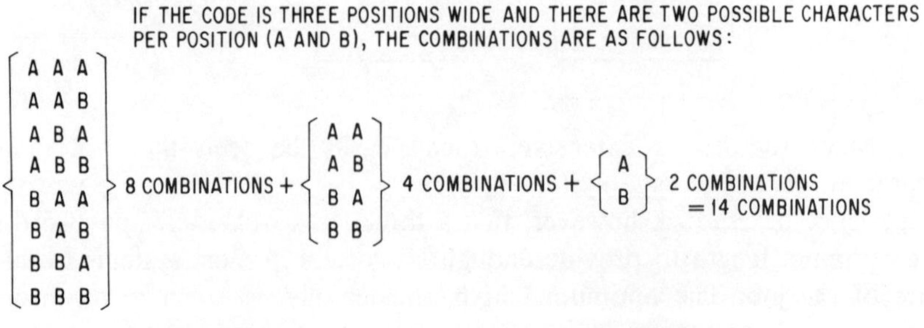

IF THE CODE IS THREE POSITIONS WIDE AND THERE ARE TWO POSSIBLE CHARACTERS PER POSITION (A AND B), THE COMBINATIONS ARE AS FOLLOWS:

$$
\begin{Bmatrix} A\ A\ A \\ A\ A\ B \\ A\ B\ A \\ A\ B\ B \\ B\ A\ A \\ B\ A\ B \\ B\ B\ A \\ B\ B\ B \end{Bmatrix} \text{8 COMBINATIONS} + \begin{Bmatrix} A\ A \\ A\ B \\ B\ A \\ B\ B \end{Bmatrix} \text{4 COMBINATIONS} + \begin{Bmatrix} A \\ B \end{Bmatrix} \begin{matrix} \text{2 COMBINATIONS} \\ = 14 \text{ COMBINATIONS} \end{matrix}
$$

combinations. But by using two positions and leaving the third position blank, four more combinations are possible. If only one position is filled, two more still are possible, for a total of 14 possibilities.

In this routine, the user's personal identification number, which is usually keyed in at the start of the request for access, tells the computer what to expect. Identification numbers and passwords must correlate. (From a practical standpoint, however, one- or two-position passwords might be inadvisable because it might make it easier for an intruder to come upon the correct password by simple random selection.)

In any event, the total number of realistic combinations, *T,* can be calculated as:

$$T = \sum_{i=1}^{i=w} C^i$$

where *i* represents individual positions (first, second, third, etc.), *w* is the total number of positions in the password, and *C* is the number of characters available. For example, a four-position password with a character set of two provides 30 combinations. Increasing the character set to eight raises the combination to 4,680.

The Unwitting Accomplice

A potent tool available to the illicit network user is another computer. Here the human malefactor harnesses the machine, which can be little more than a microcomputer and automatic dialer, to repeatedly dial, try a password, and retry if the password does not work.

If, for example, such a system were used to access a computer that permits five sign-on attempts before automatically disconnecting, and the terminal transmits at 30 characters per second, then the five tries could be performed in less than 10 s. Upon sensing a disconnect, the microcomputer could redial and try five more code combinations. Over a 3-day holiday weekend, with little traffic and the central computer unattended, this scheme could attempt over 40,000 passwords with nobody being the wiser.

To counter this brute force approach, provision should be made to monitor and record the repetition of sign-on attempts. Once a predetermined number of tries has been made for a given identification number, the system could be programmed to inhibit additional sign-on efforts until a system operator intervenes. The maximum number of tries can be established daily or at more frequent intervals. The threshold for a given identification number could be 10 attempts in a given hour or 20 attempts a day, depending on the individuality of the system. When the threshold is exceeded, the user is locked out of the network and receives a message requesting that he or she contact the system operator for return of service.

Automatic intervention does not eliminate the possible success of a concerted effort to gain access by numerous retries, but it does sharply reduce the probability of success. The only way in which access might be obtained is to try the maximum number of sign-on attempts short of intervention, disconnecting for the balance of the timing interval, and trying again. If this were to succeed at all, it could take months or years in a system with a small threshold, a long password, and a long time interval.

As shown in Fig. 6.4, with a three-position password drawing on 15 available characters, the probability of successful entry (a probability of 1) rises sharply if there is no intervention, and is assured by the 3,615th trial. With intervention after 20 repeated tries, however, the probability does not exceed 0.005. The diagram also shows that if the character repertoire is reduced to 10, and there is no intervention mechanism, the intruder is assured of access by the 1,110th try, two-third sooner than with a 15-character repertoire. Another factor that can have a major bearing on access security is the number of characters reserved to perform communications functions. While a large number of such characters are standardized, installations that remove characters from the character set available for passwords run the risk of increasing the access vulnerability of the system.

While the preceding discussion was primarily concerned with sign-on access, similar problems and solutions can be effected with respect to the passwords employed to protect data files.

Fig. 6.4. Intervention Impact

With intervention software, the probability of successful entry by random password selection becomes extremely small.

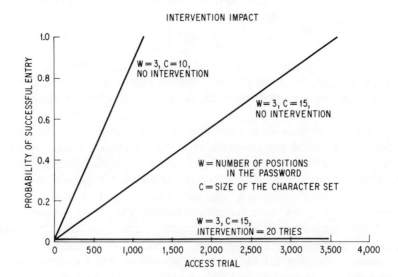

INTERVENTION IMPACT

W = 3, C = 10,
NO INTERVENTION

W = 3, C = 15,
NO INTERVENTION

W = NUMBER OF POSITIONS
IN THE PASSWORD

C = SIZE OF THE CHARACTER SET

W = 3, C = 15,
INTERVENTION = 20 TRIES

PROBABILITY OF SUCCESSFUL ENTRY

ACCESS TRIAL

Transmission Security

Although a number of methods have been developed to promote access and data base security further, unless the transmission medium utilized is secure, the user may become vulnerable to having data transmission compromised by such means as line tapping, or line monitoring. In addition, if transmission is over such store and forward systems as Telex or TWX, by courier or telegram, the message may be read by unauthorized personnel or obtained through active penetration by insiders as well as outsiders. In certain U.S. Department of Defense installations, terminal transmission is over secure transmission lines to a central facility or another terminal which makes access security their major concern. This is due to the fact that although all transmission lines on the installation are secure, personnel with different security level clearances have access to the same computer and a method of differentiating who obtains what computer resources is primarily determined by the terminal's location and the identification code of the user.

For the situation where data transmission occurs over public, non-secure facilities, a method of making the transmitted data unintelligible to unauthorized parties becomes as important as having a good access security procedure. Fortunately, numerous techniques are available for the user to make transmitted data unintelligible to unauthorized parties, with the oldest and most widely used method being the various types of manual coding processes, where through the use of code books and pads the original text is encoded before transmission and then decoded by the recipient of the message. The foundations for the various coding schemes go back thousands of years and have been used to protect a wide range of messages ranging from diplomatic and military communications from before the time of the Roman Empire thru commercial messages of industrial companies today.

Manual Techniques

In spite of the fact that most manual coding techniques can be broken by trained cryptoanalysts, they do offer a measure of protection due to the time element which may be of a considerably long period before the message is decoded by an unauthorized party. Thus, the information that company A will bid 2 million dollars on a contract whose bid is to be opened on 1 February is worthless to a competitor that decodes the message from the home office to company A's field agent after that date. In addition, manual coding schemes can also be used as a backup in the event of the failure of a coding device that the user may have installed. One of the earliest coding techniques was the so-called Caesar Cipher, which was probably known and used long before Caesar was born. Using this technique, Julius Caesar enciphered his dispatches by displacing each letter by a fixed amount. If the displacement was two, then the message INVADE ENGLAND TONIGHT would be transformed into KPXCFG GPINCPF VQPKIJV and sent by messenger to the appropriate recipient. Upon receipt of the message, a reverse transformation would develop the plain text of the message. Although this scheme may appear primitive, some encryption devices use internal circuits to perform a continuous and alternating displacement of the plain text to develop an encrypted message which could frustrate the best cryptoanalyst.

A group of encryption techniques have been developed based upon what is known as the basic checkerboard. Here, the alphabet and numerals are written into a six-by-six block with coordinates for row and column used to specify the cells. This technique can involve the use of different indices as well as a rearrangement of cell data, as shown in Table 6.2.

Again, with the advent of modern electronics it is possible to construct a device to continuously change the indices after a certain period of transmission, or to change the cells, or both.

A variation of the checkerboard technique is accomplished through the utilization of a keyword which is commonly referred to as a Vigenere cipher technique. In its simplest form, the Vigenere cipher consists of a table of alphabets, as shown in Fig. 6.5. For ease of remembrance, a meaningful phrase or mnemonic is selected as the key although this can be a major weakness, and incoherent keys which reduce the number of clues are preferable for use. Here encipherment begins by establishing a one-to-one correspondence between the characters of the plain text and the characters of the keys, with the key being partially or completely repeated if shorter than the plain text. The cipher character is then obtained from the intersection of the appropriate keyletter row and the plain text column. For example, if SECRET is used as the key to encipher the plain text message INVADE ENGLAND, the table provides a cipher text of ARXRMX WRICEGV. As shown, the cipher text is developed character by character, with the first character of the cipher text obtained from the

Table 6.2. Basic Checkerboard*

		Block 1							Block 2				
	A	E	I	O	U	V		G	H	I	J	K	L
A	A	B	C	D	E	F	A	Z	Y	X	W	V	0
E	G	H	I	J	K	L	B	U	T	S	R	Q	1
I	M	N	O	P	Q	R	C	P	O	N	M	L	2
O	S	T	U	V	W	X	D	K	J	I	H	G	3
U	Y	Z	0	1	2	3	E	F	E	D	C	B	4
V	4	5	6	7	8	9	F	A	9	8	7	6	5

* Using the above blocks, the word CODE becomes: from Block 1: AI II AO AU; from Block 2: EJ CH EI EH.

Fig. 6.5. Vigenere Cipher

A one-to-one correspondence between the plain text and the
characters of a key is used to develop the cipher text. Here, the
intersection of the plain text character I with the key character S
produces a cipher text character A.

```
PLAINTEXT     INVADE ENGLAND
              |||||| ||||||||
KEY           SECRET SECRETS
              |||||| ///////
CIPHERTEXT    ARXRHXWRICEGV
```

PLAINTEXT

```
      ↓     ↓ ↓   ↓     ↓     ↓     ↓              ↓
      A B C D E F G H I J K L M N O P Q R S T U V W X Y Z

A     A B C D E F G H I J K L M N O P Q R S T U V W X Y Z
B     B C D E F G H I J K L M N O P Q R S T U V W X Y Z A
→C    C D E F G H (I) J K L M N O P Q R S T U V W (X) Y Z A B
D     D E F G H I J K L M N O P Q R S T U V W X Y Z A B C
→E    (E) F G (H) I J K L M N O P Q (R) S T U V W X Y Z A B C D
F     F G H I J K L M N O P Q R S T U V W X Y Z A B C D E
G     G H I J K L M N O P Q R S T U V W X Y Z A B C D E F
H     H I J K L M N O P Q R S T U V W X Y Z A B C D E F G
I     I J K L M N O P Q R S T U V W X Y Z A B C D E F G H
J     J K L M N O P Q R S T U V W X Y Z A B C D E F G H I
K     K L M N O P Q R S T U V W X Y Z A B C D E F G H I J
L     L M N O P Q R S T U V W X Y Z A B C D E F G H I J K
M     M N O P Q R S T U V W X Y Z A B C D E F G H I J K L
N     N O P Q R S T U V W X Y Z A B C D E F G H I J K L M
O     O P Q R S T U V W X Y Z A B C D E F G H I J K L M N
P     P Q R S T U V W X Y Z A B C D E F G H I J K L M N O
Q     Q R S T U V W X Y Z A B C D E F G H I J K L M N O P
→R    (R) S T (U) V W X Y Z A B (C) D E F G H I J K L M N O P Q
→S    S T U V (W) X Y Z (A) B C D E F G H I J K L M N O P Q R
→T    T U V W (X) Y Z A B C D E F (G) H I J K L M N O P Q R S
U     U V W X Y Z A B C D E F G H I J K L M N O P Q R S T
V     V W X Y Z A B C D E F G H I J K L M N O P Q R S T U
W     W X Y Z A B C D E F G H I J K L M N O P Q R S T U V
X     X Y Z A B C D E F G H I J K L M N O P Q R S T U V W
Y     Y Z A B C D E F G H I J K L M N O P Q R S T U V W X
Z     Z A B C D E F G H I J K L M N O P Q R S T U V W X Y
```

intersection of the *s* character of the key SECRET with the first character
(*i*) of the plain text, and so on. Since 676 memory locations are required
for 26 characters of the alphabet, or 1296 locations for the alphabet and
digits, some devices encode data by using a fixed memory but generating
pseudorandom numbers which are used to develop a pseudorandom key.

Concurrent with the development of electromechanical devices, several methods of encoding information were developed. In 1917, Gilbert

Vernam of the American Telephone and Telegraph Company (AT&T) developed a method for insuring that the information contained in a punched paper tape would remain unintelligible to unauthorized users. In Vernam's technique, each text letter was enciphered with its own cipher letter. If the key tape was as long as the message, and its key perfectly random, the text was then theoretically unbreakable. However, the inconvenience of preparing thousands of feet of tape for high-volume traffic as well as the security problems inherent in guarding tape supplies and accounting for both active and cancelled tape rolls prevented most users from considering this technique. A practical compromise between convenience and security was the development of pseudorandom events which appear to be as unpredictable as those generated by white noise, sunspots, and other physical phenomena, but in reality are developed from a reproducible mathematical relationship. An example of this would be a program to manipulate two 18-bit registers where the product of each register's contents through a predetermined process is extracted into two numbers which return to the registers where the process is repeated again. Thus, the 36 bits of the two registers could produce a period length of $2^{36} - 1$ before returning to a repeatable pattern. Due to the continuing shrinkage of the size as well as a reduction in the costs of integrated circuits, pseudorandom keying devices have become available to the commercial user at realistic prices. The key lengths of some of these devices have become so long that it appears that the communications equipment whose transmission security they are safeguarding may become obsolete before the end of the first key period.

In addition to a number of firms which manufacture encoding devices solely for use by intelligence agencies, the U.S. Armed Forces cryptologic agencies, and other governmental users, several industrial firms have actively entered the market and manufacture a family of security devices for commercial users. These manufacturers produce a family of devices designed to operate with a wide variety of terminals to include facsimile devices. These encryption devices utilize a built-in key generator which is similar to a multilevel register device. Using propriety encryption techniques, the user selects the code family by turning appropriate rotary switches inside the device to a specific setting. Then, the specific code in each family is user selected by thumbwheel switches on the device's front panel whose access is obtained thru the unlocking of a steel door. Depending upon manufacturer, up to 32 trillion key settings or codes are available to the user. One device that offers 32 trillion code settings has those settings arranged as 16 million code families, with 2 million codes in each family. Using this arrangement the user's security officer can develop various code administration techniques in hierarchical arrangements.

Security devices available for the commercial market operate either off-line or on-line. The off-line devices preceded the development of the on-line devices and are primarily used with punched paper tape transmission over the Telex and TWX networks. The off-line systems are used to prepare enciphered message tapes prior to transmission over teleprinter circuits with the device connected to an auxiliary off-line teleprinter which provides the paper tape and keyboard/printer functions with the operator typing the clear message into the keyboard of the teleprinter and the encryption device simultaneously punching the encoded tape. Some encryption devices also permit a two-pass operation to be used where a clear tape is punched by the operator and then read by the device at high speed to punch the encoded tape. The encoded tape is then transmitted by the subscriber over the network to the recipient as any punched paper tape normally would be transmitted. At the receiving end the punched paper tape of the receiving terminal is decoded off-line by reading it into the encryption device at that end and having the plain text printed at the connected teleprinter which is now turned to the off-line mode of operation. This is shown in Fig. 6.6. Since the header of the message contains routing and destination information it obviously cannot be encoded. Thus, the off-line device has either switches or buttons which allow the user to start and stop the encoding of information at the appropriate points within the message.

New Developments

Recent advances in electronics to include large-scale integrated circuits and microprocessors have produced a technology base for the development of a family of data security devices. These devices normally employ the National Bureau of Standards (NBS) data encryption standard algorithm which provides a set of rules for performing the encryption and decryption of data which reduces the threat of code breaking by illegal personnel to virtually an insignificant possibility. This is due to the fact that if the data is intercepted, the time required to decipher the encoded information would require many hundreds or thousands of years of machine time.

Fig. 6.6. Off-line Encoding (top) and Decoding (bottom)

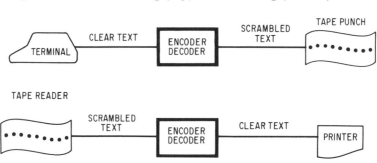

Table 6.3.   Modulo 2 Addition and Subtraction

Modulo 2 addition				Modulo 2 subtraction			
0	0	1	1	0	0	1	1
+ 0	+ 1	+ 0	+ 1	− 0	− 1	− 0	− 1
0	1	1	0	0	1	1	0

New encryption devices use a feedback-shift register and associated circuits or a microprocessor to generate a pseudorandom bit sequence following the NBS algorithm. To make the transmitted data appear to be a random stream of ones and zeros, modulo 2 addition is employed to add the data to an apparently orderless bit stream developed by a pseudo-random number generator.

Modulo, or modulus, is a capacity or unit of measurement, and a modulo sum is a sum with respect to a modulus while the carry is ignored. When a two-digit decimal counter is used, it is a modulo 100 counter. Such a counter cannot distinguish the numbers 99 and 199. When 9 is added to 8, the sum is 17, but assuming that the modulus is 10 in this case, the modulo sum is 7. In modulo 2 addition, one and zero and zero and one result in one, and both one and one and zero and zero make zero. Modulo 2 addition and subtraction are illustrated in Table 6.3.

When the bit sequence or key text generated by the pseudorandom number generator is added by modulo 2 addition to the original information, or clear text, the result is an apparently random stream of ones and zeros referred to as the cipher or encoded text. This encoded data is then transmitted to its destination where another encoder/decoder using an identical key text performs modulo 2 subtraction on the encoded data to develop the original clear text, as illustrated in Table 6.4.

Another method employed to effect data security which eliminates the requirement of hardware devices is through the utilization of software packages that can be installed on many computers and which utilize the

Table 6.4.   Modulo 2 Addition Keeps Data Secure

Encoding																
Source (clear) text	1	0	1	1	1	1	0	1	1	1	1	0	0	0	1
Pseudorandom (key) generator	1	0	0	0	1	0	1	0	1	1	0	0	1	0	0
Modulo 2 addition (encoded) text	0	0	1	1	0	1	1	1	0	0	1	0	1	0	1
Decoding																
Encoded text	0	0	1	1	0	1	1	1	0	0	1	0	1	0	1
Pseudorandom (key) generator	1	0	0	0	1	0	1	0	1	1	0	0	1	0	0
Modulo 2 subtraction (clear) text	1	0	1	1	1	1	0	1	1	1	1	0	0	0	1

NBS algorithm. These software packages can be utilized with most programming languages, including such languages as FORTRAN and COBOL through the use of CALL statements and result in a data file being encrypted. Once encrypted, the file can be transmitted to another location where another software package is available on a computer to enable the user at that location to decode the file. While this method eliminates hardware, users remotely located from the computer still face the threat of having their data intercepted if they are building a data file, since the file is not protected until it is stored and encrypted.

A problem associated with using software to encode and decode data according to the NBS data encryption algorithm is the overhead associated with the required processing. To alleviate this overhead most methods of implementing the algorithm have been through the utilization of standalone devices incorporating microprocessors to encode and decode data.

On-line Applications

With the commercial development of automatic cipher synchronization techniques, continuous on-line encryption devices are no longer the exclusive preserve of government agencies and the military and intelligence communities. These on-line encryption devices are capable of operating with both asynchronous and synchronous data streams at various data rates. In the on-line asynchronous mode of operation the encryption device uses the start-stop pulses of the individual characters to develop the synchronization between the sending and the receiving units. Plain text, which can be typed on the terminal's keyboard or read from a paper tape reader, is automatically encrypted on a character-by-character basis, with the encrypted data transmitted via the communications channel to the receiving unit where it is automatically deciphered and furnished to the receiving terminal. For synchronous transmission, the encryption devices are automatically synchronized in time by a short character sequence typed by the user or through the depression of an INITIATE button on the front panel of one of the devices. Once synchronization has occurred, the two units step under the control of crystal-controlled clocks, which keep the units in synchronization. Figure 6.7 shows typical on-line encryption device application.

As shown in Fig. 6.7, on-line encryption for terminal-to-terminal transmission over such common carrier facilities as TWX and Telex can be accomplished by the installation of an encoder/decoder between the terminal and the terminal's associated modem. Thus, clear text originating at the terminal is scrambled by the encoder and passed to the modem which transmits the data over the common carrier's facility. At the receiving end, scrambled data passes through the modem to a decoder which now produces clear text that is passed to the terminal at this end.

Fig. 6.7. On-line Encryption Device Applications

Terminal-to-terminal transmission via message switching systems such as Telex or TWX can be secured by interfacing security devices between the modem and each terminal.

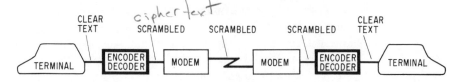

In Fig. 6.8, a typical time-sharing application for an encryption device is shown. In this example, the terminal which required the security measures associated with encryption devices is connected via a leased line to a time division multiplexer (TDM). Since this is a dedicated port connection, there is no problem in determining what port of the demultiplexer a similar encoder/decoder should be interfaced to. In Fig. 6.9, the terminal user now dials a rotary over the switched telephone network in order to connect to the multiplexer. For this configuration, the terminal may be connected to any port on the multiplexer, which means that at the other end a method to determine which port of the demultiplexer has the scrambled data is necessary. The encoder/decoder selector performs this function by sampling the output of each of the demultiplexer's ports and switching the port that has the scrambled data to the encoder/decoder,

Fig. 6.8. Time-sharing Encryption Application

Terminals connected to a time-sharing system through multiplexers must have a dedicated port to effect secure communications.

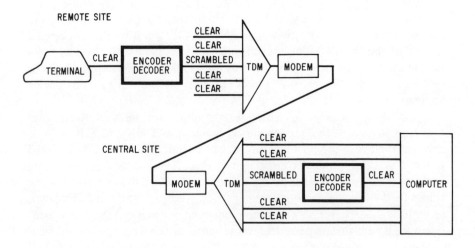

Fig. 6.9. Data Security for Time-sharing Systems

To transmit encoded information via the switched network through a multiplexer, a selector must be employed at the computer site to switch the scrambled output of a TDM channel into a decoder to produce clear text.

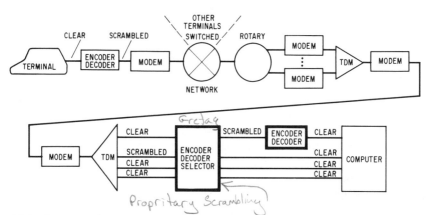

which then decodes the scrambled text and passes it to the computer. This selector in effect performs limited switching and acts as a transparent device, passing the data from the other ports directly to the computer.

Before selecting an encryption device the user should examine in detail the application requirements and develop a set of specifications which will aid in the selection process. Table 6.5 contains a checklist of some common encryption device specifications which should be considered.

Although some devices are code transparent, many are not. Since some devices are manufactured for specific applications, such as for use on the Telex or TWX network, the character sets to include the crypto and plain text character sets should be examined. Similarly, the transmission speed supported should also be examined since some devices only support teletype operating speeds where some other devices can operate at speeds up to 1 million bps.

The operational mode of encryption devices falls into three categories: off-line, or on-line asynchronous and on-line synchronous, with the mode selected dependent upon the user's requirements.

Table 6.5.   Encryption Device Specification

Character set supported	Message key
Transmission rate supported	Key code change
Operational mode	Power supply
Crypto character set	Terminal interface
Plain text character set	Alarm circuitry
Carrier compatibility	

The crypto character set and plain text character set can vary from the Telex character set through the extended binary-coded decimal interchange code (EBCDIC) character set of 256 characters. The character set selected will depend upon the terminal character set, the computer's character set, and/or the character set supported by the communications facility used. Carrier compatibility is an important feature when the user wishes to transmit encrypted messages over a commercial network such as Telex or TWX. Since certain control characters perform unique functions, carrier compatibility alleviates problems by the suppression of the generation of control characters during the encoding process as well as by sending the plain text control characters in the clear.

As mentioned previously, the message key and key code change determine the number of coding variations as well as the total codes available. Like most devices used in data communications, encryption devices have a wide range of interface options which the user must properly select from to match the terminal's requirements.

To prevent transmission from being compromised if the device should fail, some encryption devices have built-in alarm circuitry which monitors the key generator output and will inhibit data transmission upon detection of encoding failure.

6.2. Speed and Code Converters

Due to the rapid growth in the utilization of terminals for remote computing and message transmission applications, new terminal products have outpaced developments in many other areas of the computer communications field. Users who previously purchased what was state-of-the-art equipment in many cases may face costly network redesign problems if they desire to take advantage of new terminal developments. Other users who previously purchased terminals for specific applications may now have to obtain additional terminals as new applications materialize. A large portion of terminal problems are a result of the speed or code limitations of the user's existing equipment.

To reduce the time and cost involved in network redesign as well as to permit terminals procured for specific applications to become multifunctional, several conversion devices have been designed and manufactured with the problems of the terminal user in mind. These devices not only increase the flexibility and extend the life of existing terminals but can also be utilized during a network design or redesign effort to economize costs by reducing the number of computer ports and multidrop lines which may be required by a user's network without the incorporation of such a device. Although intelligent concentrators and front-end processors can also be programmed to perform these functions, quite often the memory and software processing overhead required warrants the consideration of a standalone device.

Operation

Basically, speed and code converters are built around a hardware data regenerator or microprocessor. For the former, the addition of plug-in assemblies expands the device functions to include speed and code conversion. For the latter, its adaptability is achieved by software and firmware programming for each application. Most speed converters are designed to operate with asynchronous, slow-speed terminals. When data is transmitted from a computer to a terminal at a higher data rate than the terminal can accept, the speed converter buffers the data in its memory and retransmits it at the slower rate to the terminal. Since asynchronous transmission in a human-machine interaction environment usually consists of short messages to the computer and medium length responses to the terminal, memory for such devices are normally 4,000 words or less. Some speed converters designed for synchronous operations have storage capacities up to 40,000 characters of information. When transmission occurs from the terminal to the computer, the data rate from the terminal is "stepped up" to the computer's data rate by the speed converter.

Like speed conversion, code conversion permits terminals designed to operate with one type of code to communicate with other terminals or a computer that operates in a different code. As data is transmitted from the terminal to the computer in one code format, the code converter translates each character to the code acceptable to the computer. Conversely, data transmitted from the computer in one code is converted by the device on a character-by-character basis into the terminal's code.

By combining the functions of speed and code conversion, a speed and code converter both translates the code of a transmitted character and changes its transmission speed according to the plug-in assemblies used in the device or the software and firmware programming developed for the particular application.

General Use of Converters

Consider the situation where an inventory of 110- and 150-bps terminals exists. Suppose a user wishes to obtain a 300-bps terminal due to existing requirements. A method of economizing the number of computer ports and multidrop lines to service the new terminal and maintain support for existing terminals is through the use of speed converters.

As illustrated in Fig. 6.10, top, the user who has a mixture of 110- and 150-bps terminals connected to the computer and who uses multidrop lines for communications will require a minimum of two computer ports and two multidrop lines to service the remote terminals. Two different types of modems, one to support 110-bps and the other to support 150-bps transmission are required at the computer site as well as at the remote sites, depending upon the speed of the terminal at each site. The two

Fig. 6.10. Adding Higher Speed Terminals

The network in the top portion has a mixture of 110- and 150-bps terminals and requires at least one computer port and multidrop line to service each type of remote terminal. Furthermore, two different modems are required at the computer site. With the installation of code converters, a standard speed can be obtained and only one multidrop line and one central site modem may be required, as shown in the lower portion.

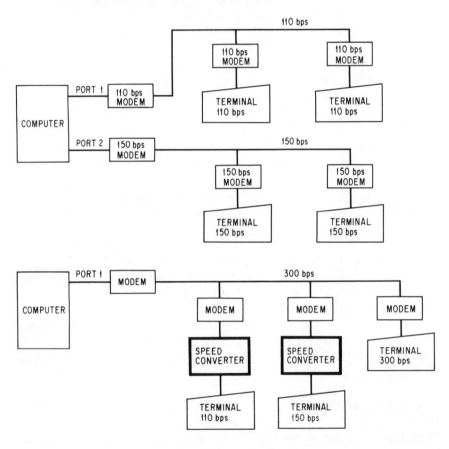

different transmission rates could also cause a large investment in spare modems if the user purchased modems and desired to stock spares at each site.

If the user now desired to install 300-bps terminals at a few remote locations, he or she would normally have to add an additional multidrop line, computer port, and enough 300-bps modems to service this new requirement. Through the installation of speed converters for each of the 110- and 150-bps terminals, all terminals may now be serviced on a common 300-bps multidrop line. In addition to reducing the number of lines required, only one modem and one computer port are now required at the central site. Since all modems in the network would now be speed standardized, a reduction in modem spare parts may now be practical. The network after the installation of speed converters is illustrated in the bottom portion of Fig. 6.10.

Like speed converters, code converters permit different types of terminals to be mixed on a multidrop line. Code converters, like speed converters, can be utilized in a variety of ways. Code converters can be very useful during the transition period of system upgrading, such as when a user gradually replaces a large number of older Baudot terminals with more modern ASCII or EBCDIC terminals. In this case, depending upon the number of existing terminals and the conversion sequence, the user can either use code converters to make the 5-level Baudot-coded terminals interface an 8-level (7 bits plus a parity bit) ASCII code transmission line or let newly installed 8-level ASCII-coded terminals interface the existing 5-level Baudot-coded transmission line until the time is right for switchover to ASCII transmission on the line. This is shown in Fig. 6.11. In Fig. 6.11A, the existing system operates by the computer transmitting 5-level Baudot code on the multidrop line to the 5-level Baudot code terminals interfaced to that line. As shown in Fig. 6.11B, the user can convert transmission to 8-level ASCII code by installing ASCII to Baudot code converters between each 5-level Baudot code terminal and the transmission line. Another option the user can consider is shown in Fig. 6.11C. Here the user can continue to transmit in 5-level Baudot code and still service the new ASCII terminal by the installation of a Baudot to ASCII converter between the new terminal and the transmission line. When all terminals have been upgraded to ASCII terminals or the user decides that it is time to switch transmission to ASCII, the appropriate action can then be taken to change the transmission code. It should be noted that although this example leaves the reader with the impression that code converters are useful during transmission switchover or during the period when all terminals on a multidrop circuit are being upgraded, the user can also elect to retain existing terminals through the permanent utilization of code converters.

Specific Application Example

By combining the functions of speed and code conversion, users may be able to satisfy two or more discrete applications on one terminal by the use of a speed and code converter. One particular area where different types of terminals may be employed is for access to the various message switching systems in operation today as well as the utilization of terminals to communicate with time-sharing computer systems.

Fig. 6.11. Implementing Code Conversion

Through the incorporation of code converters, terminals with different codes can share the use of common multipoint lines and a common modem at the computer site.

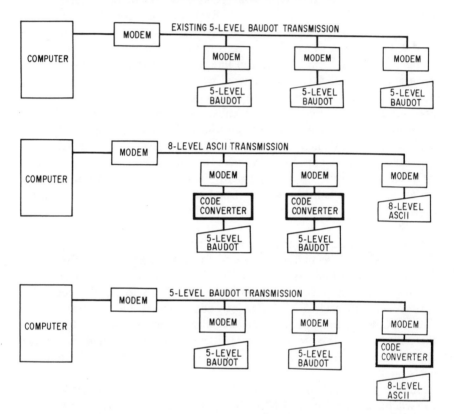

Both TWX and Telex are switched network service offerings provided by Western Union. TWX was developed by AT&T but was sold to Western Union in 1971. Of the two classes of service offered on TWX, one at 45 bps uses the 5-level Baudot code and the other operating at 110 bps uses the 8-level ASCII code. Through the use of speed and code conversion equipment located at the switching office of Western Union, terminals operating at the two different speeds can communicate with each other. In 1956, Western Union introduced Telex service in the United States. This service originated in Germany in 1934 and was expanded into an international communications service. For Telex, transmission is limited to 50 bps using the 5-level Baudot code.

Through the use of a speed and code converter it becomes possible for the user of the Telex network to obtain the more readily available Teletype models 33 and 35 or equivalent for use on the Telex network. In addition, since these terminals can be used on the TWX network as well as for data transmission to most time-sharing computers, more efficiency and greater flexibility is obtained.

Functionally, a speed and code converter provides the means by which the 8-level ASCII code of Teletype models 33 and 35 terminals can have their transmission speed and code converted to the 5-level Baudot code and 50-bps speed of the Telex network. The ASCII even parity serial code of 11 bits (1 stop, 8 character bits, and 2 stop bits) of the Teletype models 33 or 35 terminals are converted by the speed and code converter from a transmission rate of 110 bps into a Baudot serial code of 7.5 bits (1 start, 5 character bits, and 1.5 stop bits) at a speed of 50 bps, and vice versa. The ASCII control "O" character is translated to perform the Baudot figures (FIGS) function, and the ASCII control "N" character is used to perform the Baudot letters (LTRS) function. Since most any ASCII terminal can be interfaced through a converter, even cathode ray tubes (CRT) can be used to transmit messages to the Telex network as well as being used on the TWX network or for time-sharing operations. This is illustrated in Fig. 6.12.

6.3. Data Access Arrangements

Acting as a protective device between customer-provided equipment and the switched telephone network, data access arrangements (DAA) or data couplers have a long history and evolution as a result of numerous court decisions.

In what is now referred to as the Carterphone decision, the FCC ruled that non-Bell System transmitting and receiving equipment could be attached to the telephone network. Contained in the ruling was a requirement that a protective device be furnished, installed, and maintained by the

Fig. 6.12. Combining Speed and Conversion
Speed and code converters may enable a mixture of terminals to access various communication systems.

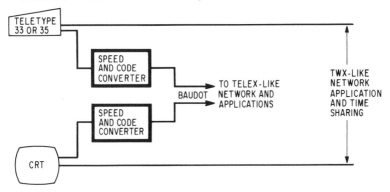

telephone company. This device was to act as an interface between the non-Bell System equipment and the network to provide protection for telephone company personnel and equipment from the possibility of hazardous voltages applied from the customer-furnished equipment, limit abnormally high frequency and signal levels, and prevent line seizure except in response to ringing. While data communications users were now permitted to interconnect the products of any vendor to the telephone network, users were also responsible for compliance with the data access arrangement requirements.

A new series of court cases resulted in an interconnect equipment registration program which modifies the requirements for data access arrangements. Under the FCC interconnect equipment registration program, customer-provided equipment that is registered as a result of meeting a series of operational characteristics can be interfaced via a plug to a telephone company jack for connection to the switched network. Unregistered equipment can be used providing that it is interfaced with the telephone company jack through a registered data coupler provided either by the telephone company or by an independent manufacturer. Figure 6.13 illustrates the effect of the FCC registration program when various types of transmitting and receiving equipment are interfaced to telephone company facilities.

When the user desires to transmit data over a leased line (Fig. 6.13A), no data access arrangement is necessary regardless of the type of

Fig. 6.13. FCC Registration Program Requirements

Data couplers may be required based upon the type of communications equipment installed and the line it is connected to.

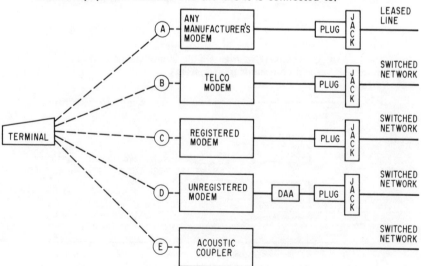

modem used. This is due to the fact that the leased line is for the exclusive use of that user, and any interference caused by nontelephone company equipment on that line should only affect that user. For the user who obtains telephone company equipment (Fig. 6.13B), the interface is via a plug, and no DAA is required since such telephone company equipment is registered. A similar interface arrangement occurs when any vendor-registered modem (Fig. 6.13C) is connected to the switched network. When an unregistered modem (Fig. 6.13D) is connected, a registered data coupler must be provided to interface the telephone company jack. For users who install terminals with built-in acoustic couplers (Fig. 6.13E), neither a DAA nor a plug-jack connection is required since the interface to the telephone line is via the telephone headset and both the terminal's and coupler's power supplies are segregated from the line.

Types of DAA

There are three types of data access arrangements available. The DAAs or data couplers should be identified by the telephone company ordering codes when the user requests installation from the telephone company or from an independent vendor since such equipment is standardized by those codes. The coupler ordering codes are CDT, CBS, and CBT, with the basic differences between each model depending upon the mode of operation (manual or unattended), the presence or absence of a built-in power supply, and the type of line control. The basic differences between each type of data access arrangement are listed in Table 6.6.

The CDT data access arrangement is designed for use with devices which can only originate or can originate and answer calls but only through manual operation. When using a CDT coupler, the operator dials the desired number and the receiving operator answers. Upon verification that the equipment at both ends are ready for data transmission, the operators depress the data keys on their telephone sets, and the modems which are connected to the CDT DAA may then transmit and receive data. Once transmission is completed, both operators hang up their telephones and the connection is broken, as illustrated in Fig. 6.14. Since control is manual, the CDT coupler is wired so that the telephone set controls the line. Likewise, being powered by the telephone company line alleviates the necessity of the user supplying a power source.

CDT couplers are also required when manual dial-backup for leased lines are employed using unregistered modems, as shown in Fig. 6.15. To effect switching between the leased line and the dial-up or switched network will require the installation of a fallback switch at each end of the link. If the leased line should become inoperative, the fallback switches are turned to the secondary position which permits access to the switched network through the CDT coupler.

The CBS and CBT couplers are designed to operate with devices that

Table 6.6. Data Access Arrangement Comparison

DAA type	Mode	Principal use	Line control	Power source
CDT	Originate only or manual originate/ answer terminals only	AC Analog devices	Telephone set controls line	By telephone company lines
CBT	Manual originate/ automatic answer terminals only	Devices employing contact closures for control leads	Coupler controls line	Optional
CBS	Manual originate/ automatic answer terminals only	Devices employing EIA RS-232 interface	Coupler controls line	Customer 3-pronged wall outlet

in addition to having manual originate capability can automatically control the originating and answering of data calls. For the automatic originating of calls a separate automatic calling unit will be required to provide this capability. The two major differences between the CBS and CBT data access arrangements are the type of control leads furnished and the source of power. The CBT coupler is designed to provide contact-type control leads, while the CBS coupler provides EIA RS-232 voltage-type control leads. Users requesting the CBS coupler receive a power transformer external to the coupler's housing and must supply a three-pronged wall outlet power source while the CBT coupler can operate with the telephone company lines power source, the dc voltage from the modem, or from an external power supply operated by conventional ac power. The utilization of CBS and CBT couplers are illustrated in Figs. 6.16 and 6.17.

Fig. 6.14. Manually Operated CDT Utilization

Data transmitted manually through a customer provided, unregistered modem must pass through a CDT coupler prior to accessing the switched network.

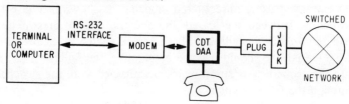

Fig. 6.15. Manual Dial Backup Operation

By turning both fallback switches to their secondary position, data may be transmitted through the CDT couplers when backup operations are required.

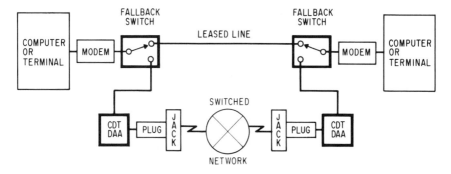

Fig. 6.16. CBS Coupler Permits Automatic Operations

By exchanging RS-232-type signals, a CBS coupler permits automatic dialing, answering and disconnecting so that the terminal or computer may operate unattended. The site at the opposite end of the transmission path must be similarly equipped with a CBS coupler. In addition, automatic answering capability must be built into the modem.

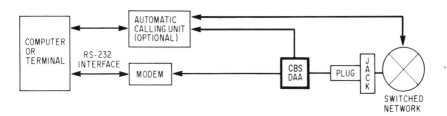

Fig. 6.17. CBT Coupler Requires External Power Source

The CBT coupler requires an external dc power source which can usually be obtained from the modem. If the connection is impractical or the capability is not available, either the telephone company can furnish the power supply or the user can provide the external power supply.

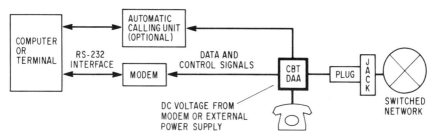

When data access arrangements are obtained from the telephone company, charges are typically 25 to 40 dollars for installation, plus 5 to 15 dollars per month for the lease of such equipment, since the DAAs are tariffed on a state-by-state basis, and pricing varies considerably. Although only available from telephone companies on a lease basis, couplers are available for purchase from a number of communications companies. Telephone company tariffs should be checked in order to determine which method of procurement is most advantageous.

6.4. Speech Plus Data Units

When the operator of a computer, remote batch terminal, or some other type of data transmission equipment experiences difficulties in the intiation or transmission of data, a common procedure is to telephone the other site and attempt to alleviate the problem. If the equipment at each site is connected by a leased line to dedicated modems, the telephone call must be made over the switched network. For this situation, not only is the leased line left unutilized until the problem is resolved, but the company may face the prospect of a costly long distance telephone bill. Similarly, those sites that rearrange equipment configurations to differentiate between daytime and nighttime operations may require one or more calls each day between sites to clarify the configuration used, the service expected, or the initiation times and procedures to be followed.

In addition to being able to arrange wideband channels so that the remaining capacity not used for data transmission can be used for simultaneous individual voice communications, users of a single voice-grade leased line circuit can configure their equipment to take advantage of alternate or simultaneous voice data transmission. Using proper equipment, this alternate or simultaneous voice data transmission can occur over the same leased line which is normally used for data transmission at speeds up to 9,600 bps.

Supplementing alternate voice data transmission services which can be obtained from the telephone company for leased line facilities is a range of devices manufactured by commercial communications companies. These voice adapters provide the user with alternate or simultaneous voice data transmission capability and can be used in a wide range of applications.

Types of Unit

A device known as a voice adapter can be obtained as a base unit which supports a standard telephone headset. Several different models are available which can be interfaced to different speed modems to provide alternate or simultaneous voice and data contact between points connected by a leased line. By incorporating all summing and switching circuits within the adapter and its associated data set, the necessity of obtaining auxiliary switching equipment which is normally used to perform this function is eliminated. Voice adapters must be interfaced to modems at each end of the leased line, as shown in Fig. 6.18.

Voice adapters are equipped with a pushbutton switch and, depending upon the model, a selector switch. The pushbutton switch permits the user to signal the distant end of the leased line when voice communications are desired. In addition to causing a tone to be produced and transmitted to the opposite end of the leased line, a connection is available on some models which can be used to drive an external relay. This external relay in turn can be used to operate a remote indicating device such as a lamp or bell which upon receipt of the tone alerts the operator at the other end of the line that voice coordination is requested. The selector switch, depending upon operating mode selected, permits full voice communications, simultaneous voice with 2,000-bps or 2,400-bps data transmission, or simultaneous teletype (up to seven 75-bps channels) and either 2,000- or 2,400-bps data transmission. Two typical applications where voice adapters could be employed are shown in Fig. 6.19.

In Figure 6.19A, if data transmission occurs at 9,600 bps, the voice adapter would be used to provide an alternate voice link between the two sites. Since 2,000- or 2,400-bps transmission would probably be inefficient for this type of network configuration, alternate voice with a return to full 9,600-bps data transmission via a voice adapter is selected. In Figure 6.19B, if the CRT normally communicates with the CPU at 2,000 or 2,400 bps, simultaneous voice data transmission can be used. In this example, the bandwidth required by the voice communication does not degrade the transmission speed requirements of the CRT.

Users considering voice adapters will find that they are simple to install and no special power is required. By attaching the connector of the voice adapter cord to a connection on the associated modem, power is furnished for the adapter from the modem's power supply, and the voice adapter becomes ready for use.

Fig. 6.18. Installing Voice Adapters on Leased Lines

By interfacing voice adapters to the modems at each end of the leased line, alternate or simultaneous voice and data transmission may be accomplished.

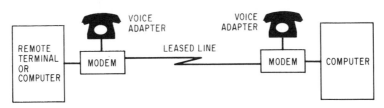

Fig. 6.19. Alternate and Simultaneous Voice and Data

Top: Alternate voice or data. Bottom: Simultaneous voice and data. Depending upon model selected and data transmission requirements, voice adapters may be used for alternate or simultaneous voice communications.

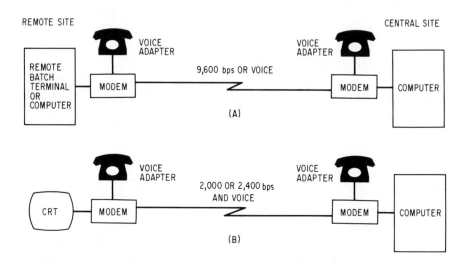

A second type of device is known as a speech plus data terminal which is used to provide an audio channel in conjunction with a number of telegraph channels that are transmitting at any bit rate up to 600 bps or a mixture of bit rates up to 2,400 bps. This type of terminal uses amplifiers to combine and then separate voice signals from the data signals. Currently, up to eight teletype channels can be operated in addition to a voice channel on such devices.

Building a System

Due to the introduction of voice digitizers it is now possible to build a speech plus data system by incorporating that device with a TDM. Basically, a voice digitizer analyzes an audio signal and converts it into a digital serial bit stream for transmission over an analog or digital transmission medium. At the receiving location, a similar unit reconstructs the audio signal for output. The key feature of the voice digitizer is that it converts a natural voice quality audio tone into a 2,400-bps bit stream, thereby permitting the audio signal to be transmitted over a leased line without consuming more than a small fraction of the total bandwidth of the line. Figure 6.20 illustrates a typical application for such a device.

At the remote location there are eight 300-bps teletype terminals, one 4,800-bps remote job entry (RJE) terminal, and one 4,800-bps CRT. Due

Fig. 6.20. Building a Speech Plus Voice System

Since the output of the voice digitizer is a 2,400-bps serial bit stream it can be multiplexed for transmission along with the data streams produced by either the RJE or the CRT and the eight low-speed interactive terminals.

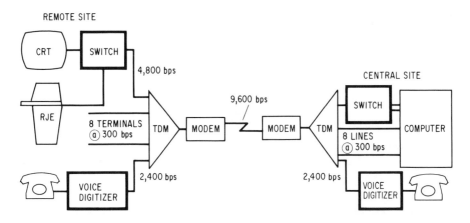

to system operation requirements, the RJE is only used to pull high-speed batch processing results from the central computer during random times throughout the day, based upon terminal user requirements. When the RJE is not operating, the CRT is normally employed at a similar 4,800-bps speed. Both the RJE and CRT share access to the multiplexer via a fallback switch. Here, the voice digitizer permits the RJE operator to keep in frequent contact with the central computer site personnel so that they may be informed when the remote site will use the RJE. When this occurs, the central site technical control center personnel must switch the high-speed port from the CRT port to the port on the front-end processor that supports the RJE protocol. If the remote location is very distant from the central site, the frequent telephone calls required could become a considerable cost element. By using the voice digitizers, long distance toll charges are eliminated.

chapter 7
integrating components

As shown from the examination of components presented in this book, numerous factors govern their employment. Even after such devices are selected and installed, a review of the network and its components should be accomplished on a periodic basis.

In addition to changes in user requirements, new communications tariffs must be examined to determine their impact on the network. While at one particular time the utilization of specialized components may not be economical, a revision in a tariff may warrant the use of such components at a later date. Similarly, a requirement to support additional time-sharing users on a computer system where all ports are used would warrant the investigation of using such devices as modem-sharing units, line-sharing units, or port selectors, as an example.

While the combinations of communications components that can be used present an almost unlimited number of possibilities, careful analysis of user requirements and tariff structures will enable the system designer to reduce the number of such devices for consideration. Although the chapter in this section is primarily concerned with integrating inverse multiplexers and multiport modems, the systems designer can similarly integrate other components to respond to user requirements in a cost effective manner.

7.1. Inverse Multiplexing with Multiport Modems

With a little imagination, the user of a small- to medium-size data communications system can fit several data streams into a voice-grade line, even if some of the signals already exceed the 9,600-bps limit of voice-grade facilities. Thus, the user can avoid the high cost of wideband service while enjoying similar advantages. The trick is to combine an inverse time division multiplexer (TDM) with a multiport modem for remultiplexing data.

Simply put, the combination of multiport modem and inverse TDM is a means of splitting high-speed data streams into two lines and multiplexing them with other data streams to circumvent the limits of narrowband lines. At the receiving end, another multiport modem/inverse multiplexer system reunites the various signal components and routes them to their destinations. An inverse TDM provides the advantage of wideband transmission to any point where two voice-grade lines are available, at a fraction of the wideband cost (Chapter 3, Sec. 3.3) when the distances between transmission points exceed approximately 50 miles. In addition, an inverse multiplexer permits a user to reduce the number of computer ports required for data transmission, since it accepts data from a single computer port at speeds up to 19,200 bps.

An inverse multiplexer splits an incoming data stream into two paths (one for odd bits, one for even bits) for transmission over two voice-grade lines and reassembles the data stream at the original composite speed at the receiving end, as shown in Fig. 7.1.

The advantages obtainable with multiport modems were examined in Chapter 2, Sec. 2.4. Basically, a multiport modem consists of a high-speed synchronous modem with a built-in, limited-function TDM. Although multiport modem capabilities vary by manufacturer as well as by the modem's aggregate speed, all are similar in that they can service two to four synchronous data streams, multiplexing these streams onto a single line, as shown in Fig. 7.2.

For many network applications, the system designer can take advantage of both the inverse multiplexer and the multiport modem to configure a network. The combination of both devices can provide flexibility and an economy of operation that may not be available when using more conventional communications, and the system designer can take advantage of both the inverse multiplexer and the multiport modem to configure a network. In certain cases, a mixture of these devices can be used to reduce computer loading and still maintain cost-effective line utilization. At the

Fig. 7.1. Inverse Multiplexing

Basic inverse time division multiplexing splits data streams into odd and even bit streams at the send station and recombines them at the receive station.

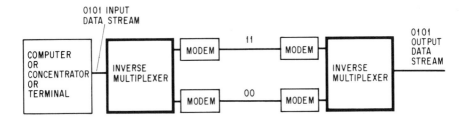

Fig. 7.2. Multiport Modem

Multiport modems have the ability to multiplex from two to four
synchronous data streams into a single line for transmission
over voice facilities.

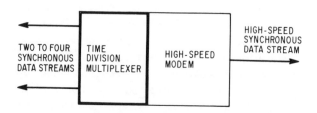

very least, the remultiplexing configurations made possible by a combination of these devices ought to be looked at by the system designer as a
possible alternative solution to his or her network design problem. A
typical data communications application where inverse time-division and
multiport modem components would be used is shown in Fig. 7.3.

Here, if the concentrator services 128 low-speed teletypewriter terminals transmitting at 110 bps, by allowing for overhead, the concentrator-
to-computer transmission speed could become 14,400 bps. This exceeds
the capacity of a single 3002-type voice-grade line, so that if the user
wishes to transmit from a single port of the remote data concentrator to a
single port of the central-site computer, he or she is faced with installing
wideband facilities, which are tariffed at $16.20 per mile for the first 250
miles, $11.40 per mile for the next 250 miles, and $8.15 per mile for
every mile thereafter. Alternately, the user may have two of the telephone
company's high- or low-density circuits and a pair of inverse multiplexers
to split the transmitted data over the two lines. When inverse multiplexers
are used, the break-even point is reached after the transmission distance
exceeds 50 miles or so based upon the leased line charges presented in
Table 3.6, plus a monthly lease rate of $1,275 for the system, including a
pair of inverse multiplexers and four 7,200-bps modems.

Postinstallation Economy

If such an installation must be expanded or modified, use of conventional
equipment and methods could be costly. One example could be a growing
demand that the concentrator serve additional terminals at the remote
location. If the concentrator's CPU utilization factor is high, a second
concentrator may have to be installed at the remote site at a cost of
several thousand dollars per month. In addition, the installation of another
line may be required between the remote location and the central site to
provide a communications path for the second concentrator. This line
would also be costed at the rates shown in Table 3.6. When terminals must
be added at a remote site, a configuration such as that shown in Fig. 7.4

Fig. 7.3. Typical Remultiplexing Operation

The combination of multiport modems with inverse multiplexers (remultiplexing) offers the user wideband services over two voice-grade lines.

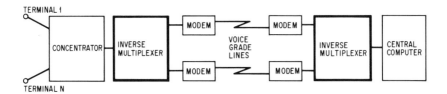

may be more appropriate. This solution would depend on such factors as the types of terminals already serviced by the concentrator, the types of remote terminals to be installed, the utilization factor of the existing lines, and the central-site computer's utilization factor.

For this type of configuration, the limiting factor is the remote concentrator utilization, rather than line utilization between the concentrator and the central computer. Thus, although additional terminals can be handled by existing lines, the installation of multiport modems makes it unnecessary to add a more expensive second concentrator. Installing multiport modems is a better solution than adding multidrop lines or installing multiport modems that only service additional terminals.

Through the installation of multiport modems, rather than conventional ones, two new 2,400-bps channels can be connected through modem-sharing units to serve as many as 12 additional polled terminals, which can be serviced at the remote location over the two type-3002 lines. In addition, line utilization is increased because the speed of each has been increased from 7,200 bps to 9,600 bps, and the two lines provide a communications path for the 128 terminals shown in Fig. 7.3, as well as the dozen 2,400-bps polled terminals that are shown in Fig. 7.4.

If only six additional terminals are needed at the remote site, yet the concentrator is reaching its saturation point in servicing only 128 low-speed terminals, the user could also remove six terminals from the concentrator, upgrade these to 2,400-bps cathode ray tubes (CRT), and have them serviced through a second modem-sharing unit. In that way, the user would be reducing the concentrator's loading. The system designer could provide service capability to the 12 polled terminals by installing two additional ports at the central computer and by interfacing the output of the multiport modem's 2,400-bps channels to these new computer ports.

Cost Consideration

The configuration shown in Fig. 7.4 entails the addition of two modem-sharing units at a typical lease price of $25 per month per unit and two synchronous computer ports at approximately $40 per month per port,

Fig. 7.4. Remultiplexing with Multiport Modems

This example of an alternate remultiplexing configuration allows the servicing of as many as 12 polled terminals by means of just two modem-sharing units.

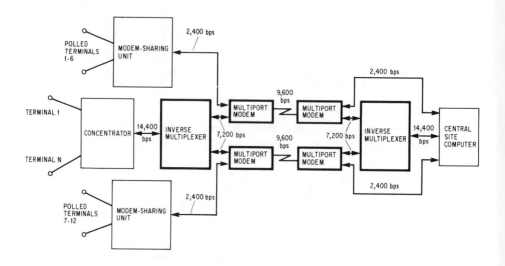

plus the costs of upgrading the four 7,200-bps modems to four 9,600-bps multiport modems, which may add approximately $45 per month per modem. These costs should be compared to (1) the cost of installing two multidrop lines at the appropriate rate schedule shown in Table 3.6, depending upon circuit type, (2) adding four 2,400-bps modems at $70 per modem per month, (3) adding two synchronous computer ports at $40 per month per port plus the two modem-sharing units, or (4) directly connecting the 12 polled terminals to three 9,600-bps multiport modems.

To implement the latter choice, the user would need six multiport modems (three at each end) at $220 per month per modem, as well as three leased lines. At the main computer site, the user would also need 12 synchronous computer ports. The two alternate configurations that can be used to service the twelve 2,400-bps polled terminals are shown in Fig. 7.5. Table 7.1 compares the monthly cost for all three configurations necessary to service systems involving the use of 12 extra 2,400-bps polled terminals. As shown, replexing with multiport modems can effectively support a network upgrade at one-fifth to one-tenth the cost of the two alternative methods considered in the table.

Table 7.1.   Additional Costs for Servicing Twelve, 2,400-bps Terminals

Reflexing with multiport modems (Fig. 7.4)
1. Upgrade 4, 7,200-bps modems to 4, 9,600-bps
   multiport modems $45/mo. × 4 modems $ 180.00
2. Add 2 modem-sharing units @ $25/mo.   50.00
3. Add 2 synchronous computer ports @ $40/mo.   80.00
                                                                 _____
                                                                 $ 310.00

Servicing by multidrop lines (Fig. 7.5A)
1. Add 4, 2,400-bps modems @ $70/mo. $ 280.00
2. Add 2 modem-sharing units @ $25/mo.   50.00
3. Add 2 synchronous computer ports @ $40/mo.   80.00
4. Add 2 leased lines, e.g., Washington, D.C. to
   Macon, Ga. (560 miles), schedule 2 rate @ $543.80   1,087.60
                                                                 _____
                                                                 $1,497.60

Servicing by multiport modems only (Fig. 7.5B)
1. Add 6, 9,600-bps modems @ $220/mo. $1,320.00
2. Add 12 synchronous computer ports @ $40/mo.   480.00
3. Add 3 leased lines, e.g., Washington, D.C. to
   Macon, Ga. (560 miles), schedule 2 rate @ $543.80   1,631.40
                                                                 _____
                                                                 $3,431.40

Fig. 7.5. Alternate Service Methods

Top: Serviced by multidrop lines. Bottom: Serviced by multiport
modems. Alternatives to remultiplexing shown here involve the
expense of either two computer ports and two modem-sharing
units or 12 ports and three multiport modems. Both require
extra leased lines.

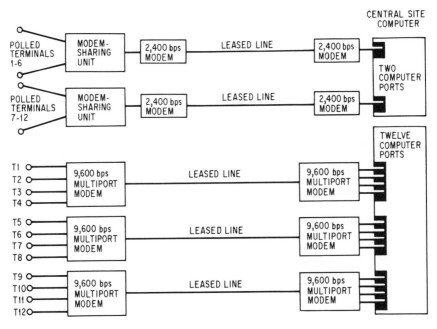

Remote Terminal Service

A variation of the configuration shown in Fig. 7.4 entails the installation of multiport modems with a data communications equipment (DCE) option at the remote site. When additional terminals are required at locations distant from the primary remote site, through the use of the DCE option, one can interface two low-speed modems to the multiport modems, allowing distant interactive terminals at a secondary remote site to be added to the system, as shown in Fig. 7.6.

Another interesting configuration could be developed through the installation of TDMs, multiport modems, and a pair of inverse multiplexers. For the configuration shown in Fig. 7.7, the basic CPU-to-CPU wideband transmission is accomplished at 14,400 bps over two voice-grade channels by the utilization of inverse multiplexers. Up to sixteen 300-bps interactive terminals can be serviced at the remote CPU location by installing two eight-channel multiplexers. By transmitting the output of the multiplexers into 2,400-bps ports of the multiport modems, no additional lines would

Fig. 7.6. Multiport Modems with DCE Option

Remultiplexing with the addition of a data communications equipment (DCE) option, employing a separate, low-speed modem interface, allows the servicing of terminals distant from the main remote site.

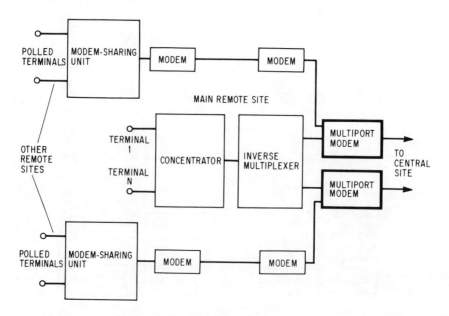

Fig. 7.7. Adding TDMs to a Remultiplexing Configuration

Two 8-channel TDMs added to the multiport modems permit
access by 16 low-speed terminals at no increase in line costs.

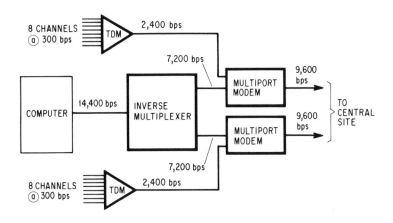

be required between the remote site and the central computer. Again, line
utilization would be increased.

Flexibility Equals Savings

As shown in the preceding examples, the use of multiport modems and
remultiplexing data permits the system designer to consider numerous configurations to satisfy operational requirements. Since the objective in using
an inverse multiplexer is to obtain wideband transmission speeds, only two
2,400-bps ports of all the various multiport modem combinations available
are shown. This configuration permits a remote concentrator or remote
CPU to achieve 14,400-bps transmission and also allows the remaining
4,800-bps capacity of the two lines to be shared by different devices
through different configurations. Although the transmission speed of the
remote concentrator or remote CPU can be further reduced (with a re-
sulting increase in the remaining transmission capacity through the multiport modems), this increase would not normally be attempted because it
defeats the purpose of using inverse multiplexers. For those cases where the
highest channel speed is 9,600 bps, the inverse multiplexer can be removed
and the configuration developed by considering addition of various communications components to multiport modems. For those who have installations that require wideband service capabilities only at certain times, the
utilization of up to four ports on each multiport modem may be considered
during those periods when the service of the inverse multiplexer is not
required.

chapter 8
manufacturers
directory

Like most industries, the data communications industry consists of a small number of firms that manufacture a wide variety of data communications components and a large number of firms that specialize in a few or one particular component.

The purpose of this directory is to provide readers with points of contact to obtain specific technical specifications for those components they may wish to examine in more detail for their particular applications. Due to the dynamic nature of the industry and the lack of a periodically published directory, it is possible that some vendors may have been omitted from the following pages. For additional information concerning recently introduced equipment it is suggested that the reader scan the new product announcement sections of such magazines as *Computer Decisions, Datamation, Data Communications, Electronics,* and *Telecommunications.*

Manufacturer	Acoustic couplers	Automatic calling units	Data access arrange- ments	Data communi- cation switches	Digital service units
American Telephone and Telegraph 195 Broadway New York, NY 10007		X	X		X
Anderson Jacobson 1065 Morse Avenue Sunnyvale, CA 94086	X				
Atlantic Research Corporation 5390 Cherokee Avenue Alexandria, VA 22314				X	
Carterphone Communications Corporation 1111 West Mockingbird Lane Dallas, TX 75247	X		X		
COM DATA Corporation 8115 North Monticello Avenue Skokie, IL 60076	X				
Cooke Engineering 900 Slaters Lane Alexandria, VA 22314				X	
Digicom Data Products, Incorporated 1441 Kill Circle San Jose, CA 95112	X				
Elgin Electronics, Incorporated Walnut Street Waterford, PA 16441			X		
Frederick Electronics P.O. Box 502 Hayward Road Frederick, MD 21701				X	
General Data Comm Industries 131 Danbury Road Wilton, CT 06897			X		
General Electric Company Waynesboro, VA 22980	X		X	X	
GTE Lenkurt 1105 Country Road San Carlos, CA 94070					X
International Data Sciences, Incorporated 100 Nashua Street Providence, RI 02904				X	
Multi-Tech Systems, Incorporated 3406 University Avenue, SE Minneapolis, MN 55414	X				

Manufacturer	Acoustic couplers	Automatic calling units	Data access arrangements	Data communication switches	Digital service units
NU DATA 32 Fairview Avenue Little Silver, NJ 07739		X			
OMNITEC DATA 2405 South 20th Street Phoenix, AZ 85034	X				
PULSECOM 5714 Columbia Pike Falls Church, VA 22041			X		
RANCAL-MILGO, Incorporated 8600 NW 41st Street Miami, FL 33166				X	
SPECTRON Corporation Church Road and Roland Avenue Moorestown, NJ 08057				X	
T-Bar Incorporated 141 Danbury Road Wilton, CT 06897				X	
TELCON Industries, Incorporated 5701 NW 31st Street Ft. Lauderdale, FL 33309		X			
Tele-Dynamics 525 Virginia Drive Fort Washington, PA 19034	X		X		
TIMEPLEX, Incorporated 100 Commerce Way Hackensack, NJ 07601		X			X
Universal Data Systems 4900 Bradford Drive Huntsville, AL 35805		X	X		
U.S. Robotics, Incorporated P.O. Box 5502 Chicago, IL 60680	X				
VADIC Corporation 505 East Middlefield Road Mountain View, CA 94043			X		

Manufacturer	Group-band modems	Group-band multi-plexers	Inverse multi-plexers	Limited distance modems	Line drivers	Line restoral units
American Telephone and Telegraph 195 Broadway New York, NY 10007	X		X			
ASTROCOM Corporation 120 West Plato Blvd. St. Paul, MN 55107				X		
AVANTI Communications Corporation Box 205 Broadway Station Newport, RI 02840	X			X	X	
CODEX Corporation 15 Riverdale Avenue Newton, MA 02195	X	X	X	X		X
Computer Transmission Corporation 2352 Utah Avenue El Segundo, CA 90245		X		X		
COMPUTROL Corporation Berkshire Industrial Park Bethel, CT 06801				X		
COMTECH Laboratories, Incorporated 135 Engineers Road Smithtown, NY 11787		X				
Cooke Engineering 900 Slaters Lane Alexandria, VA 22314				X		
Data-Control Systems, Incorporated P.O. Box 584 Danbury, CT 06810				X		
DEI-Teleproducts 563 North Citracado Parkway Escondido, CA 92025				X		
Digital Communications Associates, Incorporated 135 Technology Park Norcross, GA 30092	X					
Gandalf Data, Incorporated 190 Shepard Avenue Wheeling, IL 60090				X		
General Data Comm Industries 131 Danbury Road Wilton, CT 06897		X			X	

Manufacturer	Group-band modems	Group-band multi-plexers	Inverse multi-plexers	Limited distance modems	Line drivers	Line restoral units
GTE Lenkurt 1105 Country Road San Carlos, CA 94070	X			X		
Harris Corporation P.O. Box 160 Melbourne, FL 32901	X					
Honeywell Avionics Division 13350 U.S. Highway 19 St. Petersburg, FL 33733	X					
Infotron Systems Cherry Hill Industrial Center Cherry Hill, NJ 08003		X				
INTERTEL 6 Vine Brook Park Burlington, MA 01803						X
MICOM Systems, Incorporated 9551 Irondale Avenue Chatsworth, CA 91311		X			X	
NESCO 2904 Corvin Drive Santa Clara, CA 95051	X					
Paradyne Corporation 8550 Ulmerton Road Largo, FL 33540			X	X		
PENRIL Corporation 5520 Randolph Road Rockville, MD 20852				X		
Prentice Corporation 795 San Antonio Road Palo Alto, CA 94303				X	X	
RANCAL-MILGO, Incorporated 8600 NW 41st Street Miami, FL 33166			X	X		
SPECTRON Corporation Church Road and Roland Avenue Moorestown, NJ 08057				X		
STELMA Telecom- munications 17 Amelia Place Stamford, CT 06902				X		
SYNTECH Corporation 11810 Parklawn Drive Rockville, MD 20852				X		

Manufacturer	Group-band modems	Group-band multi-plexers	Inverse multi-plexers	Limited distance modems	Line drivers	Line restoral units
Tele-Dynamics 525 Virginia Drive Fort Washington, PA 19034				X		
Teleprocessing Products Company 11163 West Pico Boulevard Los Angeles, CA 90064				X		
TIMEPLEX, Incorporated 100 Commerce Way Hackensack, NJ 07601		X				X
Ven-Tel 2360 Walsh Avenue Santa Clara, CA 95050				X	X	
Versitron, Incorporated 6310 Chillum Place, NW Washington, D.C. 20011				X	X	

Manufacturer	Modems			Modem/ line-sharing units	Multi-point modems	Multi-plexers		Multi-port modems
	LS	MS	HS			FDM	TDM	
American Telephone and Telegraph 195 Broadway New York, NY 10007	X	X	X		X	X		X
Anderson Jacobson 1065 Morse Avenue Sunnyvale, CA 94086	X							
ASTROCOM Corporation 120 West Plato Blvd. St. Paul, MN 55107	X							
AVANTI Communications Corporation Box 205 Broadway Station Newport, RI 02840				X				
Carterphone Communications Corporation 1111 West Mockingbird Lane Dallas, TX 75247	X							
CODEX Corporation 15 Riverdale Avenue Newton, MA 02195			X	X	X		X	X
Coherent Communications 85D Hoffman Lane South Central Islip, NY 11722	X	X				X		
COM DATA Corporation 8115 North Monticello Avenue Skokie, IL 60076	X	X				X		
Computer Transmission Corporation 2352 Utah Avenue El Segundo, CA 90245	X						X	
COMTECH Laboratories, Incorporated 135 Engineers Road Smithtown, NY 11787							X	
Digital Communications Associates, Incorporated 135 Technology Park Norcross, GA 30092							X	
Digital Communications Corporation 19 Firstfield Road Gaithersburg, MD 20760							X	
Electrodata, Incorporated P.O. Box 46130 Bedford, OH 44146				X				

Manufacturer	Modems			Modem/ line- sharing units	Multi- point modems	Multi- plexers		Multi- port modems
	LS	MS	HS			FDM	TDM	
Gandalf Data Incorporated 190 Shepard Avenue Wheeling, IL 60090	X							
General Data Comm Industries 131 Danbury Road Wilton, CT 06897	X	X	X	X	X	X	X	X
General Electric Company Waynesboro, VA 22980	X							
GTE Information Systems, Incorporated Four Corporate Park Drive White Plains, NY 10604		X						
GTE Lenkurt 1105 Country Road San Carlos, CA 94070	X	X				X		
Harris Corporation P.O. Box 160 Melbourne, FL 32901						X		
IBM Corporation Thomas J. Watson Research Center Yorktown Heights, NY 10598		X						
Infotron Systems Cherry Hill Industrial Center Cherry Hill, NJ 08003	X	X					X	
INTERTEL 6 Vine Brook Park Burlington, MA 01803		X	X		X			X
Kaufman Research 99 Sylvian Way Los Altos, CA 94022				X				
Livermore Data Systems, Incorporated 2050 Research Drive Livermore, CA 94550		X						
MICOM Systems, Incorporated 9551 Irondale Avenue Chatsworth, CA 91311				X			X	
MI² Data Systems, Incorporated 1356 Norton Avenue Columbus, OH 43212	X							
OMNITEC DATA 2405 South 20th Street Phoenix, AZ 85034	X							
Paradyne Corporation 8550 Ulmerton Road Largo, FL 33540			X	X	X			X

Manufacturer	Modems			Modem/line-sharing units	Multi-point modems	Multi-plexers		Multi-port modems
	LS	MS	HS			FDM	TDM	
PENRIL Corporation 5520 Randolph Road Rockville, MD 20852	X	X		X	X			X
Prentice Corporation 795 San Antonio Road Palo Alto, CA 94303		X				X		
PULSECOM 5714 Columbia Pike Falls Church, VA 22041	X					X		
QEI, Incorporated 60 Fadem Road Springfield, NJ 07081						X		
RANCAL-MILGO, Incorporated 8600 NW 41st Street Miami, FL 33166		X	X	X	X			X
RFL Industries, Incorporated Boontown, NJ 07005							X	
RIXON, Incorporated 2120 Industrial Parkway Silver Springs, MD 20904		X						
Rockwell International 3370 Miraloma Avenue Anaheim, CA 92803		X						
SKEI Corporation 1015 East Broadway Columbia, MO 65200				X				
SPECTRON Corporation Church Road and Roland Avenue Moorestown, NJ 08057				X				
Stelma Telecommunications 17 Amelia Place Stamford, CT 06902						X		
SYNTECH Corporation 11810 Parklawn Drive Rockville, MD 20852		X		X				
TELCON Industries, Incorporated 5701 NW 31st Street Ft. Lauderdale, FL 33309							X	
Tele Data Management, Incorporated 644 Wagner Road Glenview, IL 60025		X						
Tele-Dynamics 525 Virginia Drive Fort Washington, PA 19034	X	X				X		

Manufacturer	Modems			Modem/ line- sharing units	Multi- point modems	Multi- plexers		Multi- port modems
	LS	MS	HS			FDM	TDM	
Tele-Signal Corporation 185 Oser Avenue Hauppauge, NY 11787		X						
Timeplex, Incorporated 100 Commerce Way Hackensack, NJ 07601	X	X					X	
Universal Data Systems, Incorporated 4900 Bradford Drive Huntsville, AL 35805	X	X						
U.S. Robotics, Incorporated P.O. Box 5502 Chicago, IL 60680	X							
VADIC Corporation 505 East Middlefield Road Mountain View, CA 94043	X							
Ven-Tel 2360 Walsh Avenue Santa Clara, CA 95050	X							
Western Union Information Systems 82 McKee Drive Mahwah, NJ 07430			X				X	

Manufacturer	Parallel extenders	Port-sharing units	Port selectors	Security devices
Alden Electronic Alden Research Center Westborough, MA 01581				X
American Satellite Corporation 20301 Century Boulevard Germantown, MD 20767				X
American Telephone and Telegraph 195 Broadway New York, NY 10007			X	
ASTROCOM Corporation 120 West Plato Blvd. St. Paul, MN 55107		X		
CODEX Corporation 15 Riverdale Avenue Newton, MA 02195		X	X	
Computer Linguistics, Incorporated 26 Computer Drive East Albany, NY 12205				X
COMTECH Laboratories, Incorporated 135 Engineers Road Smithtown, NY 11787				X
DATOTEK, Incorporated 13740 Midway Road Dallas, TX 75240				X
Digital Communications Corporation 19 Firstfield Road Gaithersburg, MD 20760			X	
General Data Comm Industries 131 Danbury Road Wilton, CT 06897		X		
IBM Corporation Thomas J. Watson Research Center Yorktown Heights, NY 10598				X
Infotron Systems Cherry Hill Industrial Center Cherry Hill, NJ 08003			X	
INTERTEL 6 Vine Brook Park Burlington, MA 01803		X		
MICOM Systems, Incorporated 9551 Irondale Avenue Chatsworth, CA 91311		X		

Manufacturer	Parallel extenders	Port-sharing units	Port selectors	Security devices
Motorola, Incorporated P.O. Box 1417 Scottsdale, AZ 85252				X
Paradyne Corporation 8550 Ulmerton Road Largo, FL 33540	X			
Rewau Enterprises, Incorporated 1705 Sheffield Drive Ypsilanti, MI 48197		X		
Rockwell International 4311 Jamboree Road Newport Beach, CA 92663				X
Saber Laboratories, Incorporated 1150 Bryant Street San Francisco, CA 94103				X
Stelma Telecommunications 17 Amelia Place Stamford, CT 06902		X		
SYNTECH Corporation 11810 Parklawn Drive Rockville, MD 20852		X		
Technical Communications Corporation 56 Winthrop Street Concord, MA 01742				X
Timeplex, Incorporated 100 Commerce Way Hackensack, NJ 07601			X	

Manufacturer	Speed/code converters	Speech/data devices
CODEX Corporation 15 Riverdale Avenue Newton, MA 02195		X
Coherent Communications 85D Hoffman Lane South Central Islip, NY 11722		X
COM DATA Corporation 8115 North Monticello Avenue Skokie, IL 60076	X	
C&W Technical Services, Incorporated 12 Spielman Road Fairfield, NJ 07006	X	
Digital Communications Corporation 19 Firstfield Road Gaithersburg, MD 20760	X	
DMC 2300 Owen Street Santa Clara, CA 95051	X	
E-Systems, Incorporated P.O. Box 6118 Dallas, TX 75222		X
Frederick Electronics P.O. Box 502 Hayward Road Frederick, MD 21701	X	
GTE Information Systems One Stamford Forum Stamford, CT 06904	X	
GTE Lenkurt 1105 San Carlos Road San Carlos, CA 94070		X
International Computer Products 2925 Merrell Road Dallas, TX 75229	X	
Lane Telecommunications, Incorporated 6906 Harwin Drive Houston, TX 77036	X	
MICOM Systems, Incorporated 9551 Irondale Avenue Chatsworth, CA 91311	X	
MI^2 Data Systems, Incorporated 1356 Norton Avenue Columbus, OH 43212	X	
NESCO 2904 Corvin Drive Santa Clara, CA 95051	X	
Paradyne Corporation 8550 Ulmerton Road Largo, FL 33540		X

Manufacturer	Speed/code converters	Speech/data devices
Rancal-Milgo, Incorporated 8600 NW 41st Street Miami, FL 33166	X	X
SIDERAL Corporation P.O. Box 1042 Portland, OR 97207	X	
Sykes Datatronics, Incorporated 375 Orchard Street Rochester, NY 14606	X	
SYNTECH Corporation 11810 Parklawn Drive Rockville, MD 20852	X	
SYSCOM 3058-B Scott Boulevard Santa Clara, CA 95050	X	
TELCON Industries, Incorporated 5701 NW 31st Street Fort Lauderdale, FL 33309	X	
Time and Space Processing, Incorporated 10430 North Tantav Avenue Cupertino, CA 95014		X
Triformation Systems, Incorporated 3132 SE Jay Street Stuart, FL 33494	X	
Universal Technology, Incorporated 871 Allwood Road Clifton, NJ 07012	X	

index

ACB (asynchronous communications base), 165–166

Access line, 5

Acoustic coupler, 4, 9, 18, 30–32, 233
modem compatability, 31–32

Alternate routing, 133, 135, 137

American Standard Code for Information Interchange (ASCII), 21, 24–26, 98, 178–179, 180, 205, 212, 229, 231

Analog-digital signal conversion, 33

Analog versus digital transmission, 8

Analog extension, 8–9, 19, 81–83

Analog loop-back self-test, 53–55

Analog transmission, 2–4, 8, 18–19, 76–77

ASCII, 21, 24–26, 98, 178–179, 180, 205, 212, 229–231

Asynchronous communications base, 165–166

Asynchronous transmission, 11–14, 17, 35–36, 126, 157, 225

Automatic answering unit, 195–197

Automatic calling unit, 197–210
classes, 201
interfacing, 200–206
types of units, 198
utilization, 199–200

Automatic equalization, 40, 64–65, 76

Automatic request for repeat, *see* Error control procedures

Basic telecommunications access method (BTAM), 86

Baudot code, 21–22, 98, 229–231

BCD (binary-coded decimal), 21–23

Bell System modem
acoustic coupler compatibility, 31–32
modem compatibility, 43–51
103/113 series, 31–32, 43–45, 48
108 series, 44
201 series, 45, 48–49
202 series, 45–46, 49–50
203 series, 46, 50
208 series, 47, 50
209 series, 47, 50
212A series, 47, 50

Binary-coded decimal (BCD), 21–23

Binary mode transmission, *see* native mode transmission

Binary synchronous communications (BISYNC), 28, 110–111

Bipolar signals, 8, 66, 78

BISYNC (binary synchronous communications), 28, 110–111

Bit-stream synchronization, *see* synchronous transmission

Broadcast address, 16

BTAM (basic telecommunications access method), 86

Bypass switch, 171–172